Rural Development and the Construction of New Markets

This book focuses on empirical experiences related to market development, and specifically new markets with structurally different characteristics than mainstream markets. Europe, Brazil, China and the rather robust and complex African experiences are covered to provide a rich multidisciplinary and multi-level analysis of the dynamics of newly emerging markets.

Rural Development and the Construction of New Markets analyses newly constructed markets as nested markets. Although they are specific market segments that are nested in the wider commodity markets for food, they have a different nature, different dynamics, a different redistribution of value added, different prices and different relations between producers and consumers. Nested markets embody distinction vis-à-vis the general markets in which they are embedded. A key aspect of nested markets is that these are constructed in and through social struggles, which in turn positions this book in relation to classic and new institutional economic analyses of markets. These markets emerge as steadily growing parts of the farmer populations are dedicating their time, energy and resources to the design and production of new goods and services that differ from conventional agricultural outputs. The speed and intensity with which this is taking place, and the products and services involved, vary considerably across the world. In large parts of the South, notably Africa, farmers are 'structurally' combining farming with other activities. By contrast, in Europe and large parts of Latin America farmers have taken steps to generate new products and services which exist alongside ongoing agricultural production.

This book not only discusses the economic rationales and dynamics for these markets, but also their likely futures and the threats and opportunities they face.

Paul Hebinck is Associate Professor at Wageningen University, The Netherlands, and Adjunct Professor at the University of Forth Hare, Faculty of Agriculture and Science, Alice, South Africa.

Jan Douwe van der Ploeg is Professor of Transition Studies at Wageningen University, The Netherlands, and Adjunct Professor of Rural Sociology at China Agricultural University in Beijing, China.

Sergio Schneider is Professor of Rural Sociology and Development Studies at the Federal University of Rio Grande do Sul (UFRGS), Porto Alegre, Brazil.

Routledge ISS studies in rural livelihoods

Routledge and the Institute of Social Studies (ISS) in The Hague, The Netherlands have come together to publish a new book series in rural livelihoods. The series will include themes such as land policies and land rights, water issues, food policy and politics, rural poverty, agrarian transformation, migration, rural-oriented social movements, rural conflict and violence, among others. All books in the series will offer rigorous, empirically grounded, cross-national comparative and inter-regional analysis. The books will be theoretically stimulating, but will also be accessible to policy practitioners and civil society activists.

1 **Land, Poverty and Livelihoods in an Era of Globalization**
   Perspectives from developing and transition countries
   Edited by A. Haroon Akram-Lodhi, Saturnino M. Borras Jr. and Cristóbal Kay

2 **Peasants and Globalization**
   Political economy, agrarian transformation and development
   Edited by A. Haroon Akram-Lodhi and Cristóbal Kay

3 **The Political Economy of Rural Livelihoods in Transition Economies**
   Land, peasants and rural poverty in transition
   Edited by Max Spoor

4 **Agrarian Angst and Rural Resistance in Contemporary Southeast Asia**
   Edited by Dominique Caouette and Sarah Turner

5 **Water, Environmental Security and Sustainable Rural Development**
   Conflict and cooperation in Central Eurasia
   Edited by Murat Arsel and Max Spoor

6 **Reforming Land and Resource Use in South Africa**
   Impact on livelihoods
   Edited by Paul Hebinck and Charlie Shackleton

7 **Risk and Social Change in an African Rural Economy**
   Livelihoods in pastoralist communities
   John G. McPeak, Peter D. Little and Cheryl R. Doss

8 **Public Policy and Agricultural Development**
   Edited by Ha-Joon Chang

9 **Social Conflict, Economic Development and the Extractive Industry**
   Evidence from South America
   Edited by Anthony Bebbington

10 **The Ecotourism-Extraction Nexus**
   Political economies and rural realities of (un)comfortable bedfellows
   Edited by Bram Büscher and Veronica Davidov

11 **Rural Livelihoods, Regional Economies and Processes of Change**
   Edited by Deborah Sick

12 **Rural Development and the Construction of New Markets**
   Edited by Paul Hebinck, Jan Douwe van der Ploeg and Sergio Schneider

Rural Development and the Construction of New Markets

**Edited by Paul Hebinck,
Jan Douwe van der Ploeg and
Sergio Schneider**

Routledge
Taylor & Francis Group

LONDON AND NEW YORK

First published 2015
by Routledge

2 Park Square, Milton Park, Abingdon, Oxfordshire OX14 4RN
52 Vanderbilt Avenue, New York, NY 10017

Routledge is an imprint of the Taylor & Francis Group, an informa business

First issued in paperback 2019

British Library Cataloguing in Publication Data
A catalogue record for this book is available from the British Library

Library of Congress Cataloging in Publication Data
Rural development and the construction of new markets / edited by
Paul Hebinck, Jan Douwe van der Ploeg and Sergio Schneider.
    pages cm
    Includes bibliographical references and index.
    1. Agriculture–Economic aspects. 2. Rural development. 3. New
    agricultural enterprises. 4. Agricultural industries. 5. Produce trade.
    I. Hebinck, Paulus Gerardus Maria. II. Schneider, Sergio. III. Ploeg,
    Jan Douwe van der.
    HD1415.R87 2014
    338.1′9091724–dc23   2014008578

ISBN: 978-0-415-74634-2 (hbk)
ISBN: 978-0-367-86929-8 (pbk)

Typeset in Times New Roman
by Wearset Ltd, Boldon, Tyne and Wear

Contents

List of figures   ix

List of maps   x

List of tables   xi

List of contributors   xii

Preface and acknowledgements   xiv

1 **The construction of new, nested markets and the role of
  rural development policies: some introductory notes**   1
  PAUL HEBINCK, SERGIO SCHNEIDER AND
  JAN DOUWE VAN DER PLOEG

2 **Newly emerging, nested markets: a theoretical introduction**   16
  JAN DOUWE VAN DER PLOEG

3 **The visible hand in building new markets for rural
  economies**   41
  PIERLUIGI MILONE AND FLAMINIA VENTURA

4 **Family farming, institutional markets and innovations in
  public policy: food and nutritional security as a driver for
  governmental intervention**   61
  CLAUDIA SCHMITT, RENATO MALUF AND WALTER BELIK

5 **Participatory systems of certification and alternative
  marketing networks: the case of the Ecovida Agroecology
  Network in South Brazil**   79
  GUILHERME RADOMSKY, PAULO NIEDERLE AND
  SERGIO SCHNEIDER

6 **The construction of new nested markets and rural development in China**   99

HUIFANG WU, BAOYIN DING AND YE JINGZHONG

7 **Rural governance and the unfolding of nested markets in Europe**   115

HENK OOSTINDIE EN RUDOLF VAN BROEKHUIZEB

8 **Smallholder irrigators and fresh produce street traders in Thohoyandou, Limpopo Province, South Africa**   131

KGABO MANYELO, WIM VAN AVERBEKE AND
PAUL HEBINCK

9 **Beyond land transfers: the dynamics of socially driven markets emerging from Zimbabwe's Fast Track Land Reform Programme**   149

PROSPER MATONDI AND SHEILA CHIKULO

10 **In the shadow of global markets for fish in Lake Victoria, Tanzania**   168

MODESTA MEDAR, PAUL HEBINCK AND HAN VAN DIJK

11 **Reconsidering the contribution of nested markets to rural development**   190

SERGIO SCHNEIDER, JAN DOUWE VAN DER PLOEG AND
PAUL HEBINCK

Index   206

Figures

2.1	A conceptual representation of the newly emerging constellations	18
2.2	Multi-tiered processes of exchange	21
2.3	The socio-material infrastructure of the market for Texel lamb	25
3.1	Governance structure of transactions	43
3.2	The flow of resources, consolidation of business processes and creation of new products	46
3.3	The case of care farms	47
3.4	The case of food products with low emissions of greenhouse gases	49
3.5	The case of local quality products	51
3.6	The 'big bang' of the nested market	52
3.7	The organizational innovation cycle of transaction relationships	54
3.8	Collective action and policy development	55
5.1	Schematic representation of the Ecovida Agroecological Network	82
5.2	Ecovida Agroecology Network Seal	83
7.1	Trends in CAP expenditure since 1980	116
7.2	The rural policy performance triangle	124
10.1	Nile perch export weights (fillets) and export earnings (in US$) in Lake Victoria, Tanzania.	172
10.2	Nile perch export supply flow diagram	177
10.3	Local, regional and continental fish supply and distribution networks	181

Maps

8.1   Location of Dzindi Irrigation Scheme and Thoyandou   134

9.1   Agroecological zones and the location of the Lowveld in
         Zimbabwe   150

10.1   Lake Victoria and the location of field research sites   170

Tables

6.1   The different constituent common pool resource elements   106
8.1   Number of street traders who purchased fresh produce from
      farmers at Dzindi by category (June 2009)   137
10.1 Intensification of fishing in the Lake Victoria Fishery,
      2000–2012   174
10.2 Nile perch and Tilapia cold store and selling facilities in
      Mwanza   184
11.1 A comparison of the general agricultural and food markets
      and the newly emerging markets   198

Contributors

Baoyin Ding, PhD student, College of Humanities and Development Studies, China Agricultural University, Beijing, China.

Claudia Schmitt, Professor, Department of Agricultural Development and Society, Federal State University of Rio de Janeiro, Rio de Janeiro, Brazil.

Flaminia Ventura, Professor, Department of Engineering and Environment, University of Perugia, Italy.

Guilherme F.W. Radomsky, Professor, Department of Sociology, Federal University of Rio Grande do Sul, Porto Alegre, Brazil.

Han van Dijk, Professor, Sociology of Development and Change, Wageningen University, The Netherlands; Senior Researcher, African Studies Centre, Leiden, The Netherlands.

Henk Oostindie, PhD student, Rural Sociology, Wageningen University, The Netherlands.

Jan Douwe van der Ploeg, Professor, Rural Sociology, Wageningen University, The Netherlands; Adjunct Professor of Rural Sociology at China Agricultural University in Beijing, China.

Kgabo W Manyelo, MSc, Tshwane University of Technology, Pretoria, South Africa.

Modesta Medar, PhD student, Sociology of Development and Change, Wageningen University.

Paul Hebinck, PhD, Associate Professor, Sociology of Development and Change, Wageningen University, The Netherlands; Adjunct Professor at the University of Fort Hare, Alice, South Africa.

Paul A. Niederle, Professor, Department of Sociology, Federal University of Rio Grande do Sul, Porto Alegre, Brazil.

Pierluigi Milone, Professor, Department of Engineering and Environment, University of Perugia, Italy.

Prosper Matondi, PhD, CEO Ruzivo Trust, Harare, Zimbabwe.

Renato Maluf, PhD, Department of Agricultural Development, Federal State University of Rio de Janeiro, Brazil.

Rudolf van Broekhuizen, MSc, Rural Sociology, Wageningen University, The Netherlands.

Sergio Schneider, Professor, Department of Sociology, Federal University of Rio Grande do Sul, Porto Alegre, Brazil.

Sheila Chikulo, PhD student, Sociology of Development and Change, Wageningen University, The Netherlands; Senior Researcher, Ruzivo Trust, Harare, Zimbabwe.

Walter Belik, Professor, Department of Economics, Federal State University of Campinas, Campinas, Brazil.

Wim van Averbeke, Professor, Department of Crop Science, Tshwane University of Technology, South Africa.

Wu Huifang, Assistant Professor, College of Humanities and Development Studies, China Agricultural University, Beijin, China.

Ye Jingzhong, Professor, College of Humanities and Development Studies, China Agricultural University, Beijing, China.

Preface and acknowledgements

This book grew out of a series of conferences held in Rome (2009) and Porto Alegre (2011) to debate the role of markets in rural development. These conferences were organized under a comparative research project on rural development processes in Brazil, China and the European Union carried out by the Graduate Programme of Rural Development of the Federal University of Rio Grande do Sul (PGDR/UFRGS), the College of Humanities and Development of China Agricultural University (COHD/CAU, China) and the Rural Sociology Group of Wageningen University (WUR, The Netherlands). The aim was to compare and explore the range of rural development experiences with markets across the world. The outcomes of the Rome conference found their way into a special issue of *Revista di Economina Agraria* (2010, vol. 65, issue 2) which contains papers addressing rural development processes in China, Brazil and the European Union with a view to identifying policy dimensions and what actually constitutes rural development policy.

This edited volume brings together a selection of papers presented at the Porto Alegre Conference held in 2011. As a follow up to the Rome conference, this meeting focused on empirical experiences related to market development, and specifically new markets which have 'structurally' different characteristics to 'mainstream' markets. The conference included the sharing of a broad set of experiences of such markets in Europe, Brazil and China and included an attempt to incorporate the rather robust and complex African experiences into the comparative analysis. An additional dimension of the Porto Alegre Conference was the focus on family farming across the globe. Family or peasant farming is, after all, the mainstay of many of the world's rural economies. This book makes an important contribution to the broader debate on rural development in that it explores (empirically and theoretically) the links between family farming or fishing and the emergence of new markets. The seminar's position paper stated that 'family farming has a fundamental contribution to make to key problems we face nowadays in rural areas worldwide: reducing rural poverty and social inequality, generating more sustainable rural livelihoods and fostering environmental resilience'. This contributes to our understanding of these processes by providing a better understanding of the role that markets play within them. It also shows the very different ways in which farmers access markets, an important contribution to the debates that will take place in this, the International Year of Family Farming.

The editors chose the papers on the basis of their originality and their contribution to the debate on how to explore markets, specifically the plethora of newly emerging markets. Taken together, the chapters provide a rich multidisciplinary and multi-level analysis of the dynamics of newly emerging markets. The chapters not only discuss the economic rationales and dynamics of these newly emerging markets but also their likely futures and the threats and opportunities facing them.

Lisa Thomson and Emily Kindleysides, the Routledge handling editors, have always provided extremely fast and appropriate assistance to the editors. Two anonymous reviewers provided a critical review of the draft manuscripts. They identified inconsistencies in the texts that we were able to iron out through further exchanges with the contributing authors.

We acknowledge the support of National Council for Scientific and Technological Development of Brazil (CNPq), part of the Ministry of Science and Technology, for their financial support to the researchers, with grants for the field work and data collection as well as for scholarships to enhance scientific productivity. CAPES, the Brazilian Federal Agency for the Support and Evaluation of Graduate Education also provided support, notably to Sergio Schneider and Claudia Schmitt in order to support academic cooperation between the Brazilian Universities and Wageningen University since 2007. This cooperation has stimulated the exchange of students and scholars and fostered scientific production. CAPES, the NCPQ and the Brazilian Ministry of Foreign Affairs contributed financially to the organization of the Seminar held in Porto Alegre in 2011 and the field visits.

The series editors of the Routledge ISS Studies in Rural Livelihoods, Max Spoor, Cristóbal Kay, Haroon Akram-Lodhi and Saturnino M. Borras Jr., trusted us with the production of a book without prescribing its contents and arguments. We are grateful for this.

Nicholas Parrott (www.textualhealing.nl) and Liz Cross did the language editing and proofreading for each chapter with great care, pointing out inconsistencies and proposing more eloquent solutions for thorny language issues. They managed extremely well to bridge the diverse styles of writing in the book and have made a most valuable contribution.

Cuijk/Wageningen/Porto Alegre
Paul Hebinck, Jan Douwe van der Ploeg and Sergio Schneider

1 The construction of new, nested markets and the role of rural development policies

Some introductory notes

Paul Hebinck, Sergio Schneider and Jan Douwe van der Ploeg

Steadily growing parts of the farmer populations of this world are dedicating part of their time, energy and resources to the design and production of *new* goods and services that differ from conventional agricultural outputs. The speed and intensity with which this is taking place, and the products and services involved, vary considerably across the world. In large parts of the South, notably Africa, farmers are 'structurally' combining farming with other activities (e.g. casual labour, trading and, to a degree, the 'production of nature'). By contrast, in Europe and large parts of Latin America farmers have taken steps to generate new products and services (e.g. nature management, quality production etc.) which exist along-side conventional agricultural production – at least initially. At the level of theory and policy the activities associated with the making of these new products and services have been grouped together under the heading of *multifunctionality* (van der Ploeg *et al.* 2010) or as *multiple livelihoods* (Francis 2002, Hebinck and Lent 2007). Both form essential aspects of the more general processes of *rural development*.[1] In multifunctional farming, farmers are involved in more activities ('functions') than just producing classical commodities, such as milk, potatoes or meat, which are then delivered as raw materials to food industries and large retail organizations in order to be converted into, and sold as, food. Multifunctional farming embraces the maintenance of landscapes, contributions to biodiversity, the production of high quality products and regional specialties, on-farm processing, the provision of agro-tourism facilities, enlarging the accessibility of the countryside, the production of energy and the retention of water. Some of these activities are funded (some observers would say subsidized) through government schemes (especially when they relate to the production of public goods), while others are remunerated through the market. There are also some functions for which no payment is available. Multiple livelihoods is a way of expressing the phenomenon and process whereby farmers, or rather rural dwellers, whether small or large scale, combine various ways of making a living. These processes imply (to differing degrees) an occupational shift and a temporal and/or spatial relocation of rural dwellers away from strictly agricultural based modes of livelihood.[2]

Of course, there always have been, at farm or field level depending on context, activities that are additional to the main economic activity. However until, say, 20 years ago, their number and significance was in decline. In Europe it was thought that the fully specialized farm was the most 'modern' and ideal one, and the most profitable. It is remarkable that since processes of deregulation and the gradual globalization of markets became established (in some areas a bit earlier, in marginal areas a bit later) this decline has been reversed into an upward tendency. This is partly due to neo-liberal government policies and decisions to let the market rule (Kydd and Dorward 2001) which has exerted downward pressures on farmers' incomes. In the European Union the initial response of farmers to deregulation, globalization and the ensuing squeeze on agriculture (Marsden 1998) was to search for new products and services that offered a higher value added; this took place on a large scale during the 1990s. In more recent years, since the early 2000s, rural producers have began to organize new markets to ensure that the value added does actually end up on their farm, increasing their income. Similar processes can be seen in Brazil and China. In Africa and other parts of the South it can be argued that globalization, the deregulation of markets and the ensuing squeeze on farmers' incomes has had a two-pronged effect. On one hand it has led rural producers to look for ways to expand their livelihoods beyond just agriculture; on the other hand, they have continued to operate on and deal with markets that largely fall outside the influence of governments and *conventional* supply and demand mechanisms. There are many vibrant roadside markets, street markets in (peri-) urban areas, cross-border trade and vehicle-based markets in Africa and the African chapters in this book bear witness to their expansion and growth.[3]

The making of new products and services and the re-orienting of livelihoods at least partly away from agriculture is a multi-faceted and richly chequered set of responses to the tightening of the price squeeze that agricultural sectors have been suffering from since the 1990s. It is remarkable to note that engagement in multifunctional activities is not limited to a few specific places. It is taking place nearly everywhere. In Europe this process is widely spread, fairly well documented and has been extensively theoretically elaborated. But it is also taking place in Canada, the USA, New Zealand and Australia to a considerable extent, whilst there are many widespread examples from the Global South. China and Brazil are notable and exemplary cases in this respect. In certain parts of Africa, notably in the Western Cape, Gauteng and the Midlands (South Africa) and other peri-urban agricultural areas close to metropolises such as Nairobi, Dar es Salaam and other major capital cities, similar processes are taking place, often supported by a burgeoning middle and upper classes. Elsewhere in Asia, Africa and Latin America old, renewed and new cases of multifunctionality can also be found, albeit less frequently. This nearly global nature of the (re-)emergence of new, additional activities at farm and/or household level evidently reflects the global tendency towards deregulation, while the differences in degree reflect differences in governance systems (some being favourable to multifunctional farms, others a hindrance), historical repertoires (some places have strong traditions centred on 'mixed farms', in other places it is a somewhat new phenomenon) and town–countryside relations. A final remarkable feature to recall here is that since the 1990s the range of new products and services really has exploded and now includes products and services that were previously 'unthinkable'.

The reversal towards the making of new goods and services and the reorienting of livelihoods was quickly followed by a second trend: *the construction of new markets*. The actors involved in these activities (e.g. farmers, fishermen and traders) discovered, sooner or later, that making new goods and services and channelling them into the mainstream commodity markets (i.e. into already existing patterns for marketing) had little effect on ameliorating their own incomes and wellbeing. The new products and services may offer considerable added value, but this was appropriated by other actors in the existing marketing channels. Worse still, existing trading companies were sometimes not even remotely interested in commercializing these new products or services. Thus multifunctional farmers and other rural producers started to construct and/or to strengthen their own outlets, their own channels to reach consumers and to sell their products. Some of these markets build on long, historically deeply-rooted experiences, as there has never been a society without markets; others are relatively new constructions.[4] In all this, the emphasis quickly shifted from the individual level to joint efforts – and in some places patterns of cooperation with consumer organizations and/or state agencies have been developed which have considerably strengthened these newly created markets.

In this book we analyse such newly constructed markets as *nested markets*.[5] Although they are specific market segments that are *nested* in the wider commodity markets for food, they have a different nature, different dynamics, a different redistribution of value added, different prices and different relations between producers and consumers. That is to say, nested markets embody distinction vis-à-vis the general markets in which they are embedded. This distinction may be located in one or several different dimensions, as illustrated throughout this book.

Nested markets emerge out of social struggles, and their reproduction over time is the object of complex and sometimes extended social struggles. Understanding these struggles and, consequently, the nature and dynamics of nested markets, requires five focused and interrelated theoretical steps which have methodological implications.

1   Instead of seeing markets as a 'system' (one that regulates itself in ways described in neo-classical economics), markets need to be conceptualized in terms of 'market places' (Shanin 1972). Markets are sites for social interaction (Watson and Suddert 2006). The market is a specific place (or arena) where particular transactions take place between specific buyers and sellers, who exchange specific goods and services according to specific rules. This allows us to understand markets as institutionally regulated and embedded in historical and cultural repertoires. It also explains why different markets (for one and the same product) may co-exist alongside each other, each with different *modi operandi*. Formerly, the two positions were known in economic anthropology as the formalist and the substantivist approach (Granovetter 1992, Lie 1997, Brycesson 2000).

2   The notion of market needs to be stripped of any a priori normative framing. The market is neither intrinsically 'good' (as claimed in neo-liberal discourse), nor intrinsically 'evil' (as posed by the radical left), as Abramovay (2004) puts it. It all depends on the outcomes, the efficiency, the space allowed to individual actors, the degrees of freedom entailed, the distributive effects created, and so on. What is needed is a theoretically well-grounded empirical inquiry (and that is exactly what is excluded through a priori framing).

3   One needs to accept that markets might become not only the *focus*, but also the *locus* of social struggles. According to orthodox Marxist views, social struggles occur at places of *production* and not, in the first place, in places of *distribution* (i.e. the markets). If struggles in the markets occur, they are of secondary, if not minimal, relevance. Orthodox Marxist reasoning has it that societies cannot be radically altered through changes in the markets. Indeed such changes are seen as suspect, since they only can generate redistributive effects. In this book we try to go beyond this view by focusing on the complex dialectics of today's social struggles: changes in the sphere of production (i.e. making new products and services that potentially embody a range of benefits for the producers) induce changes in the sphere of circulation (i.e. the construction of new, nested markets), while the latter allow for further changes at the place of production. The two are becoming increasingly tied together, the one leading to and allowing for the other and vice versa.

4   We also need to go beyond the conventionalization thesis (Guthman 2004, Coombes and Campbell 1998) which essentially argues that radical changes made in the production and marketing of food will inevitably be taken over or appropriated by large retail organizations and food processing industries, thus neutralizing any potential for further change. Organic production (and its partial take over by big food empires as has occurred in California, for example) is often presented here as proof of this argument. This conventionalization thesis is, we think, based on the theoretical misconceptions discussed above. It essentially perceives the food market as a *monolithic system* – one that *cannot be beaten*, and which inevitably turns out to be *evil*.

5   We also have to briefly reconsider the now ample literature on 'short food circuits' (or 'alternative food circuits'). What is crucially missing from this literature is the notion of *market places* (see above). It is about *circuits*, bringing products or services from the producer to the consumer through the shortest possible social and/or geographical distance. Yet such analysis often neglects to engage with the fact that such circuits are intrinsically part of a new market (and that consequently, the associated struggles and development do not stop once this shortest possible distance is reached). The same occurs with the notion of 'alternative' which tends to refer solely to normative embedding and then mostly moves to discuss whether or not the claimed normative objectives have actually been reached and whether or not they constitute an adequate normative framework (Goodman and DuPuis 2002).

'The double movement'

From an historical perspective, the emergence of new, nested markets can be understood as part of the 'double movement' as discussed by Polayni (1957). This describes the emerging dominance over time of untamed markets and then a swing of the pendulum in the other direction towards taming the market and aligning it with social and ecological priorities. The processes of deregulation, liberalization and globalization that we have witnessed over the last decades clearly represent a move away from any control of state and civil society over the markets. This applies generally and, more specifically, to the agricultural and food markets. Yet, when the performance of agricultural and food markets is left uncorrected ('undisturbed' as economists say) this generates a wide, though variable, range of consequences that societies find unacceptable. *'(L)eaving the fate of soil and people to the markets would be tantamount to their annihilation'* (Polayni 1957: 89). Markets and the way they operate, including some and excluding others, favouring some (product) characteristics and marginalizing others have long been subject to criticism and contestation, sometimes giving rise to various, contrasting counter-developments. Karl Polanyi (1957: 132) labelled these counter developments as constituting one part of the 'double movement' that is intrinsic to any society.

This book focuses on the dynamics of 'counter-development': the social struggles, strategies and attempts of local actors (e.g. farmers, traders, consumers, collectives) to actively respond to 'failures' of the global markets they are confronted with. While these struggles and strategies are extremely diverse, they share a common feature: they increasingly hinge on the creation or development of nested markets (van der Ploeg *et al.* 2012). These are new markets whose *modus operandi* is 'structurally' different from the markets governed by global players, such as supermarkets and global commodity trading companies. These new nested markets are usually established through processes of social struggle, shaped by local governance frameworks and cultural repertoires and are often created around locally available resources. Thus, the 'double movement' comes to the fore here as the *simultaneous presence* of global markets in which these newly constructed markets are nested, and also as the *complex and often contradictory interactions* between the two. Here conventionalization is indeed possible but not inevitable. A further unfolding, strengthening and multiplication of nested, and increasingly interlinked, markets is equally possible. Within this open-ended interaction the newly constructed, nested markets provide a countervailing power to the hegemonic institutions that control the global markets.

Rural development – expressed in policies and practices – is essentially an attempt to redress market failures (notably linked to the functioning of global commodity markets) that occur in agriculture, food production and the countryside (van der Ploeg *et al.* 2012). The creation of new, nested markets is an essential ingredient of this attempt. Such markets often emerge as actively constructed responses to specific market failures. Thus, at the conceptual level, rural development can be viewed as a socio-material process of transition that involves re-modelling distributive mechanisms (for products, services and added value) – a process that leads to the re-shaping of agriculture, food production, rural livelihoods and the countryside. These, as O'Connor *et al.* (2006) argued, cannot be conceptualized solely as an outcome of state rural development policies although, if well designed and implemented, these policies can be very important. There is a need (at both the conceptual and policy level) to recognize the role, endeavours and practices of local actors, groups and individuals and civil society at large in shaping these development processes (Long 2001, De Sardan 2006).

The contributors to this book are all involved in rural development (as academics, practitioners and, sometimes, as both) in the EU, China, Brazil and southern Africa. For some years we have been organizing seminars and meetings to explore the commonalities and differences in rural development processes in these very different settings.[6] One of the key questions to emerge from our comparative analysis of rural and market development processes in these places is the influence that state policies, social movements and civil society have on the construction of new, nested markets. This key question raises additional questions about the interfaces between rural development policies, civil society actors and social movements. The encounters at these different interfaces are often decisive in determining the success (or failure) of the many grassroots activities that abound in the agricultural sector, in the countryside and among consumers (Milone and Ventura 2010).

On the comparative approach

The chapters in this book deal with different socio-geographical constellations, the choice of which has been inspired by the insight that rural development processes critically require a strong state, a strong civil society, strong social movements, or a combination of these actors. In Europe rural development is typically driven by civil society actors (farmers, consumers and NGOs engaged with nature, biodiversity, landscape, etc.) and is, to a modest degree, supported by rural development policies. In Brazil strong social movements have triggered and developed impressive processes of rural development which, at a certain point, were strongly supported by the state (although it seems that the pendulum is currently swinging back again). In China the strong state, and the capillary presence of the Communist Party in the countryside, have been decisive in strengthening rural development in the twenty-first century. Nonetheless, the state often builds on peasant initiatives. Finally, southern Africa provides a contrast. In general terms there is no strong state (especially in the countryside, where the state lacks influence and capacity), there is no strong civil society nor are there strong social movements involved in rural development, except for a few that address the land question.

Studying these four strongly differing geographical areas and institutional contexts can provide important lessons about the creation of new, nested markets and the role that state policies play in supporting their emergence. For instance, in Brazil, the state supports school food programmes, which involve state food procurement policies that are also designed to strengthen family farms in Brazil. In South Africa earlier barriers to black producers entering markets have been removed by post-apartheid agrarian policies. The expectation of change is high and intense and the state is pulling together many resources to make change happen. But the realities are extremely complex and very different from post-apartheid aspirations (Hebinck and Cousins 2013). In South Africa, small family-based traders have created their own rural and peri-urban markets and manage to eke out a living on the margins of the main markets controlled by supermarkets. Similarly, in Zimbabwe a plethora of new markets have emerged in the wake of the Fast Track Land Reform, most of which are in places and spaces where the state is absent. To paraphrase James Scott (1998), these are emerging markets that are not or hardly 'seen by the state'. In Brazil the opposite is true. The public procurement policy that requires that family farming supplies a minimum of 30 per cent of food purchased has created new market opportunities for this group of farmers. These differences raise further questions: how are these markets created and supported? Who plays a key role? Who are the enablers and what are the obstacles? How can the new markets be up-scaled and the obstacles addressed? The chapters of this book explore in some detail the nature of relations between these markets and their broader political and economic environment, and how new markets are crafted when existing ones do not resonate with the interests and future perspectives of family farmers, peasants or other local actors.

The connections between policies and markets

Rural development policies are a strange and contradictory phenomenon. They reflect the need for the state to have some influence in the realms of agriculture, food production and the countryside. But it is a presence that is handicapped, right from the outset. Rural development policies alone cannot 'reconquer' the territory that has been lost through deregulation. Nor (because of globalization and neo-liberalism) can they copy previous modes of regulation and intervention. Yet this does not imply that rural development policies are impotent or unimportant.

We believe that rural development policies offer much promise for the construction of nested markets. The comparative research and analysis that we are engaged in allows for the identification of the potential of such policies and of the obstacles that hinder their implementation and success. Our approach differs in one fundamental way from previous comparative reviews of agricultural policies (see for example, Ellis and Biggs 2001, Ashley and Maxwell 2002). We see the successful implementation and further development of rural development policies as critically dependant on the permanent and multi-layered involvement of civil society. This applies especially when rural development policies aim to support the creation of new, nested markets.

The agrarian policies of the past were basically designed by experts and often coercively imposed by the state. Scott (1998) effectively illustrated how this became a weakness of such policies. By contrast, current rural development policies involve and need to include civil society in all its aspects: peasants, traders, consumers, rural inhabitants, social movements, etc. This has two important methodological consequences. First, we have to put rural development *practices* centre stage. Rural development is not a meta-narrative that is translated from policy into practice. Nor is it a domain solely for the state and experts. Rather, it is fashioned by a multitude of heterogeneous practices that are initiated and developed in response to market failures. Policy making is one of these practices and the more it intertwines with the practices of others – including individual farmers, cooperatives, social movements, civic initiatives, etc. – the more effective it becomes. In short, the study and analysis of rural development policies should not take these policies as the starting point of rural development, but instead should see them as one of the, often highly contradictory, outcomes of the complex encounters between many different practices. More specifically, rural development policies are co-produced through the many multi-levelled encounters between the heterogeneous practices of policy making and the many rural development practices that occur within civil society. The second methodological consequence follows from this. If we focus on the multiple interfaces between different practices, we necessarily have to focus on the role of the actors involved. It is not possible to study rural development policies, their mechanisms and their impact if we ignore the farming families who design and create novel ways to produce food, manage environmental resources, aggregate value and produce wealth. The same applies to those actors (including consumers) engaged in new, nested markets and to social movements seeking to change the socio-political horizon.

The next generation of rural development policies – the need to go further

Comparative research on rural development policies is still in its early stages. A new set of theoretical references and methodological guidelines, which take this new context, processes and policy reorienting into account, need to be developed. In this endeavour three discernible possibilities can be identified as the 'seeds and shoots' of the next wave of rural development policies. The first envisages further improvements to rural development policies coming from the 'inside', led by competent officials working within the main state agencies. Such a possibility is crucially dependent on the presence of, and pressure exerted by, social movements (of whatever form) in the countryside. The joint development (sometimes overt, sometimes covert) of new initiatives and proposals might also play an important role within this approach.

A second possibility lies in the interface between rural policies (and associated agencies) and strong regions and/or social movements. Considerable transformative capacity can emerge at these interfaces, with the potential to transform both policy and practice in a dialectical and mutually reinforcing way. Such interfaces allow 'forward movements' that go beyond the usual limits of rural policy. It is important here that the state provides the legal space and sufficient resources to enable such experimentation.

The third possibility is provided by 'institutional voids'. These can open up new fields of action where there are, as yet, *'no clear rules and norms bestowing to which politics is to be conducted and policy measures are to be agreed upon. To be more precise, there are no generally accepted rules and norms according to which policy making and politics is to be conducted'* (Hajer 2003: 175). When rural initiatives (or social movements) are among the first to enter such an institutional void, they can develop convincing novel settings (of whatever type) and gain considerable momentum. Within the realm of policy making (i.e. within the responsible state agencies) institutional voids might also be used as a source for innovation and change (see, for instance, McGee 2004).

These three positions are well known and can all be recognized in the current debates about the next generation of rural development policies. What we propose here is to consider these three positions as the three driving forces in what we call a 'policy cycle'. This cycle starts from the third position. Social movements, rural groups and/or enterprising individuals try to go beyond limiting, and sometimes paralysing, policies by entering into the 'unknown' or the 'non-prescribed' – that is to say they move into an institutional void. If their practices produce promising constellations this can induce a useful interface with the established authorities (the second position). This allows for a twofold transformation: the improvement of policies and the strengthening of the practices. This is then followed by a third stage in which policy will try to encapsulate and mainstream the new (and probably disseminated) initiatives. This requires further improvements in policy and will also lead to a process of standardization. This might then trigger a new cycle.

Within this policy cycle it is crucial that (a) the activities, procedures and agendas at different levels (e.g. the state, the region and grassroots initiatives) are well aligned and (b) that the required simultaneity is secured. Beyond this there is always a need for (c) intermediaries or brokers to make the required connections. When such conditions are met, collaborative innovation might well occur and thorny problems can be effectively addressed. Such collaborative innovations might result in the creation of consistency and synergy which, as demonstrated in the European ETUDE programme, are strategic for rural development (Vihinen and Kull 2010).

We have the impression that many of the rural development policies currently being deployed stem from such a policy cycle. We also think that any further unfolding (i.e. a 'new generation') will critically depend on new cycles.

It is certain that these new cycles will not be inspired by targeting classical goals, such as specific productivity increases, etc. Instead, sustainability, self-organization and self-governance, food sovereignty and synergy will need to be the guiding principles and axes along which rural development initiatives and rural development policy will be articulated and mutually reinforce each other.

The book

This book is divided into 11 chapters, including this introductory chapter that sets the scene and a synthesis chapter that draws some major conclusions and lessons from the two theoretical and seven empirical chapters. The two theoretical chapters create the conceptual clarity of the phenomenon of 'nested markets'; the empirical chapters draw on recent research on the experiences of markets per se and nested markets in particular in a broad variety of spatial contexts. Together these chapters provide ample material from which to draw our conclusions about processes of rural development and market practices.

Chapter 2 also helps set the scene for the book. Comparative analyses of rural development experiences across the globe indicate that rural development increasingly occurs through the construction of nested markets. Van der Ploeg argues that it is necessary to revisit the notion of 'market' in order to conceptualize these newly emerging or nested markets. Despite the wide ranging differences in such markets, they share common characteristics. These commonalities are theoretically elaborated and the argument is supported by reference to a few examples of new, emerging experiences that help define the *nested* nature of these markets. Coming to grips with processes of *nesting* is essential in order to be able to document the experiences and dynamics of such markets. The features of established nested markets and the processes that give rise to the new ones are then drawn together in order to further elaborate the concept of the nested market.

Chapter 3 continues the discussion on how to conceptualize these markets. Milone and Ventura critique early theories about markets, from Smith and Pareto to new-institutional perspectives on markets, and build a new conception. Their chapter raises an essential point for understanding and appreciating the notion of a nested market: that they are made and constructed by people through collective action. Collective actions require human capital, a strong social capital and communication and information systems through which objectives and actions can be shared. This implies the need to create and strengthen tools for further enhancing human and social capital at a territorial level. Building cohesion at the local level enables communities and territories to pursue sustainability goals that have been defined and planned at the international level.

Chapter 4 explores two distinct, though interrelated, experiences with markets that hinge on institutional food purchases in Brazil. Both the Food Acquisition Programme and the National School Meals Programme are federal programmes with a nationwide scope but they follow quite distinct institutional trajectories. These programmes use different mechanisms for incorporating family farmers as suppliers of foodstuffs for public programmes but have the common feature of providing a stable market. The analysis focuses on the political and institutional dynamics that have allowed the family farming sector to receive preferential treatment in Brazil's public procurement. At the same time, it examines how these programmes have been implemented, specifically in balancing supply and demand and ensuring quality and availability. This involves a delicate balancing act: prioritizing purchasing from a specific group of suppliers while ensuring the achievement of food and nutritional security as a universal right.

Chapter 5 explores the role of collective action in the making of nested markets. The case of the Ecovida Network in Brazil deals with a group of family farmers cultivating crops according to agroecological principles. They are organized on a territorial basis and their mode of organization goes beyond sharing information and technical knowledge. Accessing and defending markets through self-labelling is an essential element. They use a participatory eco-labelling process to create a social-material infrastructure that supports this specific market. The authors examine the problems, benefits and drawbacks of such a construction. One of the challenges they currently face is the changing nature of the social relationships between the actors involved and what this might mean for prolonged cooperation and collective action.

Chapter 6, which focuses on experiences with nested markets in China, explores an interrelated phenomenon. Farmers in China also find it very difficult to improve their levels of income through engagement with the emergent large commodity markets for food. As a result, many Chinese farmers are engaging in new activities that meet new societal demands (attractive and accessible countryside, high quality food products) which also improve their incomes. These activities are underpinned by new market circuits that are nested in the general commodity markets. This chapter shows that these new, nested, markets are sometimes constructed by state agencies and sometimes by farmers themselves, working in close cooperation with urban actors. Two examples of such markets are explored. One is related to agritourism and highlights the important role of the state – especially when the level of intervention moves from the farm to the landscape level. The second example concerns the processing of sweet potatoes into glass noodles, a high quality food product that is much appreciated as gift during Chinese festivals. Farmers from a mountain village have established their own nested market, a process that involved labour migration and experts from China Agricultural University. The two cases differ in many respects. Nonetheless, both underpin the need to involve external actors when seeking to construct new nested markets. This applies especially at the early stages. Once a nested market is well-established, farmers can continue to manage it independently.

The issues and problems of multi-level territorial governance are discussed in Chapter 7. Van Broekhuizen and Oostindie link this with the dynamics of the unfolding of nested rural markets in Europe. Multi-level governance in rural Europe implies new meso-level institutional arrangements. These arrangements are used to implement the rural development policies initiated by the EU. Lessons from Sweden, Italy, Germany, Ireland and the Netherlands are used to develop an analytical tool, the 'rural policy performance triangle', which explores and explains the effectiveness of rural policy. This is then used to explore the experiences of farmers from the Laag-Holland region in the Netherlands with a view to understanding the underlying sets of mechanisms that influence the unfolding of nested rural markets.

Chapter 8 discusses a widely shared view among government, expert and academic circles in South Africa: that smallholder farmers need to be linked to mainstream markets, notably supermarkets. Supermarkets are the dominant suppliers of food to urban and peri-urban consumers and are extending their influence to smaller market towns. They are perceived as an ideal vehicle for rural development and for achieving the objectives of post-apartheid policies (supporting black empowerment and enhancing the lives of smallholder farmers). Yet a critical reflection on their role shows that they are not the ideal institution for meeting these goals as, for many reasons, it is difficult for small scale producers to acquire 'preferred supplier' status). This chapter explores the dynamics of other kinds of markets, such as street markets, that have emerged over time. These differ from the mainstream South African fresh produce network (the supermarkets) in terms of the relationships between producers, traders and consumers, the quality control and price setting mechanisms, and, most importantly, the distribution of benefits. From a developmental perspective the *alternative* fresh produce network is significant, because it generates high levels of local employment and offers better access to fresh produce for people living in the locale than supermarkets do. These alternative markets are seen as nested markets, the development and expansion of which has been accompanied by a change in policy from one that was highly interventionist and regulatory to one which is almost completely *laissez-faire*.

In Chapter 9, Matondi and Chikulo explore the role of markets in Zimbabwe. The central argument that runs through the chapter is that the recent land reform processes have boosted the emergence of new markets that can be viewed as nested. The chapter focuses on a region in Zimbabwe, the Lowveld, where land reform has created a radically different agrarian structure. The previous land owners, who were almost exclusively white large scale commercial farmers specialized in a few commodities and dominated the landscape for years. The market structures resonated with their interests and mode of production. When a group of new landowners, predominantly women, settled on the land, the institutional landscape was gradually transformed so as to better fit their approach to making a living in a new landscape that differed from that to which they were accustomed. The chapter explores these experiences in constructing markets which bear no resemblance to the mainstream market dynamics that existed before. The significance of the Zimbabwean case is that it underpins that new, 'nested' markets have the ability to enhance the autonomy of local social actors while they learn to master a new situation of autonomy through fostering a market culture which is very different from the previous state-controlled agribusiness relations.

Chapter 10 deals with fish markets in and around Lake Victoria in Tanzania. This case is significant because the commodity in question – fish – is a mobile resource; one that competes with other similar resources. The significance lies also in the processes of commoditization that were fuelled by the introduction of a predatory fish, the Nile perch. Nile perch feeds a global market, meeting global consumer demands and invokes Northern concerns about health and sustainability. All this shapes the way that fishing takes place, the trading opportunities that exist and how the fisheries are organized. The market is dominated by a few export processing facilities who exert tight control over fishing, fishermen, fish handlers and capital. A range of domestic, regional and local markets exist in the shadow of this global market: some of these are recent, while others have strong historical roots. These markets are dynamic and sustain a range of local livelihoods but are often ignored in economic analyses. These markets embody the counter-developments that Polanyi (1957) refers to: they differ from the global markets in that the added value is distributed differently, and this will have significant effects on rural development in and around the lake.

The last chapter ties together and elaborates on the main arguments developed in the various chapters. It also addresses the policy domain and identifies a number of key themes for the role of public policy in the construction and further unfolding of nested markets that can support rural livelihoods and rural development processes more effectively.

Notes

1 Multifunctionality is usually defined at farm level and multiple livelihoods are generally identified at the level of the homestead or household. Rural development is understood as a wider process that is articulated at the landscape or regional level. The development of multifunctionality and multiple livelihoods are one of the mechanisms that constitute the new and alternative process and trajectories of rural development.
2 This process is often understood as de-agarianization (Bryceson 2002a, 2002b). It is debatable whether this should be understood as being a structural, irreversible process or as a temporal one, which implies there are options and feasible trajectories for re-agrarianization (Hebinck and Van Averbeke 2007, van der Ploeg 2008). One the main theses of this book is that the construction of newly emerging 'nested' markets are part of a process that counters de-agrarianization and perhaps even contributes to a trajectory of re-agrarianization.
3 A recent publication (Kambewa *et al.* 2013) makes this point empirically.
4 Again, direct selling is far from a completely new phenomenon. It has been part of farming for many centuries. In the second half of the twentieth century direct selling became increasingly marginalized. The Second World War, the modernization of agriculture and the emergence of new veterinary diseases all contributed to this marked decrease. Since the mid-1990s this trend has been reversed. The construction of new, nested markets now goes far beyond direct selling. It involves joint actions, building new socio-material infrastructures and this allows far larger volumes to be traded.
5 This concept was first applied to the analysis of rural development processes by van der Ploeg *et al.* (2010, 2012). Previously the term had been used to describe markets as a 'nested institution' (Ostrom 1992, 2005). It builds on the notion that all markets are institutionally embedded and governed (Granovetter 1992). Consequently, the making of new, nested markets is about constructing new forms of governance.
6 The first meeting, in 2010, was hosted by ISMEA in Rome and organized by the Rete Rurale. The main contributions to this seminar were published as a special (English language) issue of the *Rivista di Economia Agraria* vol. 65. no 2, 2010). Subsequent seminars have been organised in Porto Alegre (2011) and Beijing (2012). This book draws on the proceedings of the Porto Alegre seminar.

References

Abramovay, R. (2004) 'Entre Deus e o Diabo – mercados e interação humana nas ciências sociais', *Tempo Social – Revista de Sociologia da USP*, 16: 35–64.

Ashley, C. and Maxwell, S. (2002). Rethinking rural development, *Development Policy Review*, 19: 395–425.

Bryceson, D. (2000) 'Peasant theories and smallholder policies: past and present', in D. Bryceson, C. Kay and J. Mooij (eds) *Disappearing Peasantries? Rural Labour in Africa, Asia and Latin America*, London: Intermediate Technology Publications.

Bryceson, D. (2002a) 'The scramble in Africa: reorienting rural livelihoods', *World Development*, 30: 725–739.

Bryceson, D. (2002b) 'Multiplex livelihoods in rural Africa: recasting the terms and conditions of gainful employment', *Journal of Modern African Studies*, 40: 1–28.

Coombes, B. and Campbell, H. (1998) 'Dependent reproduction of alternative modes of agriculture: organic farming in New Zealand', *Sociologia Ruralis*, 38: 127–145.

De Sardan, O. (2006) *Anthropology and Development: Understanding contemporary social change*, London: Zed Press.

Ellis, F. and Biggs, S. (2001) 'Evolving themes in rural development 1950s–2000', *Development Policy Review*, 19: 437–448.

Francis, E. (2000) *Making a Living: Changing livelihoods in rural Africa*, London: Routledge.

Goodman, D. and Dupuis, M. (2002) 'Knowing food and growing food: beyond the production–consumption debate in the sociology of agriculture', *Sociologia Ruralis*, 42: 5–22.

Granovetter, M. (1992) 'Economic action and social structure: the problem of embeddedness', in M. Granovetter and R. Swedberg (eds) *The Sociology of Economic Life*, Boulder: Westview Press.

Guthman, J. (2004) *Agrarian Dreams. The Paradox of Organic Farming in California*, Berkeley: University of California Press.

Hajer, M. (2003) 'Policy without polity? Policy analysis and institutional void', *Policy Sciences*, 36: 175–195.

Hebinck, P. and Cousins, B. (eds.) *In the Shadow of Policy: Everyday practices in South Africa's land and agrarian reform*, Johannesburg: Wits University Press.

Hebinck, P. and Lent, P. (eds) (2007) *Livelihoods and Landscape. The people of Guquka and Koloni and their resources*, Leiden/Boston: Brill Academic Publishers.

Hebinck, P. and Van Averbeke, W. (2007) 'Livelihoods and landscape: people, resources and land use', in: P. Hebinck and P. Lent (eds) *Livelihoods and Landscape: The people of Guquka and Koloni and their resources*, Leiden/Boston: Brill Academic Publishers.

Lie, J. (1997) 'Sociology of markets', *Annual Review of Sociology*, 23: 341–360.

Kambewa, E., Konlambigue, M., Wennink, B. and Wongtschowski, M. (2013) *Do All Roads Lead to Market? Lessons from AGRA's market access programme*, Amsterdam: Royal Tropical Institute and Alliance for Green Revolution in Africa.

Kydd, J. and Dorward, A. (2001) 'The Washington Consensus on poor country agriculture: analysis, prescription and institutional gaps', *Development Policy Review*, 19: 467–478.

Long, N. (2001) *Development Sociology: Actor perspectives*, London: Routledge.

Marsden, T. (1998) 'Agriculture beyond the treadmill? Issues for policy, theory and research practice', *Progress in Human Geography*, 22: 265–275.

McGee, R. (2004) 'Unpacking policy. Knowledge, actors and spaces', in K. Brock,

R. McGee and Gaventa, J. (eds) *Unpacking Policy: Knowledge, Actors and Spaces in poverty reduction in Uganda and Nigeria* Kampala: Fountain Books.

Milone, P. and Ventura, F. (2010) *Networking the Rural: The future of green regions in Europe*, Assen: Royal van Gorcum.

O'Connor, D., Renting, H., Gorman, M. and Kinsella, J. 2006. *Driving Rural Development: Policy and practice in seven EU countries*, Assen: Royal Van Gorcum.

Ostrom, E. (1992) *Crafting Institutions for Self-governing Irrigation Systems*, San Francisco: ICS.

Ostrom, E. (2005) *Understanding Institutional Diversity*, Princeton NJ: Princeton University Press.

Polanyi, K. (1957, 1st published 1944) *The Great Transformation*. Boston: Beacon Press.

Scott, J. C. (1998) *Seeing like a State: How certain schemes to improve the human condition have failed*, New Haven: Yale University Press.

van der Ploeg, J. D., Jingzhong, Y. and Schneider, S. (2010) 'Rural development reconsidered: Building on comparative perspectives from China, Brazil and the European Union', *Rivista di Economina Agraria*, 65: 164–185.

van der Ploeg, J.D., Jingzhong, Y. and Schneider, S. (2012) 'Rural development through newly emerging, nested, markets', *Journal of Peasant Studies*, 39:133–173.

Vihinen, H. and Kull, M. (2010). 'Policy implications to support rural development webs', in: P. Milone and F. Ventura (eds), *Networking the Rural, the future of green regions in Europe*, Royal Van Gorcum: Assen.

Watson, S. and Studdert, D. (2006) *Markets as Sites for Social Interaction. Spaces of diversity*. Bristol: The Policy Press.

2 Newly emerging, nested markets

A theoretical introduction

Jan Douwe van der Ploeg[1]

Comparative analysis of very different politico-economic spaces (China, Brazil and the European Union) indicates that rural development increasingly occurs through the construction of nested markets (van der Ploeg *et al.* 2010). Evidently, such rural development processes differ strongly (at least as far as their immediate objectives are concerned) as does the nature, dynamics and scope of the nested markets themselves. Nonetheless, these newly emerging markets also contain some very important common characteristics (van der Ploeg *et al.* 2012). In this chapter I aim to theoretically elaborate on these commonalities. I will illustrate my argument with a few examples of new, incipient experiences. I include these examples because they help to illustrate the process of *nesting* far more clearly than the better documented longstanding experiences. Features of the established nested markets and the processes that give rise to the new ones are then drawn together in order to further elaborate the concept of the nested market. Before doing so it is worth revisiting the generally held notion of 'the market'.

Markets are the places where, or the structures through which goods and services are exchanged. Markets connect producers and consumers – directly or indirectly – and in straightforward or highly complex ways. They are the places where transactions and the associated flows of commodities occur. These places might be contained in the local. They may as well extend to the global level. In that case we are facing complicated networks that organize commodity flows that go from one time-space location to another, often through complex and interrelated transactions. Equally the markets involve social relations, which can either be directly visible or highly anonymous. These relations pattern the flows of goods and services through time and space. These patterns are adapted to, and follow, specific socio-material infrastructures. Goods and services flow in specific ways, according to specific conditions and there are specific benefits and costs (transaction costs) related to these patterns. The distribution of transaction costs between the different parties and actors involved often differs and can be object of dispute, negotiation and re-negotiation.

Yet, these patterns can also contain 'structural holes': a term that refers to the flows that do *not* materialize and to the relations that are *not* created (or are being blocked, for whatever reason). The construction of new, nested markets can help to bridge such structural holes. New, nested markets can re-pattern the flow of a commodity and rearrange the sequence and nature of the transactions. When this occurs, complex market figurations emerge, in which (approximately) similar products and goods are moved, distributed and traded in contrasting ways, each following a different pattern. These patterns very often enter into competition with each other, with some expanding whilst others decline. But the characteristics of expanding patterns might also be taken over by the threatened patterns as a survival mechanism.

Rural development is a many faceted and highly dynamic process: over time it has changed its focus and direction. For example, in Europe, the emphasis was initially (from 1990 onwards) on the production of new goods and services alongside the standard agricultural activities. Multifunctionality emerged as a key word. For many farming families, engagement in new activities (such as agro-tourism, the production of regional specialties, the provision of care services, management of the landscape and biodiversity, etc.) proved to be a useful response to the squeeze on agriculture, and multifunctional farming also met several new needs of society as a whole. Although it evidently is impossible to draw a clear line of demarcation, it might be argued that from around 2000 the emphasis shifted. Now there is an increased attention on the *marketing* of the new goods and services. Distributing them through the general markets turns out to be increasingly counterproductive, if not outright impossible. Thus, a wide array of new mechanisms for distributing these products and services has been developed.

By now, there is an extensive and rich literature on new agro-food chains, short circuits and the like. This literature, however, misses a crucial point: that it is not, or not only, the *shortening* of the chains between producers and consumers (often carried forward under the logo of the local) that explains the current dynamics of rural development. It is, instead, the creation of *new markets* that function alongside or within the general agricultural and food markets and the subsequent creation of economic space that lies at the heart of current processes of rural development.[2] I will analyse these new markets here in terms of 'nested markets'. These are markets that are nested within the wider markets. They are part of the wider markets but differ from them in terms of their dynamics, their interrelations, forms of governance, price differentials, distributional mechanisms and overall impact.

A comprehensive overview

It is difficult to discuss the phenomenon of newly emerging, nested markets in a linear way. There is no one single starting point and a subsequent sequence of effects. Nor is there one, overall, ordering principle. Instead there are several different, but interacting, components that mutually shape each other and which only create the relevant differences when they are simultaneously present and operated together in a skilful way. Therefore, I opt to first present an overall view (synthesized graphically in Figure 2.1), then discuss the constituent elements individually and, finally, return to the constellation as a well-composed whole.

Figure 2.1 summarizes how the squeeze on agriculture (that follows from the patterns that govern the general agricultural and food markets) induces multi-functionality in farming: the multifunctional farm is an actively constructed response to this squeeze.[3] This applies in economic as well as in socio-cultural terms. A crucial factor in the success of the multifunctional farm is the construction of distinctiveness: the new products and services need to be different from the ones already circulating in the general agricultural and food markets. Achieving 'distinction' is fundamental. Products (or services) that are distinctive have the potential to realize a better price (or other, probably non-monetary, benefits). Of course, it is not only farmers who are looking for distinction. Distinction has many sources. In this text, though, I will limit myself to farm-related (or farm-based) distinction.

In turn, these distinctive products (and services) are distributed through, and valorized by, new nested markets. Just 'pouring' them into the general markets would be counterproductive (and often impossible): it would either frustrate the aim of getting better farm-gate prices or backfire through consumer prices being far too high (a consequence of the huge difference between producer and consumer prices within the general agricultural and food markets). Next, the nested markets critically require the development of socio-material infrastructures that make the products and services flow. These infrastructures are not only different from the ones reigning in the general commodity markets for food and agricultural products – *they strategically bridge the structural holes that characterize the latter.*

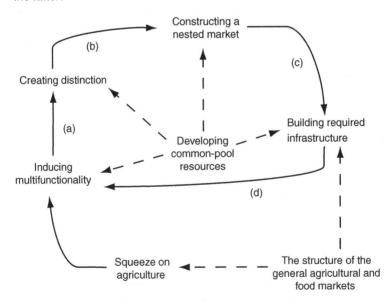

Figure 2.1 A conceptual representation of the newly emerging constellations.

Once adequate socio-material infrastructures have been developed they can considerably strengthen the impact and further development of multifunctionality at the farm level, possibly creating a new virtuous circle (composed by relations a, b, c and d in Figure 2.1). Additional income is earned, which might trigger the design and development of a wider array of new products and services (or greatly improve the existing ones); the nested markets become consolidated, thus allowing for more turn-over and/or a wider assortment of products and services; the same markets allow for further market research (mostly occurring through learning-by-doing) that may result in further growth; and the reputation that is gained helps to enlarge the distinctiveness of the involved products and services.

Common-pool resources play a key role in these dynamics. As indicated by the dashed arrows, distinction is constructed and functions as a common-pool resource. The distinctiveness of new products and services is neither private property, nor a common good. It is a common-pool resource that links many different stakeholders: farmers, processors, distributors, clients and – sometimes – local and regional authorities and NGOs. The distinction entailed in a particular product relates back to the distinctiveness of producers, their resources and the way production is organized. The same distinction is also transferred to the consumers who acquire the product or service. They distinguish themselves, as it were, through its acquisition and consumption. The nested markets and the embodied socio-material infrastructures are also common-pool resources, as I will argue further on.

The position of the general agricultural and food markets in Figure 2.1 is twofold: on the one hand they induce the search for multifunctionality and the creation of new markets; on the other *they allow for it*, due to the presence of *structural holes*. This implies, in the first place, that the development of multifunctionality (or in more general terms: the process of rural development) cannot be reduced to voluntarism. It does not solely depend on the willingness and other individual attributes of the involved actors. It is rooted in, and emerges from, the imperfections of the general commodity markets (imperfections that show up here as 'structural holes'). Second, this double relationship points to a very important socio-political feature: that these complex and interlocking markets increasingly constitute an important arena for socio-political struggles.

Distinction

Distinction can be constructed along different dimensions. It might be created along the price dimension. That is, the products might be distinctively cheaper (or far more expensive). I will focus here on products that are cheaper than those channelled through the general agricultural and food markets. A good example is the *mercati contadini* (peasant markets), which are dotted all over the city of Rome. Farmers transport their produce directly to these markets. A key feature of these markets is the provision of digitally provided information[4] (sometimes printed, sometimes on an electronic display board) comparing the average selling prices in the surrounding supermarkets and the average price on the farmers' market itself. The latter is referred to as *prezzo amico*, i.e. the price paid between friends. On the whole the prices on these farmers' markets are some 20 to 30 per cent below the supermarket level. Nonetheless, this price is still far higher than the farmer would receive if selling to traders that provide the companies operating in the general market. The creation of these peasant markets is being actively supported by local and regional authorities.

A second import dimension is product quality. Alongside well-known quality products with a long history (such as *Parmigiano-Reggiano* cheese and *Chianina* meat in Italy, *boerenkaas* in the Netherlands) that are rooted in longstanding, and often extended, nested markets, there is a wide and steadily expanding range of newly constructed quality products. A third dimension on which distinctiveness might be acquired is through the process of primary production. Organic products are a point in case. In more general terms a distinctively different process of production can create distinctive products. A fourth and fifth dimension emerge in the social organization of time and space. Freshness makes a product distinctive compared to products that embody long time lapses between production and consumption. Local origin (and, consequently, short transportation distances) represents distinctiveness on the spatial dimension. Exotic products do the same, but are, by contrast, often associated with long distances. And finally we might identify a sixth dimension: availability. When a product is difficult to find its scarcity can provide a specific distinctiveness: as not everybody is able to find and/or acquire it.

In practice these dimensions of distinction will very often combine and do so in many ways. Together, these dimensions can be seen as spanning a six-dimensional space that allows for many different positions, each representing specific forms and levels of distinction. This makes distinction a matter of degree: the number of dimensions involved and the specific position on each of them will continuously differ (Barjolle *et al.* 1998; Casabianca *et al.* 2005; Rocchi and Romano 2006).

There is yet another space where the distinction embodied in specific products plays a major role; this is the field composed by the transactions that help to pass the distinctive product between different actors. A distinctive product requires consumers who are able to appreciate the distinction that is incorporated in the product. This distinction passes from the product to those who buy it through the transaction by which the product is acquired. The purchasers show themselves, as well as others, that they have the necessary cultural capital to recognize and acquire distinction. The same applies to those who produce (and process and distribute) the product. They are distinctive producers (processors etc.) because they are able to build distinction into the product; consequently they often receive positive feedback from their consumers. It might be argued that this creates reciprocal relationships of symbolic giving-and-receiving that ties producers and consumers together in a social network.

Theoretically, distinction assumes multi-tiered chains of exchanges. The two-way flow of products, going one way, and money, going the other, is embedded in a wider set of relationships, summarized in Figure 2.2. The central tier (level 2) illustrates the material exchanges and aspects of distinction: products for money and vice versa. Distinctiveness is a socio-material feature. It is socially defined (see level 1), and then materially built into the product by the primary producer and the processor. But the distributors and consumers also relate to the 'material' side. If they mishandle the product (lack of care, exposure to heat, improper preparation or whatever), the distinctiveness is lost. Level 1 (closely intertwined to the other levels)[5] illustrates the exchange of information, expectations, possibilities and the associated feedback and 'feed forward' mechanisms. Level 1 therefore illustrates the social definition of the qualities that together create the distinction that consumers (and producers) are looking for (for an extended analysis see Meulen and Ventura 1994, and Meulen 2000). Without a properly functioning level 1 the required distinction cannot be materially constructed and the associated transactions at level 2 would not be possible. However, and this is especially important in longstanding nested markets, these processes can become strongly institutionalized. This gives the product and its producers a vested reputation, with trust becoming the main characteristic of the relations between consumers and producers.

Level 3 represents a shift away from levels 1 and 2. It focuses on actors and culture, not on the product or transactions; it shows how distinction is transferred from the producers, via the product, towards the consumers and how this transfer is connected with a reverse flow of appreciation that attributes distinction to the producer. Level 3 implies that the social identity of clients and consumers is jointly defined by the specific transactions and the circuits in which they occur.

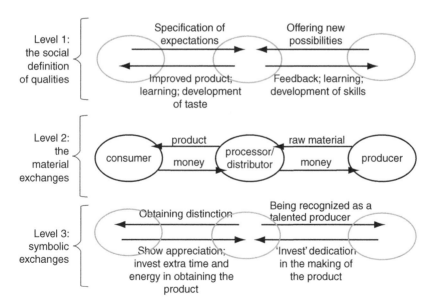

Figure 2.2 Multi-tiered processes of exchange.

On level 3 distinction translates into new connections between people, places and practices (Wijffels 2011).

Taken together level 1 and level 3 constitute a social network.[6] Level 2, the actual transactions, is embedded (or 'nested') in, and crucially dependent on, such a social network. It is the social network (composed by and through the *social* definition of qualities and the associated symbolic exchanges, including trust and reputation) that make the distinctive processes materially flow. They provide, as it were, the river bed that makes the water flow (and which allows the salmon and trout to swim upstream to spawn). In short, level 2 transactions are 'social network based exchanges' (Fafcamps 2004: 17).[7]

Figure 2.2 also raises another set of considerations. Several of the activities that occur on levels 1 and 3 can be understood, within a neo-institutional framework, as transaction costs (Saccomandi 1998). For example, within the general food markets, the 'specification of expectations' occurs through market research, which examines what consumers want and how they perceive specific products. This kind of market research is relatively costly. In new, nested markets, however, it occurs through the small-talk that occurs during shopping. The distributor (who is sometimes the same person as the producer) is directly informed by the customers. For the actors involved these small dialogues are often pleasurable exchanges but they can also be highly informative. The same applies to 'offering new possibilities'. In conventional circuits this occurs through advertising. In nested markets it is the producer (or distributor) who directly informs clients and word-of-mouth campaigns will probably follow. Within the general food markets, expensive advertising campaigns (and sometimes take-back operations whenever products contain defects) are needed to establish reputation. In stark contrast, the reputation of producers in nested markets is sustained by their direct visibility and the transparency of the process of production (sustained, for instance, by organized farm visits). In short: whereas the general agricultural and food markets are largely characterized by relatively high transaction costs, such costs tend to be relatively low in the nested markets which commercialize distinctive products. They sometimes even go below zero: that is, they are converted into positive benefits. Searching for distinction can be, on occasion, a joy – experienced as a positive contribution to the definite transaction. This is the case with many elderly people who turn the act of shopping into pleasure by e.g. biking to a nearby farm shop, finding out about the quality of the meat and the way the cattle has been raised and then preparing a nice dinner where they can tell their guests about the lovely meat they got from 'their farmer' (as they often say). Now, this may sound terribly romantic, but it helps to highlight how *transaction costs within social networks tend to be low or can even be converted into benefits*. This applies not only to the cycling elderly (who may be more numerous in the Netherlands than elsewhere), but to a very wide range of people and situations. *In this way a competitive advantage is created.*[8]

Nested markets and infrastructures

A nested market is a segment of a wider market. It is a specific segment that typically displays different price levels, distributional patterns of the total Value Added and relations between producers, distributors and consumers than those seen in the wider market. This segment is nested in a wider market. It is part of, but at the same time it differs from it. The market for e.g. agro-tourism services is embedded in (i.e. a segment of) the general market for tourist services. At the same time it differs from this general market – not only because the services being produced and consumed are distinctively different, but also because the way they are *distributed* is distinctively different. The same applies to regional products, high-quality products, organic products (at least partly) as well as to care-services offered by farming families and decentralized forms of bio-energy production. To make the point clear: distinctive products are not mainly (or exclusively) marketed through existing markets and the associated market-chains. Their distribution, i.e. the way they flow through time and space, from producers to consumers, and the way in which this flow is connected with associated flows of money and meaning (see again Figure 2.2) – all this is, in synthesis, patterned differently. In short, we are talking about different *markets*. It is precisely this point that is missed in most contributions to the debate, In her 'critical reflections', Angela Tregear (2011) discusses 'marketplace trading' only in terms of the particular socio-psychological attributes that stem from direct buyer-seller interactions (e.g. "depth, reciprocity, intimacy [...] and community vibrancy"). David Goodman (2004) does the same,[9] but from a diametrically opposed position when he refers to "the capitalist *instincts* of farmer-vendors" (italics added). All this might be true, or not. But it definitely does not define the particular *markets*.

These newly emerging and distinctively different markets are delineated by particular boundaries. Mostly these are permeable: new producers might enter, others can leave: the total number can go up or down, or remain stable. The same applies to the total turn-over realized in any particular segment and to the number of consumers. This relative permeability represents one of the main differences between niche markets and the nested markets discussed here. A niche market has fixed and non-permeable boundaries; a nested market has flexible boundaries that might very well change over time. Beyond this, a niche market often associates with rigidity (due to regulatory schemes), whilst nested markets show considerable flexibility and innovativeness.

The boundaries of nested markets are co-defined by the distinctiveness of goods and services, the social networks through which they flow and the created competitive advantages. Other possible elements that may help to delineate boundaries, include certification, the particular organization of time and space, links with social movements and the particular socio-material infrastructure of these markets. Every particular nested market is characterized by a specific combination of these elements and this combination can change over time. It develops, indeed, just as a nest is built: the available pieces of straw, feathers, twigs and debris are gathered and intertwined in a goal-oriented way until a protective shield is constructed that allows, in the end, for eggs to be laid and hatched and young birds to get their strength.

Nested markets create, and are rooted in, socio-material infrastructures that help to delineate, and simultaneously structure and sustain, the new markets. Building upon earlier work (van der Ploeg, Ye and Schneider 2012) such socio-material infrastructures can be defined as the set of specific artefacts and rules that are used to channel flows of goods and services between places and people. These artefacts and rules are tied together into a coherent and smoothly functioning whole that defines a particular pattern of connectedness. Different socio-material infrastructures can co-exist alongside each other. This also explains how different markets can co-exist and co-evolve within the same time-space constellation. A market is not only an abstract system of prices, preferences, supply, demand and automatically generated equilibriums (this would exclude the presence of a plurality of markets). A market is also about concrete transactions between concrete people who exchange concrete products according to concrete infrastructural patterns. Supermarkets for instance are selling points that belong to a wider socio-material infrastructure within which centralized purchasing, radial and just-in-time distribution patterns (based around national distribution centres and linked to 'local' supermarkets through regional hubs), long distant transport, cooling facilities and complex planning systems are key elements. Cooperating farm shops represent a strongly contrasting pattern that is not radial but circular; not centralized but governed through many interacting local *loci* of control; not disconnected from the local but linking production and consumption through short distances in time and space. Consumers' expectations of (the kind of qualities they are looking for) also differ considerably. In short, these are two contrasting socio-material infrastructures that constitute two concrete but significantly different markets: two different patterns that make commodities flow in a contrasting way.

I will try to elaborate the notion of socio-material infrastructure, and the related notion of *nesting* (i.e. *building* new, nested markets), through a discussion of lamb meat and the ways in which it is marketed, as shown in Figure 2.3.

Once Texel's lamb was an unambiguous product. It was lamb from the Texel breed, born, raised and slaughtered on the island of Texel. It was known for its distinctive quality and taste. It was the product of a particular actor-network in which local breed, local ecology (characterized by the influences of the North and the Wadden Seas), local skills, local slaughter houses, local butcheries and local restaurants all played an important, if not indispensable, role. Sometimes, when droughts caused shortage of roughage, the sheep and lambs had to be transported to the meadows of the nearby mainland of North Holland. This immediately triggered changes in the quality, taste and flavour of the lamb meat – a phenomenon that underscored the tightness of the actor-network.

In the epoch of globalization and de-regulation, many of these once unambiguous notions have been torn apart. In the case of Texel's lamb these came down to the following points.

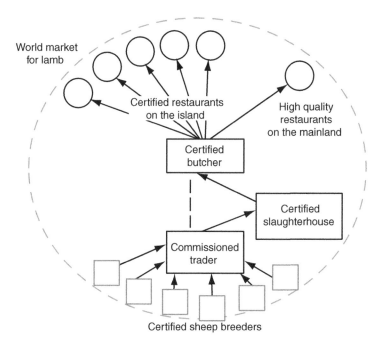

Figure 2.3 The socio-material infrastructure of the market for Texel lamb.

1   The Texel breed is now raised on a considerable scale in New Zealand. This
    implies a disconnection between the breed and local ecology, which is
    reflected in the qualities of the end product.

2   Among the massive exports of New Zealand lamb to Europe there is also a
    large flow of 'Texel's lamb' (which indeed stems from the Texel breed but
    it is raised and slaughtered in New Zealand). The meat is distributed to
    butcheries and restaurants all over the country from Rotterdam. The price is,
    on average, far lower than lamb meat originating from Texel. In some cases
    New Zealand lamb that is not from the Texel breed may also be passed off
    as Texel's lamb.

3   Restaurants (even on Texel) prepare the imported meat and present it as
    Texel's lamb, thus obtaining an lucrative (and unwarranted) extra benefit
    that relates to the low purchase price (of lamb produced in New Zealand)
    and the high selling price grounded in the notion of Texel origin.

It will be evident that these points (together with many others) create a particular
socio-material infrastructure that spans the world through a global network and
within which price differences, the capacity to link cheap production spaces to
rich consumption spaces, refrigerated ships, large slaughterhouses and storing
facilities, are major components. These combine with the indifference and/or
ignorance of the wider public about quality and origin of lamb meat, and the

difficulty in tracing back the products. As a consequence, the inferior products tend to drive out the superior ones (all along the lines of the 'lemon' scenario of Akerlof, 1970). This seriously threatened the continuity of lamb production on Texel and, consequently, of other values as well. Dikes would no longer be maintained through grazing sheep and the attractiveness of the island as a whole for tourists would get reduced qith the disappearance of sheep breeding.

In this doomful panorama, a new notion was developed: 'Real Texel's Lamb'.[10] This is again lamb from the Texel breed, raised on the island itself (according to explicit criteria developed by the actors involved), and also processed and distributed on the island (and beyond). 'Real Texel's Lamb' is not just a return to the past. It is radically new, especially in as far as it is meant to face and to withstand the cheap imports from New Zealand. To achieve this a new socio-material infrastructure was required. The novel element of it resides in the simultaneous certification of all participating *actors* instead of only certifying the *product*, as happens most of the time. It is not only the breeders who are certified, but also the slaughterhouse, the butchery and the restaurants. Thirty-six restaurants (ranging from low priced popular eating houses to starred restaurants) indicate on their menus (and on the front wall of the restaurant and web-sites) that they offer Real Texel's Lamb. This might reduce their profit per dish, but it considerably enlarges their reputation and the flow of customers. The certified butchery (that delivers to the restaurants) also sells directly to the public (returning tourists and inhabitants of the island), whilst meat is sent, on request, in cool boxes, to restaurants on the main land. All the meat sold (3,000 lambs are distributed and processed as Real Texel's Lamb; compared to the total yearly production on the island of 15,000 lambs) is obtained from certified breeders (23 in total) who follow the specifications for certification. Supply and demand are coordinated by the butcher (and a commissioned trader who operates on behalf of the butcher). All Real Texel's Lamb is slaughtered in a certified local slaughterhouse (whilst most of the other animals are slaughtered on the mainland). Taken together (as shown in Figure 2.3) these elements and their interrelations *compose a specific socio-material infrastructure* that sustains (and delineates) a new, nested market that is not only able to face down New Zealand competition but which has shown the capacity to grow from year to year and to extend into new domains through several novelties. Flexibility and stability are important features of this new pattern. At first sight such features seem to be contradictory, but here they are aligned. There is flexibility in as far as all the involved partners can also produce, process and/or trade and sell non-certified lamb products, on the condition that this is clearly indicated. There is stability in that trust, distinctive quality (here the commissioned trader, the slaughter and the butcher play a key role) and reputation make for a stable (and even growing) demand. There is further flexibility and stability due to the butchery converting the less 'noble' parts (the noble parts mainly go to the restaurants) into a range of processed products that add further value. The same combination is reflected in the use of the wool for newly developed Texel's eiderdowns (or quilts). There are additional gains in stability in that price drops are considerably cushioned, especially at the farm level. And finally there is a range of additional benefits at the level of the island as a whole (in terms of maintained scenic beauty, dike maintenance, employment, typical cuisine, etc.) which explains why local and regional authorities increasingly support the initiative.

The magnitude and strength of nested markets

Newly emerging, nested markets might seem, at least at first sight, like David pitted against the Goliath of the general markets for food and agricultural products. In mainstream thought this often translates into 'powerful and promising' versus 'insignificant and marginal'. 'As sympathetic as they may be, such small initiatives never can feed big cities (or the world, for that matter)'.[11]

The case of Real Texel's Lamb is a perfect tool to unravel the fallacy entailed in such reasoning. Compared to the total flow of lamb meat from the island, Real Texel's Lamb does indeed represent a relatively small segment (3,000 of 15,000). And when compared to the flow from New Zealand (the biggest provider of lamb meat on the world market) it is less than microscopic. This is partly (but only partly) due to the very recent start of the initiative discussed. All new things start from scratch: even the Philips conglomerate (now a global player) started in a backyard shed. The nested market for Real Texel's Lamb is unlikely to follow this trajectory. But this is not the point: Real Texel's Lamb is not intended to *replace* the general market for lamb meat; it is not meant to become the next 'global provider' with a market share equal to the one that now belongs to New Zealand lamb meat. It is a *local* initiative and due to the characteristics of the local it contains clear quantitative boundaries (that are often narrowed further by explicit criteria on e.g. sustainability). *But the juxtaposition and connection of many such markets that are nested in – and therefore confined to – the local, might come to provide a genuine alternative for the general market as it is currently constituted.*

If we examine the general markets for food and agricultural products in more detail we can see that they are far from being, as is commonly assumed, massive spot markets that cover extended parts of the globe. While some commodities (like New Zealand lamb) do indeed travel all over the world, most products' circulation is regional or local. Only 15 per cent or so of all the food produced in the world crosses international borders. The notion of a 'world market' does not imply that all products travel great distances (or that all products are produced for global exports). Nonetheless, the remaining 85 per cent is still part and parcel of the world market (or the 'general market for food and agricultural products' as I have phrased it so far). The 'world market' is primarily a metaphor that is used to describe global modes of governance that (1) impose one and the same set of global regulations and parameters on transactions, *wherever and whenever they take place*, and that (2) simultaneously centralize the value flows through a few nodes. This 'world market' (or 'general market') does not displace local transactions (or chains of interconnected local transactions), but makes them subject to an overarching set of requirements and rules (whilst simultaneously reshuffling many of the material flows). In short: what we usually refer to as 'world market' is shorthand for the subordination of local and regional processes of production, circulation and consumption of food to the needs, rules and interests of global players. The latter (together with the WTO, neo-liberal states, etc.) constitute a global mode for governing transactions – wherever these are located and regardless of the way in which they are interconnected (or not).

A few examples will help illustrate the dynamics of this constellation and show that it increasingly are, indeed, a few central nodes that order and re-order it. Let us assume a local markets in Austria for organic potatoes. Let another market be the Dutch market for organic potatoes. Exporting organic potatoes from Austria to the Netherlands would be an insane operation. If the Dutch are capable of anything it is potato growing – organic or otherwise. And due to ecological and material conditions they probably can do it far cheaper than Austrian farmers. Anyone arranging such an export operation (say a large supermarket chain) could lose some (or even a considerable amount of) money with such a transaction, but might simultaneously gain tenfold by stimulating a reduction in the price of organic Dutch potatoes.[12] It is similarly in the paper industry, where some of the main enterprises own and control large production forests. Taken in isolation these might represent permanent losses, but by bringing the raw material to the market for wood pulp at strategic moments, they might earn tenfold through provoking a slump in the price of wood pulp at a given time.

Expressed in another way, the 'world market' increasingly represents an obligatory passage point for agricultural products. Production and consumption (wherever localized) can only be linked through globally operating networks (represented by global players) – and the establishment of such a link requires the acceptance of globally defined parameters, regulations, etc.

Within this framework, the issue of the newly emerging markets can be clarified further. These new nested markets represent a 'by-pass': they relink production, processing, distribution and consumption in ways that are (at least relatively) independent from globally controlled networks. What I discussed before as 'bridges', can also be seen as 'by-passes' – in that they help to avoid a long detour (that goes via different global hubs) and provide a literal short-cut. Nested markets reconstitute, as it were, local and regional markets through short-cutting past the obligatory passage points of the general commodity markets. In this respect, they represent new and contrasting modes of governance. They are nested in new networks and distinctive qualities and are sustained by new socio-material infrastructures. This means that their strengths do not reside in their magnitude. On the contrary, their confinement often provides an element of their strength. This is due to their characteristic (again in contrast to the 'global markets') of acting like (numerous) classical *spot markets*: markets with many suppliers and many buyers interacting personally with each other.[13] The newly emerging nested markets represent, in a way, a return to the spot market. 'For all the supposed dominance of the abstract market, concrete marketplaces [again start] to flourish, not least because of popular demand' (Aldridge 2005: 39).

Infrastructures and structural holes

In the social sciences attention is normally focused on social relations, how they are patterned into specific networks (or 'structures'), the impact this has on social action and how these structural patterns are reproduced (or changed) through these actions. Social relations connect, they allow transactions, communication and flows of information to occur. Different parts of the world and different fields are interlocked through specific social relations, thus creating different forms of interdependency and interaction.

There is a flipside to social relations. That is the *lack* of social relations. These are referred to as 'structural holes' (Burt 1992). Such a hole 'is a buffer, like an insulator in an electronic circuit' (ibid.: 18). A structural hole is identical to the absence of social relations, it is a 'chasm' (ibid.: 28). Building on the Texel example, it could be argued that the processes of globalization and de-regulation have resulted in the creation of at least two such structural holes (or 'chasms'). The first structural hole was created between the meadows and dikes of Texel and the Texel sheep breed: sheep and lambs started to disappear from the island. A second structural hole emerged between the remaining sheep breeders (using the Texel breed) on Texel and the local restaurants selling Texel's lamb (that was imported from New Zealand). Following Granovetter, Burt introduces the notion of 'bridging'[14]: 'a bridge is at once two things: it is a chasm spanned and the span itself' (1992: 28). In our previous example the notion of Real Texel's Lamb (and the underlying socio-material infrastructure) clearly represents such a bridge. Bridging 'provides network benefits that are in some degree additive rather than overlapping' (ibid.:18). That is, the benefits are felt on both sides of the divide.

Historically, the bridging of structural holes has often been the result of the construction of new markets. Once, the lives of rural women in the North of the Netherlands and the luxury textile shops of the main Dutch cities were completely separate worlds. Going to shop 'over there' represented evil: it would have been an embarrassment, a squandering of one's money. And the shopkeepers in their turn would not go to the 'filthy and greedy' countryside. But then the 'walking patch-sellers' made their appearance. They typically came from elsewhere (in this case the north of Germany). They walked around with large baskets filled with all kind of patches, buttons, yarn and the like, going from farm to farm, not just once but reappearing every two months or so. In this way they constructed a new market, a market that later gave rise to national textile chains such as Peek & Cloppenburg. The role of the walking patch-sellers was crucial: they embedded the selling and buying of textiles (including the luxury cloths) into a new socio-material infrastructure. Buying nice cloth was disconnected from going to the pools of vanity (i.e. the cities of the time) and step-by-step became an ordinary part of daily life in the countryside. This new notion (ref. level 3 in Figure 2.2) became strong enough to transfer, in the end, the selling point to the cities.

Traditional communities are often very isolated from the outside world through taboos on contact. Bridging the structural holes that this creates is something that is mostly done by outsiders (Long 1977). These middlemen or traders connect previously separated value circuits.[15] By doing so they create value and trigger economic growth (Barth 1967). And, they improve their own livelihoods. To underpin this latter point Burt uses the notion of the *tertius gaudens* (the 'laughing third party'). 'The *tertius* establishes new negotiational relations; he extracts value and he adds value, strengthening the relations for later profit'. As such, the *tertius gaudens* is 'an entrepreneur in the literal sense of the word – a person who generates profit from being between others' (Burt 1992: 34). The *tertius gaudens* goes where others don't go. Structural holes are entrepreneurial opportunities and the *tertius* creates competitive advantage by bridging these.[16]

Alongside and in between the many, often highly complicated, and partly overlapping structural patterns that characterize today's economy, there is a plenitude of structural holes. This also, and maybe especially, applies to the structure of markets. Here, the holes result from the specific actions of those playing a central role in these markets and, in a way, reproducing them.[17]

The thesis I will bring forward here is that the newly emerging, nested markets discussed so far are the outcome of bridging. They are bridges that connect hitherto separated parts of the world. And those who construct these bridges might indeed be analyzed in terms of the *tertius gaudens*. That is, the multifunctional farmers of today, and especially those who succeed in creating new nested markets, are the *tertius gaudens* of our time. Before returning to these new, nested markets it might be helpful, though, to reconsider an historical example: the entrance of Japanese and Korean enterprises into the US markets during the 1970s and 1980s. The example shows how structural holes are created by vested interests and subsequently used as a new opportunity by newcomers.

Willard and Savara (1988) empirically show how the penetration of, and, in the end, the nearly complete take-over of market segments can result in the creation of a wide range of structural holes.[18] In the case of tractors, for instance, the main US industries focused on the production of large and powerful machines. This was mainly due to reports forecasting ongoing scale increases in farming and the assumed need to greatly increase labour productivity through further mechanisation. Smaller tractors for smaller farmers were seen as an unattractive and disappearing segment of the market. In retrospect it is clear that by '*defining one's market too narrowly*' (Willard and Savara 1988: 59), a structural hole was created that subsequently became a 'window of opportunity' for foreign competitors. This window included the many remaining small farmers, house owners with large lawns that need frequent mowing and enterprises that need small tractors for specialized operations. Another structural hole was created because the American industries opted for those segments that 'allow for skimming' (i.e. the imposition of relatively high prices as opposed to 'penetration prices') (ibid.: 67, 68). A third structural hole identified by Willard and Savara resulted from the 'follow the leader strategy':

If a market segment is perceived by a major competitor to be too small to be interesting, few will attempt to serve it for fear that others will follow, causing the small segment to become overly competitive and therefore unprofitable.

(ibid.: 67)

Thus, windows of opportunity were created for new competitors. Entering these 'windows' allowed the latter to avoid direct competition ('not competing head-on with market leaders' (p. 61)). 'To strike at the corners of the enemy's force' (Musashi 1974) turned out to be more beneficial. Thus, new strongholds were created that allowed, in combination with a keen development of infrastructure[19] and well-balanced price–quality relations, for the later establishment of market hegemony.

The current agricultural and food markets are accompanied by (if not result-ing in the creation of) extended and expanding structural holes. The first dimen-sion of these holes lies in the very process of value adding by the food industries and supermarket chains; this results in growing *distances* between producers and consumers. Currently, producers interact with banks, suppliers, traders, firms' representatives and drivers; but *as producers* they do not interact with consum-ers. The same applies to consumers: they may interact with cashiers in the super-market or the occasional assistant that helps to find a product – but they do not interact with producers, let alone *as a consumer*. In short: there is a structural hole between producers and consumers.

It is precisely this hole that is being bridged by new, nested markets. The newly developed institution of *farmers' markets* bring the producers to the urban centres and allows them to establish direct contacts with consumers – contacts that may well result in stable social relations.[20] The farmers' market is a socio-material infrastructure (a physical marketplace combined with a particular set of rules) that allows producers and consumers to engage in what the infrastructure provided by supermarkets makes physically impossible i.e. direct interaction. *Farm shops*, a comparable institution, bring consumers towards the producers, thus also (re-)establishing direct social relations.[21] To slightly paraphrase Bourdieu (2005:20). One might argue that both institutions are grounded on

the will to create places embedded in more or less stable social relations where different flows of merchandise, people, information, status, etc., will be concentrated; where experiments will take place, introducing and testing new products [...]. It is a collective project [...]. Such a market may become a locus of cohesion, and integration, of affection, satisfaction and routine.

A second dimension along which structural holes are apparent is the fear of renewal. Many agro-industries keep the innovations they have developed under 'lock and key'. Introducing them could be too disruptive,[22] it could break the well-established routines of the salesmen or run counter to the interests of stock-holders who prefer to stay in well-established markets that allow for 'skimming'.

This creates new windows of opportunity for those who enter the market with novel, i.e. distinctive products.

A third dimension relates to the social organization of time and space.[23] The food products that are being distributed through the general food markets increasingly travel long distances through time and space. This is especially the case in supermarket chains that are supplied through (trans) national distribution systems, where depots that organize the transfer of merchandise between arriving and departing lorries, play a major role. Extended time and space distances are unavoidable here. They are even needed to allow for the cheapest possible supply (and more generally to impose the same set of parameters in every selling point).[24] Thus, radial patterns emerge: merchandise is brought from everywhere to one or a few hubs and then redistributed to everywhere. From one perspective this system is very impressive: the art of logistics developed to a very high level. 'Ordering and tracking' allow for detailed control and ongoing adjustments. However, there is a price to pay as well: many 'fresh' products are harvested long before they are ripe in order to allow for long distance travel. This translates in undeniable losses in taste, flavour, smell and quality. Second, products are handled by non-specialized people (who are insufficiently acquainted with product qualities and the care required). Together these features create a third problem: relatively frequent and high losses. It is estimated that some 30 per cent of fruits and vegetables are thrown away. Finally, there is considerable standardization within the range of offered products: the exceptional is lost.

Together these features delineate a structural hole: fresh products 'from local gardens and fields' (Braudel, 1992:29) do not reach the market anymore. Huge differences between prices paid to fruit and vegetable growers and those paid by consumers are another aspect of this structural hole, which, in a way, increasingly translates to the normative level as well: fair trade seems to be impossible in such a situation.

Willem & Drees is a recent Dutch initiative that aims to bridge this void. It is especially interesting in as far as it is not organized alongside, or even in opposition to, supermarkets (as the farmers' markets and farm shops discussed before). It aims, instead, at a particular *symbiosis*. Willem & Drees bridges a chasm. It delivers what supermarkets themselves cannot organize (due to the particular socio-material infrastructure of which they are part). Willem & Drees provides supermarkets with *fresh* fruits and vegetables.

The organizing principle is represented by a range of partly overlapping circles that symbolize product flows that go from the local to the local (local–local). The flows remain within 'their' circle. It is telling that the selling points of the supermarket chains are referred to as 'local supermarkets'.[25] The local–local transactions (the radius of each circle is 30 kilometres, with the central point coinciding with a 'local supermarket') contrast with the local–global–local flows of the general food market. The pioneers who designed this local–local delivery system (both worked for more than 10 years as marketeers for Unilever and Heineken and are highly knowledgeable about the mechanics of markets) calculated that the break-even point for one small lorry coincides with the delivery of 30 'local supermarkets', whilst 120 allow for a regional distribution centre.[26] At the moment some 100 different products, from 75 growers, are delivered to 90 local supermarkets. The participating farmers receive prices that often are twice, sometimes even four times as high as the prices paid by the general markets. Consumer prices, on the other hand, are not far beyond those for competing products. This is because the supermarkets accept a lower margin (25 per cent versus the normal 50 per cent), because Willem & Drees is taking over the activities that are otherwise done by the supermarkets (the trade function, novel presentation, quality control, risk taking, etc.). The logistics of Willem & Drees' operation are far from simple. Quality, supply security and the local–local principle constantly need to be brought in line. It is a process that implies complex, sometimes difficult trade-offs.

Thus we have, once again, all the elements elaborated so far together in one single experience. There is distinction (grounded in freshness and taste). There are newly constructed markets (represented by the circles around the 'local' supermarkets). These markets are nested in the consumers' search for freshness, in the capacity of growers to deliver high quality, in the willingness of some supermarket chains to distinguish themselves from main chains such as Albert Heijn and in the capacity of Willem & Drees to run complex logistics. The Willem & Drees certificate (and the novel ways of presenting the products) are additional elements that help differentiate the nested market from the general one. There is also a particular socio-material infrastructure (local–local) that is decisively distinct from that of the general market (local–global–local). Finally, there is the background – a specific structural hole within the general market – that explains the rise, structure and dynamics of this particular experience. These are the same elements (summarized in Figure 2.1) that are present in, and which together explain, the other examples discussed in this text. And time and again it is clear that these new experiences function well and prosper because *all* these elements are present, cleverly tied into one seamless whole.

'To discover a gap in the market' is the everyday language used to describe market opportunities. The notions of this proverbial 'gap' and that of a 'structural hole' partly coincide. But there are important differences as well. A 'gap' is just there, awaiting somebody clever enough to 'fill' it with a new product. Once this is done, the order of the market is restored: there is no gap anymore. Instead, when we refer to a structural hole there is far more than just a coincidental and neutral gap. A structural hole is the result of the limitations implied by the strategies of the dominant players. The latter shape the market in a particular way and particular holes are an intrinsic outcome of this. The next difference relates to 'filling' versus 'bridging'. According to popular discourse (embodied in everyday language) a gap is to be filled with a new product that differs from the ones currently available. When we talk, instead, of structural holes the emphasis is on new, nested markets: on new marketplaces and new patterns for the circulation of goods, services, money, information and symbols (see again Figure 2.2) that are *actively constructed* within the existing mainstream markets. This new, nested market is, indeed, a bridge as it spans the structural hole. And, in order to be an adequate, strong and durable bridge ('a bridge made out of armoured concrete') it needs reinforcing bars, a patchwork of steel that gives both strength and flexibility. This patchwork of reinforcing bars is what I referred to as the sociomaterial infrastructure. It is a well-tied *pattern* of material and social elements (of specific practices that contain specific material and social elements) that allows for particular transactions that contrast with those occurring in the general market. Finally, there is, I think, a third major difference. After filling a gap, order is restored. Bridging a structural hole, instead, implies a reshuffling of positions. New actors pop up and vested interests might lose their positions. The well-established order is not restored, but threatened. The new markets are interstices that might expand further (Holloway, 2002). They are, in a way, permanent disorder.

One final consideration is needed. Why is it that nested markets, such as the ones discussed here, endure? How can we explain why some longstanding nested markets, as e.g. the one for Chianina meat in Central Italy, have been operating for many decades? (For a discussion of this particular nested market see van der Ploeg, Ye and Schneider 2012) Or, phrased differently: why are they not simply taken over by vested interests? The marketing of organic products, for instance, has been partly taken over by such vested interests. Will this story be repeated? I think the answer is to be found in a commonality that underlies the newly constructed, nested markets: they are grounded on common-pool resources.

Common-pool resources

Common-pool resources are not external to distinction, nested markets and/or the infrastructural patterns discussed so far. Although, for analytical reasons, they are represented in Figure 2.1 as constituting a separate field, in reality they are *internal* to distinction, nested markets and infrastructure since these features are all created, structured and developed *as* common-pool resources. They *are* common-pool resources and *function* as such (albeit to varying degrees). It is precisely this that provides them with their strength, resilience and influences how they unfold over time.

Building on the well-known work of Elinor Ostrom (1990) I define common-pool resources (CPRs) as the commonly shared and well institutionalized[27] capacity to generate joint benefits and at the same time to avoid these benefits being adversely affected 'by temptations to free ride, shirk or otherwise act opportunistically' (Ostrom, 1990:29). CPRs embrace both material as well as social elements. CPRs might consist of natural resources combined with specific rules that regulate their use; they might equally consist solely of man-made and/or non-material resources. CPRs always depend on shared notions and norms (partly institutionalized in specific rules); hence, they are grounded on, and critically assume, social networks. Equally CPRs are part of wider resource systems; only in exceptional cases do they stand alone.

A CPR is not private property. Neither is it a public good, characterized by open access. CPRs are the outcome of self-organization and self-governance.

They are both the outcome and main ingredient of collective action that aims to produce joint benefits. CPRs are subject to joint use – which is regulated through a set of shared rules.

The capacity to produce distinction is a CPR. This is argued in general terms by Arfini *et al.* (2010:14 and 14) and Bérard and Marchenay (2004) who explicitly refer to the 'collective dimension'. Real Texel's Lamb provides a good example. A specific piece of Real Texel's Lamb is, evidently, a commodity, sold and bought through private transactions. However, the *capacity* to produce Real Texel's Lamb and to position it as such in the market, is part of the resource system and is definitely a CPR. It is shared by a well-delineated (albeit permeable) group of farmers, slaughterers, butchers, cooks and owners of restaurants. And it delivers joint benefits to all of them. This capacity is dependent on the commonly defined rules that govern the production, processing and distribution of the resource units. It is a capacity that is partly embodied in the Texel breed, in the specific ecology of the island, in the craftsmanship of breeders, slaughterers, butchers and cooks; above all it is the capacity to tie these particular resources together into a coherent resource system. The certificate is both expression and integral part of this capacity.

The capacity of the Willem & Drees initiative to deliver freshness and to run the complex logistics that sustain it definitely make it a CPR: one that is shared by growers, by 'local' supermarkets and the agency itself and which produces joint benefits for all those involved.

A nested market is equally a CPR.[28] A nested market cannot be run by one individual (or one single enterprise). It is the outcome of collective action that unfolds according to shared rules (and within which different actors evidently might play distinguishable roles). A CPR (and more specifically, a nested market) is defined by, and operates through, a set of commonly shared rules. These rules (and their implementation) make a CPR into an institution – this also applies to a nested market. A nested market produces joint benefits: it makes distinctive products accessible, it results in better prices and/or more security for the farmers involved. It may also face and sanction opportunism and free rider behaviour. Consequently, there are joint rules to address such dangers (sometimes embodied in particular devices like the digital screens at the farmers' markets in Rome or the certificate of Real Texel's Lamb). The socio-material infrastructures that underlie the nested markets are, as a whole, CPRs, although the single elements may very well be private. Good understanding between consumers and producers (that might occur in the market) is a CPR, as are trust and reputation (at least, when related to products such as Real Texel's Lamb and those who produce it).

It is to be noted that the resources referred to here as CPRs (as the *capacity* to produce distinction, etc.) are essentially *non-material* (although they might very well include, or result in, material elements).[29] This is an important difference with most of the CPRs discussed by Ostrom (irrigation water, common pasture lands, fishing grounds, commonly managed forests, joint parking spaces) and others (see e.g. Jongeneel *et al.*, 2009). Material resources raise issues of rivalry and divisibility, potentially triggering a zero-sum game. When a certain group of fishermen has access to particular fishing grounds, this implies the exclusion of others. Limited access implies the actual or potential exclusion of others, simply because supply (or availability) is not unlimited. In our case, though, we are talking about *new* resources, resources that are constructed *anew*. Thus the existing stock of resources is enlarged and improved. This implies that the construction of such new CPRs is not an immediate threat for those who currently control the available resources. On the contrary, the development of these new CPRs contributes to overall development and economic growth.

The foregoing considerations all come down to one central point: *CPRs cannot be sold*. They are intrinsically tied to the collective that is its main social carrier. 'Since it is property of a collective, only appropriation for economic, social and cultural objectives is considered legitimate' (Arfini *et al.*, 2010: 15). Selling the CPR as such is excluded. A CPR is not private property, neither is it capital (in the Marxist sense).[30] This is the first reason why the CPRs discussed can 'resist' take-over. Just as distinction resists take-overs (for an extended discussion see van der Ploeg, Ye and Schneider, 2012). The second reason that explains such resistance is that the party that would hypothetically take-over a CPR needs to have the capability to maintain the *capacity to differ* at its core. Large corporations lack this capability. They represent and embody the structural hole: they are too large, too standardized, too rigid, or whatever: they cannot meet the conditions needed to reproduce the capacity to be different and/or distinctive.[31] At best, a *symbiosis* is possible (as in the case of Willem & Drees).

Notes

1 I am grateful to Aad van Tilburg and Norman Long who guided me through fields relatively unknown to me. I also want to express my gratitude to the Italian organization Coldiretti which invited me to participate in their internal debates on the marketing of agricultural products and to the Dutch Organization for Regional Specialties (SPN) which is now reflecting on new strategies to strengthen the production and marketing of regional products. The text benefited greatly from comments by Rudolf van Broekhuizen and Henk Oostindie and from language editing by Nicholas Parrott.
2 I do not aim at any simplistic bifurcation here: together, the mainstream markets and the newly emerging nested markets compose a highly heterogeneous whole that is currently characterized by several, often contrasting, trends and trajectories. In this text I explore the nested market as an ideal type, with the aim of creating some clarity in the current confusion that can even lead to some blindness in seeing and understanding such new markets.
3 In Arfini *et al.* (2010: 11) this is explicitly related to the creation and subsequent production of 'typical products', i.e. new products having a strong relation with the territory.
4 Provided by the Ministry of Agriculture (SMS Consumatori, Mipaf).
5 In reality there is, of course, just one flow that entails the different aspects distinguished in Figure 2.2. The 'separation' is only made for analytical purposes. The central point is that the 'economic relations' (or the market relations, i.e. level 2) are strongly embedded in social relations (levels 1 and 3). The flows at, and the specificities of, level 2 cannot be understood without taking levels 1 and 3 into account.

6 It might equally be argued that together levels 1, 2 and 3 constitute an actor network that entails both social and material elements (Latour, 2005).

7 Social network based exchange is 'a form of economic exchange in which contracts are primarily or exclusively enforced via first and second party punishments' (Faf-camps: 17). The notion of punishment is tied closely to the concept of reputation: 'In a reputation-enforcement mechanism, cheaters – namely agents who failed to respect their contractual obligations – are subjected to a coordinated punishment by all (or a subgroup of) other agents' (ibid.: 15).

8 The validity of this argument is proven indirectly by supermarkets that try to counter this inherent competitive advantage of nested markets, by suggesting a similar embedding. This is done by putting a recognizable and friendly farm family at the centre of their TV and other advertisements, implying, as it were, that all milk sold in the supermarket comes from this family. The magazines distributed by the large supermarkets do the same thing. It goes without saying that this is only virtual embedding – it is not about embedding in real and existing social networks.

9 In a previous debate (Goodman 2004 vs. van der Ploeg and Renting 2004) I argued, along with Henk Renting, that Goodman essentially ignores the creation of additional value and the specific way it is distributed.

10 The initiative came from the Wadden Group. This is an association that aims to promote regional products from the Wadden area (which includes the island of Texel). Crucial criteria are local origin, local processing and preferably a historical origin. Also important are a positive contribution to the regional economy and making a positive contribution to overall sustainability. Currently the Wadden Group manages the distribution of some 400 different products, and there are more than 300 producers and processors linked to the association.

11 A slightly paraphrased quote from Mr. Dijkhuizen, President of Wageningen University (Lange, 2011: 21).

12 Just as one shipment of potato crisps from Canada to the Netherlands might cause the price in north western European to decrease considerably. In the end it is just the rumour of potatoes possibly being shipped that can impact on a market elsewhere. Even if New Zealand cannot provide, due to ecological and logistical reasons, the whole of Europe with dairy products, the simple possibility of some dairy products being exported will already condition distant markets. This shows how the world market is an ordering principle rather than a material reality in which all products are shipped all over the world.

13 Here, the contrast with the notion of super market is telling. A supermarket is far from being a place where many suppliers (who are provided with merchandise by a wide range of producers and/or intermediaries) meet with many clients, offering the later the possibility to compare and to negotiate. A supermarket is the selling point of just one provider who will not permit others to operate in the same realm (with a few token exceptions).

14 In a more general sense this relates to the concept of bridging social capital that was developed later. See e.g. Thisenkopfs, Lace and Mierina, 2008.

15 'There is little gain from a new contact redundant with existing contacts. Time and energy would be better spent cultivating a new contact to unreached people' (Burt 1992: 20).

16 There is an evident flipside here: 'Foreign merchants – especially members of the great ethnic and familial trading networks, such as Jews and Armenians – come and go, able to escape local surveillance and accountability: they can always disappear into the exotic nowhere land from whence they and their goods appeared' (Slater and Tonkiss 2001: 11). Or, as Aldridge (2005: 39) phrases it: 'the merchant is a trickster, both an amiable rogue and a callous parasite'.

17 There is a change in analytical perspective here: 'In the standard economic perspective, the market is the main central institution, and the firms' black box actions

derive from markets. Here we treat the firm (which is not a black box) as the central institution. And we view markets as the outcome of corporate activities' (Anderson and Gatignon 2005: 402).

18 Their analysis is built on data from the industrial sectors for automobiles, tires, colour TVs, tractors and machinery.

19 They started using already established dealers for distribution who liked to run, along-side the US supply, a 'second line' (ibid.: 63). Equally important was that the 'new-comers' operated in more than one market.

20 In the sense that 'going to the market' and preferably to the same traders becomes a new routine that is increasingly build upon trust.

21 Of course, starting such new market forms is far from easy. Authorisations need to be negotiated and obtained: 'what are traded on the market are not [...] physical entities, but the rights to perform certain actions, and the rights which individuals possess are established by the legal system' (Coase 2005: 37).

22 This is echoed, in general terms, by Anderson and Gatignon who observe that 'new prod-ucts are outside buyer's routine' and that 'innovations arouse resistance' (2005: 417).

23 When discussing the features of products and services that carry distinction I referred to six dimensions. These same dimensions re-emerge in the discussion of structural holes. This is no coincidence. Distinctive products embody the features that character-ize the interface between the general commodity markets for food and agricultural products. Thus they help to turn the structural hole into a window of opportunity. Dis-tinctive products are building blocks used in the construction of the 'bridges' that cross the 'chasms'.

24 Theoretically, local procurement is possible in franchise chains, but it has increasingly disappearing due to fears over food scares. Local procurement is also seen as too expensive since it implies a double supply system. It also excludes control from the top.

25 I.e. supermarkets thought of as being (partly) disconnected from the general supply system.

26 Willem & Drees has been functioning for about two years. At the moment (summer 2011) four circles and one regional distribution centre are operating. There are 16 people (including intern students) working in the organization.

27 That is, the rules of the game are well specified, controlled, maintained and, if needed, enforced by sanctions. They are internalized by those who join in the collective action that underlies and reproduces the CPR.

28 This is in line with Ostrom's observations. See especially 1990: 14.

29 In Polman *et al.* (2010:309) we argued that this applies to most CPRs that play a role in current processes of Rural Development. In this vein we referred to 'the art of maintaining a beautiful landscape [...] the art of producing high quality products, the art of creating synergy (re. multifunctionality)' (italics added).

30 It produces joint benefits, not privately appropriated surplus value.

31 This is mirrored in e.g. the failure of big dairy industries to take over the production of cheeses made from raw milk (as *Parmiggiano-Reggiano*, *boerenkaas*, etc) or of large supermarket chains to take over the distribution of *Chianina* meat.

References

Akerlof, G.A. (1970) The market for 'lemons': qualitative uncertainty and the market mechanism, *Quarterly Journal of Economics*, 84: 488–500.

Aldridge, A. (2005) *The Market*, Cambridge: Polity Press.

Anderson, E. and H. Gatignon (2005) Firms and the creation of new markets, in: C. Ménard and M.M. Shirley, *Handbook of New Institutional Economics*, Dordrecht: Springer.

Arfini, F., G. Beletti and A. Marescotti (2010) *Prodotti tipici e Denominazioni Geografiche, strumenti di tutela e valorizzazione*, Gruppo 2013 Rome: Quaderni, Eizioni Tellus.

Barjolle, D., S. Boisseaux and M. Dufour,(1998) *Le lien au terroir; bilan des travaux de recherché*, Lausanne: Institut d'économie rurale.

Barth, F. (1967) Economic spheres in Darfur, in: R. Firth (ed.), *Themes in Economic Anthropology*, London: Tavistock.

Berard, L. and P. Marchenay (2004) *Les produits de terroir, entre cultures et règlements*, Psris: CNRS éditions.

Bourdieu, P. (1984) *Distinction: A social critique of the judgment of taste*, London/New York: Routledge & Kegan Paul.

Bourdieu, P. (2005) *The social structures of the economy*, London: Polity Press.

Braudel, F. (1992) *The Wheels of Commerce: Civilization and capitalism, 15th–18th century*, Volume II, Berkeley: University of California Press.

Burt, R.S. (1992) *Structural Holes: The social structure of competition*, Cambridge MA: Harvard University Press.

Cassabianca, F., B. Sylvander, Y. Noël, C. Béranger, J.B. Coulon and F. Roncin (2005) *Terroir et Typicité: Deux concepts-clés des Appelations d'Origine Coltrolée. Essay de définitions scientifiques et opérationelles*, Symposium international 'Territoires et enjeux du développement régional', Lyon.

Coase, R.H. (2005) The institutional structure of production, in: C. Ménard and M.M. Shirley, *Handbook of New Institutional Economics*, Dordrecht: Springer.

De Rooij, S., F. Ventura and P. Milone (2010) *Large farmers increasingly opt for multifunctionality*, Perugia: DEA, University of Perugia.

Fafchamps, M. (2004) *Market Institutions in Sub-Saharan Africa, Theory and Evidence*, Cambridge MA/London: MIT Press.

Goodman, D. (2004) Rural Europe redux? Reflections on alternative agro-food networks and paradigm change, *Sociologia Ruralis*, 44: 3–16.

Jongeneel, R., N. Polman and L. Slangen (2009) Changing rural landscapes: demand and supply of public services in the Netherlands, in: F. Brouwer and C.M. van der Heide (eds), *Multifunctional Rural Land Management: Economics and Policies*, London: Earthscan.

Lange, Y. (2011) De opmars van Food Valley: 'De hele wereld komt onze kant op', in: *De Groene Amsterdammer*, 21 July 2011.

Latour, B. (2005) Reassembling the social – an introduction to actor-network theory, Oxford: Oxford University Press.

Long, N. (1977) *An Introduction to the Sociology of Rural Development*, London: Tavistock Publications.

Meulen, H. van der (2000) *Circuits in de Landbouwvoedselketen: Verscheidenheid en Samenhang in de productie en vermarkting van rundvlees in Midden-Italie*, PhD thesis, Wageningen: Wageningen University.

Musashi, M. (1974) *A Book of Five Rings*, The Overlook Press, New York.

Ostrom, E. (1990) *Governing the Commons: The Evolution of Institutions for Collective Action*, New York: Cambridge University Press.

Polman, N., K.J. Poppe, J.-W. van der Schans and J.D. van der Ploeg (2010) Nested markets with common pool resources in multifunctional agriculture, *Rivista di Economia Agraria*, 65: 295–318.

Rocchi, B. and D. Romano (eds) (2006*) Tipicamente buono: concezione di qualitá lungo la filiera dei prodotti agro-alimentari in Toscana*, Milano: Franco Angeli.

Saccomandi, V. (1998) *Agricultural Market Economics: a Neo-Institutional Analysis of Exchange, Circulation and Distribution of Agricultural Products*, Assen: Royal van Gorcum.

Slater, D. and F. Tonkiss (2001) *Market Society: markets and modern social theory*, Cambridge: Polity Press.

Thiesenkopf, T., I. Lace and I. Mierina (2008) Social capital, in: van der Ploeg J.D. and T. Marsden (eds) *Unfolding Webs: The dynamics of regional rural development*, Assen: Royal van Gorcum.

Tregear, A. (2011) Progressing knowledge in alternative and local food networks: critical reflections and a research agenda, *Journal of Rural Studies*, 27: 419–430.

van der Meulen, H. and F. Ventura (1994) *La Costruzione Sociale di Qualitá*, Assisi: CESaR.

van der Ploeg, J.D. and H. Renting (2004) Behind the 'redux': a rejoinder to David Goodman, in: *Sociologia Ruralis*, 44: 235–242.

van der Ploeg, J.D., Y. Jingzhong and S. Schneider (2010) Rural development reconsidered: building on comparative perspectives from China, Brazil and the European Union, in: *Rivista di Economia Agraria*, 65: 163–190.

van der Ploeg, J.D., Y. Jingzhong and S. Schneider (2012), Rural development through the construction of new, nested markets: comparative perspectives from China, Brazil and the European Union, *Journal of Peasant Studies, 39:* 133–173.

Ventura, F. (2001) *Organizzarsi per Sopravvivere: un analisi neo-istituzionale dello sviluppo endogeno nell'agricoltura Umbra*, PhD Thesis, Wageningen: Wageningen University.

Wijffels, H. (2011) *A changing world order and the provision of global public goods, in: B. Berendsen, Common Goods in a Divided World*, Amsterdam: KIT Publishers.

Willard, G.E. and A. Savara (1988) Patterns of entry: pathways to new markets, in: *California Management Review Reprint Series*, 30: 57–76.

3 The visible hand in building new markets for rural economies

Pierluigi Milone and Flaminia Ventura

> The old, ironclad vessels of the industrial era will sink under the crashing waves, while firms that create highly nimble and networked structures and connect to external ideas and energies will gain the buoyancy they require to survive.
>
> (Tapscott and Williams, Wikinomics 2006:117)

Introduction

The market can be basically conceived as an institution with specific social rules which provide the basis for exchanges to take place. These rules lead to the definition of product characteristics, methods of use and consumer preferences, all of which are often culturally dictated. In the past, markets have generally had limited territorial boundaries, usually determined by the available technologies, infrastructures and the history and culture of a region.

These boundaries have gradually been eroded by the process of globalization, which has been driven by new technologies, particularly ICT, and the improvement of infrastructures and transportation systems. These markets are increasingly exogenously controlled by a few multinational companies which, in the food sector, have been referred to as 'food empires' (van der Ploeg 2008). Under these circumstances it is difficult to endogenously construct markets with local characteristics. These processes significantly delocalize production, disconnect productive processes from cultures and regional resources and greatly damage the resilience of the socio-economic and environmental systems of rural areas. They also deplete (or make redundant) local natural resources, creating new social costs related to their reproduction or preservation. These costs, which fall upon local communities, are directly related to the history, culture, the quality of life and sensitivity and ability of such communities to protecting and preserving their resources.

The concept of a competitive market, as an efficient place to trade, is derived from the assumption that the market is a place of *free trade* attended by a large number of small companies most of which are engaged in small scale production, exchanging goods and services in response to the local conditions of supply and demand. Neo-classical economics saw market actors as perfectly rational and unable to influence market outcomes. Adam Smith (1723–1790) coined the metaphor of the 'invisible hand' to describe the self-regulating nature of such a marketplace. He regarded the invisible hand as the 'providence' through which a free market turns self-interest into benefits for society as a whole, and private vices into public benefits (Smith 1776). Later, Walras[1] (1834–1910) and Pareto[2] (1848–1923) argued that the invisible hand was a social mechanism of market governance that provides for perfect competition in a free market.

The concept of the invisible hand was later challenged by Keynes, whose 1926 essay 'The End of Laissez-Faire' debunked the ideas that individuals possess a prescriptive 'natural liberty' in their economic activities, and that self-interest is generally enlightened. He proposed a capitalism that should be 'wisely governed' by the state, which should guide the market. In doing so, he did not propose that the state should replace firms or undertake activities that they are perfectly capable of accomplishing, but that it should make those decisions

> ...which are made by no one if the State does not make them. The important thing for government is not to do things which individuals are doing already, and to do them a little better or a little worse; but to do those things which at present are not done at all.
>
> (Keynes 1926: IV)

He argued that the economy not be left 'to the free play of private interests' (Keynes 1936), but regulated by a 'invisible hand', driven and oriented by specific public interventions.

At around the same time, the English economist Coase (1937) pointed out that a functioning market involves transaction costs. He identified these as being associated with: (a) searching and information; (b) bargaining and decision-making, and (c) policing and enforcement.[3] When these costs exceed a certain threshold, the market mechanism falls into crisis or fails as it is no longer the best mechanism for exchange. Firms facing this situation will decide to internalize their trade. This realization later led Coase (1960) to regard the firm as a productive organization, consisting of a set of contracts that can replace the market when transaction costs are too high. The concept of the firm as organizational alternative to the market was taken up by Chandler (1977), whose historical essay stated that it was not only markets that allocate resources, but also firms, complex organizations administered by professional managers. He argued that, in this sense, the firm, in particular conditions (such as market failures) usurps the role of the market in coordinating economic activities and allocating resources, replacing the 'invisible hand' with its visible administrative hand and permitted better profits.

Currently, and particularly because of the emergence of the neo-institutional approach, the market is no longer seen as the only mechanism for governing transactions. Neither is it regarded as an abstract and pure entity, free from the influence of market actors. It is, instead, perceived as a social entity in which different economic, political, and social factors interact to determine the outcome of a transaction. Agricultural markets, for example, are only a part of a wider agri-marketing system which can be defined as '…all the activities associated with the agricultural production and food, feed and fiber assembly, processing, and distribution to final consumers, including the analysis of consumers' needs, motivations, and purchasing and consumption behavior.' (Branson and Norvell 1983).

Transactions can be governed by a myriad of different, often hybrid, forms (Saccomandi 1998) that are located between two extreme poles: the market and the hierarchy (Williamson 1985). Hybrid forms of trade are intermediate governance structures that fall somewhere between these two extremes.

There are two main types of hybrid governance: quasi-organizational and quasi-market. The first can be defined as systems in which actors are part of different business units belonging to the same organization, or working in systems where shared rules delineate an organization or a stable network. A quasi-market is a structure within which the actors share cooperative patterns of behaviour or are involved in contractual relationships that (partly) replace the spot market. These hybrid forms are flexible and fluid, and can be subject to continuous and dynamic changes which reshape their boundaries, size and shape. These features determine the polymorphism of governance forms, which can constantly evolve in response to the cycle of organizational innovation (Saccomandi 1998). One example of a quasi-organization is the new system for regionally designated products (PDOs and PGIs). In these systems a consortium coordinates the productive and marketing activities, which helps to reduce transaction costs. An example of a quasi-market can be found in the current multi-annual contractual forms (as in the milk or cereal sectors) between farmers and processors. These contracts define the characteristics of the product, as well as the quantity and method of payment. These also have the objective of reducing transaction costs.

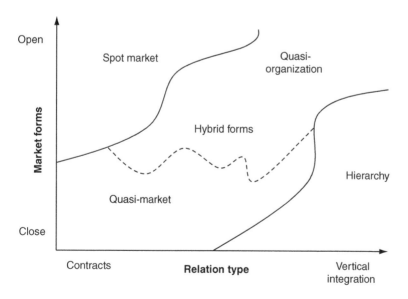

Figure 3.1 Governance structure of transactions.

The coordination and control of such systems are carried out through a 'visible hand' which extends beyond specialized management. It can take different forms and characteristics, depending on the socio-economic and institutional contexts. The visible hand can be made manifest through the involvement of institutions,[4] the emergence of a network of firms,[5] or even through lobbying.[6] The visible hand, then, is a real driving force that determines, controls and coordinates transactions and aims to achieve satisfactory trade[7] for all the actors involved and to reduce transaction costs.

Moreover, it should be noted that, the visible hand is the main influence over how the forms of governance evolve. It is particularly relevant when markets fail, usually due to one (or combinations) of three main factors, listed below.

1   Markets are often characterized by opportunistic behaviour, driven by information asymmetries and limited rationality (Simon 1947, 1957; Williamson 1985[8]).
2   Firms can generate incomes only when the markets work inefficiently. This implies gains for some and losses for others. In this sense, markets are often characterized by forms of power that benefit a few to the detriment of many (monopolies, oligopolies, contestable markets, etc.). They also often contain large 'social costs'[9] which are not explicitly recognized in the transaction, but are charged to firms.
3   High transaction costs, which drive a search for hybrid forms of transaction to reduce such costs.[10] This dynamic leads to the emergence and evolution of new markets and new forms of transaction, as discussed later in this chapter.

Markets are wild beasts. They are valuable, but often uncontrolled and fail to discern the quality of a transaction. They have values and strengths, which should be recognized. But they also need to be tamed and coordinated, rather than demonized.

This chapter investigates some hybrid forms of governance, guided by a 'visible hand', that have been identified in empirical studies. These assume different forms in different contexts. In our analysis we seek to emphasize that these forms are both a result and a cause of the success of strategies adopted by European farms to align themselves more closely to the new rural development paradigm. The strength of these new forms of transaction is now influencing the transition of the entire European food and agricultural system, in which even large firms (those with a strong market orientation) choose multi-functional strategies since these offer better prospects for their survival and prosperity (de Rooij, Ventura *et al.* 2011).

The emergence and development of nested markets

The objects of transaction and the rules of the different market structures are usually well defined and usually subject to limited rationality among traders and information asymmetries: the later due mainly to the diversity of technologies, social milieus, knowledge and power. Even in a 'consolidated' market we can find information incompleteness, although these gaps are generally filled by legal devices designed to protect traders from uncertainty and opportunistic behaviour. These socio-institutional devices are intended to minimize, or reduce, transaction costs but there are a number of cases where the effectiveness or scope of these devices may be lacking. This may occur when:

- a new product/service emerges for which there are no previous transaction experiences;
- in market niches where there is little initial interest in regulating transactions, and;
- in large markets where it is difficult to regulate transactions without incurring high costs.

Such situations can create real deviations from the typical and familiar forms of market governance and lead to the emergence of hybrid forms of quasi-organization and quasi-market that are forms of an incomplete market (Greenwald and Stiglitz 1986) that is the seed of nested market.[11] At the risk of overstating the point we might say that a transaction object in a conventional market is defined exogenously by traders, while in the nested market it is the result of interactions between various actors who participate and contribute to creating both the good or service to be traded and the market rules. This is leading farmers (particularly in Europe) to combine aspects of their production with the reproduction and improvement of the natural and environmental resources that support or enhance their business activities. In agriculture this model is often referred to as multifunctionality. It represents a revolutionary departure from conventional approaches to farming. It makes multiple usage of different but synergistic resources, which may simultaneously be inputs, outputs or production processes (see Figure 3.2) and which can determine a range of structures and organizational forms, with variable boundaries (Milone 2008). This provides an element of competitiveness and sustainability, strengthening resilience against external shocks (Stirling 2008; Leach 2008).

Nested markets are very dynamic and can evolve towards hybrid forms of quasi-market, quasi-organization, or a market within the market. They are characterized by low transaction costs: this is due to the nature of the goods or services traded and to the ways in which transactions are regulated.[12]

Nested markets emerge and develop through very diverse mechanisms. These often have their roots in the history and institutions of a region. In general three main types of new markets can be identified: 1. Completely new markets, i.e. markets for an entirely new transaction object. Public goods are a case in point. In recent years new markets have emerged to achieve environmental and social benefits: preserving biodiversity; managing the landscape; reducing greenhouse gas emissions; care farm. 2. Markets constructed through the segmentation of already existing markets. This mostly occurs though processes of product differentiation

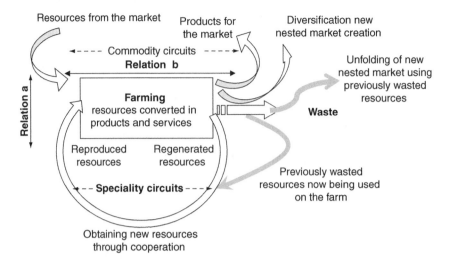

Figure 3.2 The flow of resources, consolidation of business processes and creation of new products.

(as in the case of organic, quality or traditional products). 3. Markets constructed through policies to promote the access of new segments of the population to local food production. This is most visible in the agrarian reform measures in Brazil – support for family farms by creating new markets (Schneider *et al.* 2011) – or school canteens programme in Scotland, (Morgan and Sonnino 2008).

In the following sections we outline three case studies that illustrate the mechanisms through which nested markets can emerge and develop. It is worth noting that, in all three cases, the triggers for the emergence of these markets was almost the same, the need of farmers to find new ways of earning income in the face of an ongoing price squeeze, and the new and emerging needs of the civil society, which created new forms of demand. The simultaneous emergence of these two factors creates the conditions in which a nested market can blossom. In this sense nested markets become the co-evolutionary result of the interactions between the needs of the various economic, institutional and social actors.

Care farms

Care farms provide social services for vulnerable groups of people, giving them the opportunity to work on the land. Care farming involves the therapeutic use of farming practices. Interactions between physicians, families and farms led to the realization that farms could provide a number of services that would improve the quality of therapeutic care available to disabled or traumatized people. This phenomenon led some farms to test the feasibility of such activities in providing alternative or supplementary forms of income, thereby diversifying their farming activities in a multifunctional direction.

Care farms are derived from pilot experiments based on informal, sometimes 'illegal' agreements between physicians, families, health authorities and farms. The success of such experiences has led to a highly diversified pattern of care farming, according to the socio-institutional contexts within different European countries (and regions). They are an example of a nested market that initially emerges or appears as a quasi-organization, where the types of service, rules, methods and levels of remuneration are the result of constant interactions between different actors. These interactions are mainly based on factors such as reputation, trust, shared ethical values and lead to a common response to the different needs of customers (i.e. providing services and assistance to disabled and traumatized people and their families). They also have helped stabilize the incomes of participating farm households. At the early stage of their evolution, it is not possible to formalize or institutionalize relationships, which are in a constant state of evolution and redefinition as participants search for the optimal arrangements. In Europe, the evolution of the phenomenon towards a new nested market, in which the new types of services offered by farms become the transaction object, has followed different paths (see Figure 3.3) moving from hybrid forms of quasi-organization to quasi-markets.

In the Netherlands, for example, this evolution has led to the development of a significant market in which more than 1,000 farms are currently actively involved. The participating farms and the local health authorities have to follow a set of rules and standards that specifically define the types of services provided and the terms of market access. These were formulated within the framework of a national agreement between the Ministries of Health and Agriculture and associations of agricultural producers the farmers' organizations. This formalized socio-institutional context has encouraged the dissemination of information and knowledge about this new market, facilitating access to it and increasing its size.

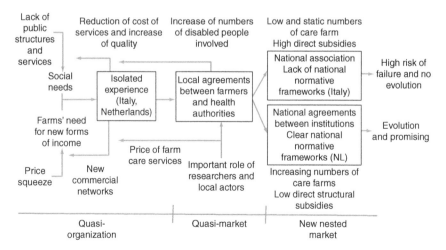

Figure 3.3 The case of care farms.

By contrast, in Italy, the governance of care farms has only been formalized in the region of Tuscany, where local institutions, researchers and farms have showed some interest in investing directly in the building the required financial and human resources. Thus, an institutional context with a purely local significance has emerged. This has acted as a catalyst for other Italian regions to develop innovative approaches. This more fragmented approach has both positive and negative aspects. On the positive side, it allows local stakeholders more flexibility to focus on specific local needs. The negative side is that these initiatives generally face higher transaction costs than those incurred in the Tuscany Region. In this sense this fragmentation is hindering the potential development of the market, increasing the risk of failures, and of care farms remaining within the framework of a quasi-market, or regressing to forms of quasi-organization.

Food products with low greenhouse gas emissions

The need to reduce greenhouse gas emissions was recognized by the Kyoto Protocol of 1997, which has been subsequently been ratified by most countries of the world. The protocol has created new opportunities for diversification and increasing the income of European farms through developing local markets offering 'low mileage' food. The markets are based on consumption segments which favour traditional techniques and territorial suitability, and allow a more rational use of resources and a reduction of dependency on external inputs, particularly from the oil industry. These elements all improve competitiveness instead of leading towards marginalization. Finally they offer the opportunity to enter new markets, such as carbon credit markets. In this case the transition has been one from initial forms of quasi-organization to quasi-market and later to new nested markets, which are acquiring a universal dimension. This took place through a progressive formal recognition of the capacity of the products to cater for new societal needs. This initially started with voluntary schemes (carbon footprints) which were subsequently scientifically validated (e.g. through DEFRA's Carbon Trust). This eventually led to new market rules being defined that were congruent with the model of the green economy promoted by the new Common Agricultural Policy (see Figure 3.4). The next step was represented by the creation of new voluntary schemes concerning the rational and appropriate use of natural resources, such as water.

Greenhouse gases

Local quality products

Another good example of a nested market is represented by the renaissance of local quality products. Proof of this phenomenon is evident all over Europe (Milone 2008; Milone and Ventura 2010, 2004; Swagemakers 2002; Roep 2002; Scettri 2001; Wiskerke and Ploeg 2004; Parrott *et al.* 2002). Here, we report

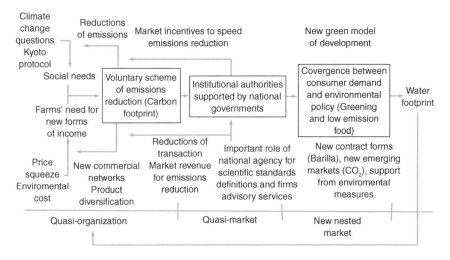

Figure 3.4 The case of food products with low emissions of greenhouse gases.

briefly on what happened in the sheep and goat farming sectors in two European regions: Abruzzo (Italy) and Provence (France). In Abruzzo, the shepherds have developed organizational and product innovations aimed at opening up new market segments. They have implemented portfolio strategies, increasing their range of products and establishing informal partnerships between each other. They are sharing the costs associated with marketing these products and the research and testing of new production processes and activities. Such strategies and forms of collaboration gave birth to economies of scope (Teece 1980; Milone and Ventura 2001) and allowed for the development of high quality products and new transaction modalities. These, and particularly the emergence of hybrid forms of quasi-market (niches, town fairs, festivals, events such as *Salone del Gusto* and Slow Food), have substantially increased farm incomes and led them to become less dependent on state aid, which now accounts for less than 20 per cent of their incomes (Milone 2008). This process was enabled by several institutional schemes, including an organic farming one that, in the early stages, provided incentives for testing new products, and later supported voluntary collective branding initiatives (including Slow Food and *Prodotti dei Parchi*) which provided guarantees about environmental sustainability, the specificity of production processes and product quality.

The second case concerns farms in the alpine areas of Provence where, since time immemorial, local shepherds have followed sustainable grazing practices which help protect the local landscape and biodiversity. These features are now recognized as having a huge social and environmental value. Following further income reductions due to the price squeeze, the shepherds established new agreements with local administrations. These provided specific incentives for more sustainable grazing practices and established new quality schemes such as

'Agneau du Sisteron PGI', and 'Label Rouge'. This process gave birth to a quasi-organization that enabled shepherds to protect their incomes and find new market niches. Changing grazing practices and closer involvement of the shepherds as guardians of the land has subsequently led to a considerable decrease in forest fires that have often represented a very real threat to these, and neighbouring coastal, areas (Franca 2008).

These farms are far more dependent on state aid than farms in Abruzzo, with an average of 70 per cent of their income coming from the public purse. However, the strength of their organization or network, which involves both public and private actors, is strengthening the economic sustainability of the initiative and leading to an exploration of new market opportunities. In both cases, the farms' transactions follow mixed forms of governance, where market forms and hybrid structures coexist and are merged by shared protocols for good practices that also define the quality of the products (often handmade) which are more strongly embedded as part of the cultural and social heritage of the territory. This includes the provision of a range of public goods, such as fire prevention in areas bordering the grazing lands, landscape protection and biodiversity preservation through grazing practices in areas with a poor mix of pasture species. New nested markets are emerging, that assume a mixed form of governance: providing both direct incentives for producing/maintaining public goods, and allowing the emergence of local products with unique quality characteristics onto into the market.

The main tools used are quality schemes that are jointly designed by the public-private partnership. These play several roles. On the one hand, they provide society and public institutions with assurances that farmers are fulfilling their commitments in terms of protection of the environment and natural resources. On the other hand, they provide consumers with information about product and production quality, which encourages purchases and loyalty. Within this mixed form of governance, the market aspect may, over time, assume more importance, thus reducing dependency on state financial assistance, but without losing the typicality of the product or the public good component involved in the production processes.

Figure 3.5 shows the development processes of these two examples, showing their differences and their shared convergence towards nested markets, which is due to similar product characteristics and transaction rules.

Common features of nested markets

The experiences described above reveal some specific characteristics of nested markets, which are summarized below.

1   The products and services sold on a nested market always have a strong component of public good. They are products and services that both meet the specific needs of individual consumers purchasing them and broader collective needs.

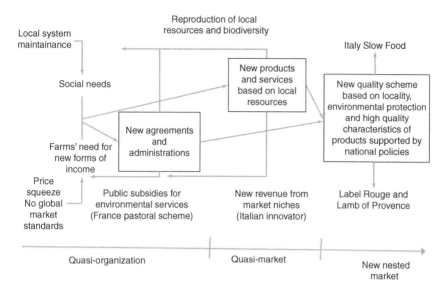

Figure 3.5 The case of local quality products.

2   The marketable component of products and services reduces social costs that would otherwise be incurred to satisfy social demand for these public goods.

3   The process of constructing a nested market is the result of interactions between two important dimensions: market governance,[13] typically the domain of firms, and the creation of new institutional arrangements[14] which allow for the protection and/or development of products and services sold in the nested market. These interactions between firms and public and private institutional players need to be continually maintained throughout the process.

The reasons and conditions that influence the emergence or discovery of a nested market are worth further empirical and theoretical discussion. Following Hirschman (1958) it can be argued that the interactions leading to the development of a nested market are the result of 'partial disturbances concentrated in space and in some policy areas that determine a provisional situation of imbalance'. Partial disturbance produces unexpected consequences that affect the expectations and behaviour of the actors involved, bringing to light 'hidden resources, scattered, or badly utilized' (ibid.). The development process becomes a public good that, rather than being consumed, grows with its use.

Nested markets, therefore, seem to emerge from unusual or unanticipated situations rather than from constant relationships or uniform sequences, the conditions that Palermo (2009) claims generate and underpin local development processes. A range of different innovative processes may emerge simultaneously within the same region, leading to the development of new markets, each with its own nature, complexity and level of risk. Eventually one of these will emerge as a better alternative than the others. This generates competition and cooperation between the different processes. Public institutions may find it difficult to identify which processes are more promising in terms generating positive externalities and providing common goods. As a result it may be difficult for them to identify which innovative actors to support, although this is a fundamental requirement for initiating the development of a nested market.

The complexity and uncertainty of the process derives from the changing nature of the structures that govern the transactions of these new products. These multiple, intermediate, forms lie between those defined by Williamson as 'market' and 'hierarchy'.

Figure 3.6 shows the various stages leading up to the emergence of a nested market: from the initial 'big bang' to continued expansion. It is clear that the initial spark occurs, as already mentioned, within the space of the innovation dynamics. It can, however, be initiated and guided by firms, by development institutions, by the dominant technological regime seeking answers to the new demands of civil society, or by the economic system itself.

Initially, actors often work independently in seeking to create innovations. It is, therefore, difficult to reproduce the initial spark. The actor generating this can vary considerably from region to region. The second stage, in which the potential and characteristics of a nested market are recognized, and attempts made to build on these, is the result of cooperation between public and private players. This involves two main elements. First, the recognition of the component of social utility of a product or service justifies providing support through direct,

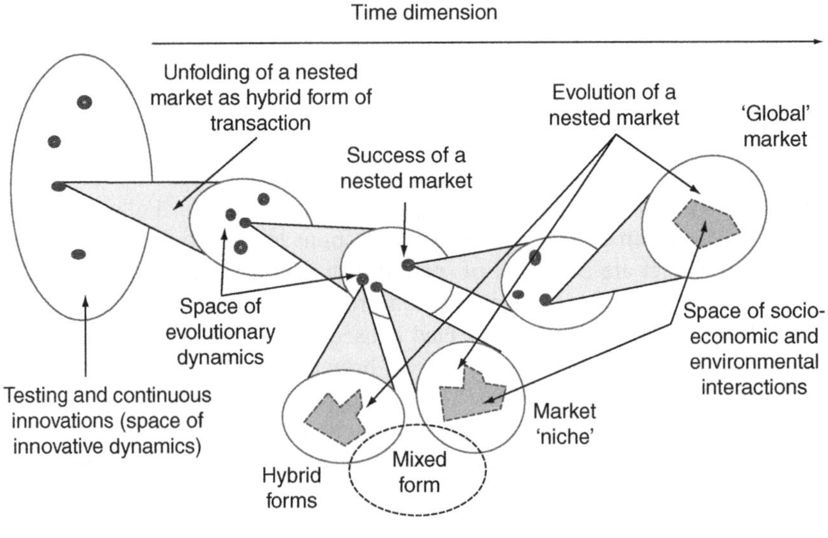

Figure 3.6 The 'big bang' of the nested market.

financial, and regulatory public interventions. Second, the market component encourages the development of strategic behaviour by firms strengthening their entrepreneurial character, capacity to innovate their competitive position in the markets. This allows the firms to move away from dependence on state aid, a move that can be planned on a provisional basis. This enables policies to pursue objectives not only intended to increase economic activity, but also to reduce the social costs related to the economic system of incentives and to enhance and protect the environment.

Finally, this evolution does not run in one single direction. Indeed, the variables of market dimension and form of governance can lead to a large number of combinations that are oriented towards: global markets (e.g. alternative energy and carbon credits); niches of global markets (e.g. PDO/PGI), mixed forms of market and hybrid forms (e.g. quality schemes with public incentives); or local markets (that might acquire global importance owing to the facilities offered by the new ICT technologies (e.g. agro-tourism and local handmade products).

A nested market may evolve towards a global market by building on the special features and standards embedded within the products and services originally exchanged in the nested market. This may greatly increase the quality of overall demand (and thus supply). At the same time, however, the conditions for new nested markets are emerging with new specificities that again will create new distances between local markets and global ones. The relevance of nested markets does not lie just in the spatial dimension or in new opportunities for product placement. Above all it resides, in the unfolding dynamics and their evolution. This is because a nested market allows for co-production between innovators and entrepreneurs, of producers and consumers, and of individual agents and their context. Thus, the nested market inherently contains the capacity that allows for dynamic adaptations to changing societal needs and/or to changing environmental or market conditions. The development from a quasi-organization to a nested market depends on the match with, as yet, not fully articulated societal demand, i.e. an ability to anticipate and be precursors of new societal needs and socio-economic trends.

In summary, a nested market can take on a considerable variety of forms of transaction governance. Even the same or (a similar) good or service can take different forms of transactional governance, depending on the socio-economic and institutional context, the interaction between market governance and the new institutional arrangements and the local environmental conditions (i.e. the availability and condition of natural resources). Also, since the context is dynamically evolving, the boundaries and forms can continuously change over time within the organizational innovation cycle of transaction relationships (see Figure 3.7).

Nested markets and rural development policies

Public institutions can play a key role in the construction and development of nested markets. Their creation and evolution over time often relies upon establishing interrelations between demand and supply, which is often obtained through public regulatory mechanisms and/or incentives. One example is this

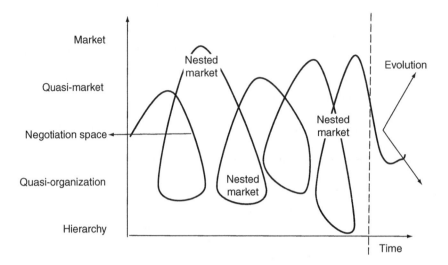

Figure 3.7 The organizational innovation cycle of transaction relationships.

care farm sector in the Netherlands. This phenomenon emerged spontaneously but needed a regulatory framework to develop. Often the critical aspect is building relations between agricultural and rural enterprises and markets. These markets may already exist, but accessing them is difficult due to a lack of knowledge and information (as in the case of carbon credits markets).

There are important interrelations between the new markets. These interrelations are based on the fact that different firms use the same (often, common pool) resources to produce different products and services. This allows for the creation of synergies between firms and an optimal use of resources.

Rural development policies can play a central role in the development of these markets (Oostindie *et al.* 2011), through a number of different mechanisms: regulatory tools (as in the case of agri-tourism, care farms, wine routes, etc.); direct incentives (for participating in quality schemes aimed at valorizing natural, environmental and cultural territorial resources (such as organic, PDO products, etc.); and lastly by giving support to individual farms providing goods and services (such as saving energy or water) that provide collective benefits.

One interesting aspect of such policies is that direct public financial intervention is usually always provisional and temporary; lasting only until the market itself recognizes the economic value of a collective good. In this sense, nested markets become resources for farms and rural areas. In these nested markets farms are not only price takers, but can be subjected to contractual power that allows them to protect and reproduce their own and locally specific, jointly used, resources, that are essential for the future of their region.

As such these markets encourage the creation of new relationships within a region. These relationships are based on the synergistic and non-competitive use of limited natural and cultural resources and give birth to new regional and trans-regional networks. Moreover, they also enhance sectoral integration as demand is not only from final consumers, but also from other economic operators, i.e wine routes or local food supply chain.

One of the major issues within rural development is competition between different sectors (residential, industry, tourism, agriculture) for the use of resources (Marsden *et al.* 2003) The development of nested markets is based on a more sustainable use of such resources, and makes economic and institutional actors more aware of the strong interdependence between these different sectors and activities. The importance of these relational aspects and territorial integration can lead to a shift in attention from individual beneficiaries and sectors to more complex structures, such as formal and informal networks, consortia, partnerships, etc., which contribute to the emergence of new goods and services, ways of trading them and of adding and distributing value.

In our analysis, this important aspect is represented by the rural web which, due to its multilevel and multi-actor nature, not only governs interrelations within a region, but also those between rural and urban areas. This facilitates the ability of rural areas and actors, particularly farmers, to satisfy new societal demands in other locations. These factors imply that development policies need to become more coherent, as they will increasingly be driven by the collective actions of multiple actors making use of both regulatory and support tools (see Figure 3.8).

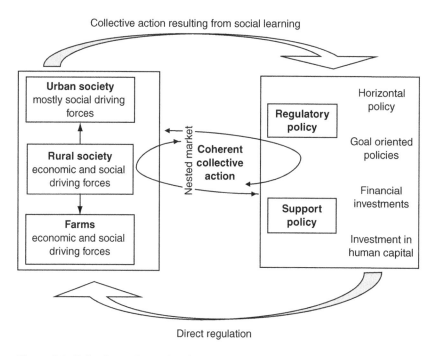

Figure 3.8 Collective action and policy development.

Collective and coherent actions require human capital, a strong social capital and communication and information systems through which objectives and actions can be shared. This implies the creation and strengthening of new tools that are not just sector specific, but which strengthen and develop human and social capital at a territorial level. This involves creating, developing and strengthening relationships that will increase consistency, at the local level, between the objectives and actions of all the dimensions of the rural web. Building cohesion at the local level enables communities and territories to pursue sustainability goals that are defined and planned at the international level.

Notes

1 Walras (1874) shows that in a perfectly competitive market it is possible to determine a balanced price system which implies an equality between supply and demand in all markets, as well as between production costs and the selling price for each item and each entrepreneur. Indeed, Walras proves the existence of a general economic equilibrium that makes Smith's 'invisible hand' redundant. Walras' work laid the foundations for the new theory of economic value, based on the concept of marginal utility.

2 The first theorem of welfare economics states that any competitive equilibrium leads to a Pareto efficient allocation of resources. This merely indicates that no one can become better off without someone becoming made worse off (Pareto 1911). The first theorem is often taken to be an analytical confirmation of Adam Smith's 'invisible hand' hypothesis (Ingrao and Israel 2006). Later, several authors showed that the basic assumptions about perfect competition are misplaced, rendering neoclassical postulates redundant in explaining the real world (Sen 1970, 1971; Scarf and Debreu 1963).

3 Transaction costs can be divided into three broad categories: search and information costs, namely costs incurred by the firm to acquire information about products and services, or to create new products; bargaining and decision costs, namely costs necessary to reach an acceptable agreement with the other party, such as the drafting of a proper contract etc.; policing and enforcement costs, incurred so that agreements are respected (often through legal proceedings).

4 For example, the regulations surrounding Appellations d'Origine and the quality policy of the EU.

5 For example, rural webs, theorized as systems through which human and non-human components in a rural area interact to create sustainable development (Marsden and van der Ploeg 2008; Milone and Ventura 2010), In economic terms, such interactions connect the production of goods and services with the use of land and other resources, creating socio-economic and institutional networks. The nodes of these networks can be spatially concentrated, (represented by the local system), but can also be connected through relational networks to geographically very distant places. These webs play a key role in strategically coordinating the relations of production and trade.

6 For example the lobbying activities of 'food empires' seeking to influence global food markets, or those carried out by movements such as Slow Food to promote high quality artisanal produce.

7 A trade is satisfactory when the parties concerned, although aware that there are more efficient equilibriums, decide to settle in favour of a social benefit or repeated transactions. According to the concept of game theory, this is a second-best solution for the individual actors, but it stabilizes trade and its mode of governance.

8 Opportunistic behaviour, made possible by information asymmetry and limited rationality, can pave the way to what Akerlof (1970) termed 'lemons', i.e. the advantage

derived from selling a used car rather than a new one. This is especially true in large markets (such as the global one). In food markets this phenomenon is leading to a strong increase in the market share for low quality products, often sold as high quality products ('lemons'), and progressive price reductions. The global markets are vulnerable because they are unable to govern trade in a way that ensures that all traders make a fair profit. Instead wealth tends to flow to just a few, leading to business failures. This has two serious consequences: it causes a loss of consumer welfare, as consumers pay more (for lower quality) products; and it increases the social costs required to protect the public interest: e.g. by setting standards and regulating production and distribution methods to maintain public health, desired nutritional levels etc.

9 Social costs are those costs that are not intrinsic to production but which firms incur in order to prevent pollution, ensure consumer protection, workers' health and safety and cover social contributions (pensions, social security etc.).

10 We refer here to forms of transaction in which limited rationality and information asymmetry are counterbalanced by factors such as reputation or institutionalization. These factors help to ensure that the rules are respected and product label information is truthful. They also help reduce transaction costs. Another contributory factor is to develop 'portfolio strategies' which align the boundaries of firms with the reputation of the territory, through collective actions or shared quality schemes. A strong reputation or the existence of collective actions reduces the need for the firm to integrate its internal production functions/activities in order to enhance its business reputation. This allows firms to be specialized but also be integrated in a territorial scheme which progressively protects and enhances the heterogeneity of enterprises, in terms of structure and functions. This can strengthen the territorial dimension and increase resilience to external shocks and changes in markets. It can also increase the potential for innovation allowing firms to function as field laboratories (Stuiver *et al.* 2003) in territorial networks where they share their experiences.

11 From a theoretical point of view, nested markets are based on different types of common pool resources, such as the agricultural landscape (van der Ploeg 2012), that are a form of common capital, often regionally defined. Nested markets are social constructs characterized by a process of 'institutionalization'. In other words, they are driven and protected by a set of rules that go beyond the logic of supply and demand and the maximization of profit and utility. In such markets, we can talk about 'collective utility', a utility that can also be shared by actors who may not be directly involved in the transaction, but who contribute to the construction of the socio-institutional context in which such innovations are introduced and developed. This aspect of institutionalization, often informal, is a particular characteristic of nested markets, setting them apart from other types of market.

12 Less information asymmetry and speculation, collective reputation, social and ethical responsibility of firms, strong role of territorial institutions that limits adverse selection phenomena.

13 The governance of markets is a dimension of the rural web, which can be defined as the institutional capacity to control and strengthen markets and to construct new markets. This capacity is related to the way in which a certain supply chain is organized and how the share, and levels, of income derived from it are distributed among the different players, from producers to consumers. The modes of market governance are influenced by a number of economic, social and political considerations, and can be grouped into three main categories: neo-liberalism, the welfare state and corporate social responsibility (CSR) (Midtun 1999, 2004, cited in Vihinen and Kroger 2008). These models imply different relations between government, civil society and the market. The relevance of the dimension of market governance does not lie as much in identifying alternative forms, but rather agreements between the players involved to avoid one actor dominating the others. On this basis it can be argued that it is less important to identify alternative forms of distribution, but rather to move, through

new models of market governance, from global and regulatory supply chains to local participatory processes (Vihinen and Kroger 2008).

14 These new institutional arrangements represent another dimension of the rural web. From a generic perspective, institutions can be understood as structures and mechanisms of social order and cooperation that govern individual behaviour. Institutions are most commonly understood as sets of regulations, laws, norms or traditions that are shaped through human interactions. They are often manifest in an organizational structure (North 1990). Institutions influence human activities, in particular economic ones, and are a real tool for regulating trade and allocating resources. Institutional arrangements also provide incentives for building trust and reputation and facilitating collective action; conditions that reduce transaction costs (Knickel *et al.* 2008). The main function of a new institutional arrangement, within the framework of sustainable rural development, is to facilitate positive interrelations and produce efficient links between the different sectors and actors within an area and to establish and build relations between the various levels of governance that affect the development of the area. From a more specifically economic point of view, a new institutional arrangement should create the conditions for developing an eco-economy, fostering cooperation between different economic sectors and actors and promoting the creation of networks, knowledge exchange, public-private partnerships, access to information, and increased local control over the distribution of profits. Finally, institutions also embody shared rules (formal and informal) concerning the use of local social and environmental resources.

References

Akerlof, G. (1970) The market for lemons: qualitative uncertainty and the market mechanism, *Quarterly Journal of Economics*, 84: 488–500.

Branson, R. and D. Norvell (1983) *Introduction to Agricultural Marketing*, New York: McGraw Hill.

Chandler, A. (1977) *The Visible Hand: the managerial devolution in American business*, Cambridge (Mass.): Harvard University Press.

Coase, H.R. (1937) The nature of the firm, *Economica*, 4: 386–405.

Coase, H.R. (1960) 'The problem of social cost', *Journal of Law and Economics*, 3: 1–44.

De Rooij, S., F. Ventura and P. Milone (2010) *Large farmers increasingly opt for multifunctionality*, Perugia: DEA, University of Perugia.

Franca, A. (2007) Rapporto finale IV Task, Progetto Interreg III C PASTOMED.

Greenwald B. and J.E. Stiglitz (1986) Externalities in economies with imperfect information and incomplete markets, *The Quarterly Journal of Economics*, 101: 229–264.

Hirschman, A. (1958). *The Strategy of Economic Development*, New Haven: Yale University Press.

Ingrao, B. and G. Israel (2006) *La mano invisibile. L'equilibrio economico nella storia della scienza*, Bari: Laterza.

Kanemasu, Y., R. Sonnino, T. Marsden and S. Schneider (2008) Testing the web: a comparative analysis, in van der Ploeg, J.D. and T. Marsden (eds), *Unfolding Webs. The dynamics of regional rural development*, Assen: Royal van Gorcum.

Keynes, J.M. (1926) *The end of laissez-faire*, London: Hogarth Press.

Keynes, J.M. (1936) *The General Theory of Employment, Interest and Money*, London: Macmillan.

Kitchen, L. and T. Marsden (2006) Assessing the Eco-economy of Rural Wales, Research Report 11, Cardiff: Wales Rural Observatory.

Knickel, K., S. Schiller, H. Vihinen and A. Weber (2008) New institutional arrangements in rural development, in: van der Ploeg, J.D. and T. Marsden (eds), *Unfolding Webs. The dynamics of regional rural development*, Royal van Gorcum, Assen.

Law, J. (1994) *Organizing Modernity*, Oxford: Blackwell.

Leach, M. (2008) Re-framing Resilience: A Symposium Report. STEPS Centre Series no. 18, Brighton.

Long, N. and J.D. van der Ploeg, (1994) Heterogeneity, actor and structure: towards a reconstitution of the concept of structure, in: D. Booth (ed.), *Rethinking Social Development: theory, research and practice*, Harlow: Longman Scientific and Technical.

Marsden, T., J. Murdoch, P. Lowe, R. Munton and A. Flynn (2003) *Constructing the Countryside*, London: UCL Press.

Milone, P. (2008) *Agriculture in Transition*, Assen: Royal van Gorcum.

Milone, P. and Ventura, F. (2000) Theory and practice of multi-product farms: farm butcheries in Umbria, *Sociologia Ruralis*, vol 40: 452–465.

Milone, P. and F. Ventura (2004) *Innovatività Contadina e Sviluppo Rurale: un'analisi neo-istituzionale del cambiamento in agricoltura in tre regioni del Sud Italia*, Milano: Franco Angeli.

Milone, P. and F. Ventura (2010) *I contadini del terzo millennio*, Perugia: AMP editore.

Milone, P. and F. Ventura (eds) (2011) *Networking the Rural*, Assen: Royal van Gorcum.

Morgan, K. and R. Sonnino (2008) *The School Food Revolution. Public food and the challenge of sustainable development*, London: Earthscan.

Midttun, A. (1999) The weakness of strong governance and the strength of soft regulation: environmental governance in post modern form, *Innovation – The European Journal of Social Science* 12: 235–250.

Midttun, A. (2004) Realigning business government and civil society: CSR model compared to the neo-liberal and welfare state models. Paper for the Third Annual Colloquium of the European Academy of Business in Society. Gent.

Murdoch, J. (1998) The spaces of actor-network theory, *Geoforum*, 29: 357–374.

North, D.C. (1990) *Institutions, Institutional Change and Economic Performance*, Cambridge NY: Cambridge University Press.

Oostindie, H., J.D. van der Ploeg, R. van Broekhuizen, F. Ventura and P. Milone (2011). Il ruolo centrale dei "Nested Markets" nello sviluppo rurale in Europa, *Rivista di Economia Agraria*, 65: 191–222.

Osti, G. (1991) *Gli innovatori della periferia, la figura sociale dell'innovatore nell'agricoltura di montagna*, Torino: Reverdito Edizioni.

Palermo, P. (2009) *I limiti del possibile-Governo del territorio e qualità dello sviluppo*, Roma: Donzelli.

Panzar, J. and R. Willing (1982) Economies of scope, *American Economic Review* 71: 268–272.

Parrott, N., N. Wilson and J. Murdoch (2002) Spatialising quality: regional protection and the 'alternative geography' of food, *European Urban and Regional Studies* 9: 241–262.

Pareto, V. (1911) *L'Economie mathematique, in Encyclopedie des sciences mathematiques pures et appliquées*, Paris: Gautiers Villars.

Roep, D. (2002) The Waddengroup Foundation: the added value of quality and region, in van der Ploeg, J.D., A. Long and J. Banks, *Living Countrysides*, Doetinchem: Elsevier.

Saccomandi, V. (1998) *Agricultural Market Economics*, Assen Royal van Gorcum.

Scarf, H. and G. Debreu (1963) A limit theorem on the Core of an Economy, *International Economic Review*, 4: 235–246.

Scettri, R. (2001) *Novità in Campagna*, Roma: IREF.

Schneider, S., S. Shiki and W. Belik (2011) Rural development in Brazil: overcoming inequalities and building new markets, *Rivista di Economia Agraria*, 65: 225–259.

Sen, A.K. (1970) The impossibility of a Paretian liberal, *Journal of Political Economy*, 78: 152–157.

Sen, A.K. (1971) The impossibility of a Paretian liberal: Reply, *Journal of Political Economy*, 79: 1406–1407.

Simon, H.A. (1947) *Administrative Behaviour*, New York: Macmillan.

Simon, H.A. (1957) *Models of Man*, New York: Wiley.

Smith, A. (1961, first publ. 1776) *An Inquiry into the Nature and Causes of the Wealth of Nations*, Methuen: London.

Stirling, A. (2008) The Dynamics of Sustainability: durability, stability, resilience and robustness. Presentation to ERSC workshop on Complexity Economics for Sustainability, Oxford, 28 November.

Stuiver, M., J.D. van der Ploeg and C. Leeuwis (2003) The VEL and VANLA environmental co-operatives as field laboratories, *NJAS – Wageningen Journal of Life Sciences*, 51: 27–40.

Swagemakers, P. (2002) *Making differences: novelty production and the contours of local co-operatives*, Studies van Landbouw and Platteland 33, Wageningen: Wageningen University.

Teece, D.J. (1980) Economies of scope and the scope of the enterprise, *Journal of Economic Behaviour and Organization*. 1: 223–247.

van der Ploeg, J.D. and T. Marsden (eds) (2008) *Unfolding Webs. The dynamics of regional rural development*, Assen: Royal van Gorcum.

van der Ploeg, J.D. (2008) *The New Peasantries: Struggles for autonomy and sustainability in an era of empire and globalization*, London: Earthscan.

Vihinen, H. and L. Kroger (2008) The governance of markets, in: J.D. van der Ploeg and T. Marsden (eds) *Unfolding Webs. The dynamics of regional rural development*, Assen: Royal van Gorcum.

Walras, L. (1874) *Elements d'économie pure, Lausanne, Corbas, trad. it. Elemnti di economia politica pura*, Torino: UTET.

Williamson, O. (1975) *Market and Hierarchies: analysis and implication*, New York: The Free Press.

Williamson, O. (1985) *The Economic Institutions of Capitalism*, New York: The Free Press.

Williamson, O. (1996) *I meccanismi del governo*, Milan: Franco Angeli.

Wiskerke, J.S.C. and J.D. van der Ploeg (eds) (2004) *Seeds of Transition*, Assen: Royal van Gorcum.

4 Family farming, institutional markets and innovations in public policy

Food and nutritional security as a driver for governmental intervention

Claudia Schmitt, Renato Maluf and Walter Belik

Introduction

Over the last decade in Brazil, a series of political, legal and institutional measures have given Food and Nutrition Security (FNS) a central position within public policy and action. The approval of the Organic Law of Food and Nutrition Security, the inclusion of the Human Right to Adequate Food in the Social Rights stipulated in the Brazilian Constitution, the restructuring of the National Food and Nutrition Security Council (*Conselho Nacional de Segurança Alimentar e Nutricional* – CONSEA) and the creation or reformulation of public policy instruments based on the principles of FNS, are the main institutional changes that have occurred in Brazil during this period. One key feature of these changes is that policies and programmes for FNS have been formulated and implemented by governmental agents working closely with civil society organizations (CSOs), and have often led to the implementation of new instruments of state intervention.

The atmosphere of political and social mobilization that existed in Brazilian society after the launch of *Fome Zero* (Zero Hunger Program)[1] by the Lula administration and the re-establishment of CONSEA,[2] led to governmental food purchases for social programmes being influenced by the principles of Food and Nutrition Security.

The Brazilian state is very committed to supporting food for social programmes and maintaining public reserves of foodstuffs. Under the Constitution, all children or youth enrolled in public or recognized private schools are entitled to receive meals from the state. The government also purchases food for social assistance programmes, hospitals, prisons and other institutions. Finally, the Federal Government's maintenance of food stocks is an important instrument for regulating internal prices and guaranteeing food security. All these actions constitute what can be called 'institutional demand'. In Brazil this is quite substantial, given the number of students who receive school meals and the demand from other sources. Until quite recently these supplies were acquired in the regular market and provided by large suppliers.

This chapter focuses on two distinct, though interrelated, experiences of incorporating FNS principles in institutional food purchases in Brazil: the creation and implementation of the Food Acquisition Programme (*Programa de Aquisição de Alimentos* – PAA) and the reformulation of the National School Meals Programme (*Programa Nacional de Alimentação Escolar* – PNAE). These are two federal programmes with a nationwide scope but quite distinct institutional trajectories. They each use different mechanisms for incorporating family farmers as suppliers of foodstuffs for public programmes.

In 2003 PAA began as a pilot programme buying food from 42,000 family farmers. After ten years, in 2012, it was buying from 185,000 family farmers, 4.2 per cent of the 4.3 million family farms registered in Brazil (IBGE 2009). The funds allocated to the programme have also significantly expanded over this period, reaching R$838 million (US$356 million) in 2012 (IPC-IG, 2013). In 2014, investments are expected to rise to R$1.9 billion (US$808 million) (Brasil 2011). Food distribution schemes organized through the PAA reached approximately 15.5 million people between 2007 and 2010 (Brasil 2010).

The PNAE offers around 46 million free schools daily to students. The Federal government transferred R$3.3 billion in 2012 (US$1.4 million) to states and municipalities to acquire this food. At least one third of these funds (R$1.1 billion, US$478 million) is required to be spent buying food directly from family farmers. However, this percentage has not yet been reached, as the new legislation is still being implemented.

Our analytical perspective focuses on the political and institutional dynamics which allows the family farming sector to receive preferential treatment in Brazil's public procurement programmes. At the same time, we examine how these programmes have been implemented, specifically in balancing supply and demand and ensuring quality and availability. This involves a delicate balancing act: prioritizing purchasing from a specific group of suppliers and ensuring the achievement of FNS as a universal right.

The first part of this chapter provides a brief literature-based review of the international debate about incorporating the principles of social justice[3] and environmental sustainability[4] within governmental procurement programmes. In the next section, the main juridical mechanisms for regulating public procurement in Brazil are discussed and their more recent evolution. After this, we outline the political and institutional processes which allow the principles of FNS to be incorporated within food purchases made under the PAA and the PNAE, including a brief comparison of the operational design of these two programmes. In the conclusions we look at the achievements of these two programmes and the challenges they face.

Sovereignty, sustainability and equity in governmental purchases: the international context

At the international level, governments and multilateral development agencies have been discussing the role of governmental procurement since the end of the 1970s. The first agreement related to this theme, resulting from a multilateral negotiation process between states, was signed in 1979, as part of the GATT negotiations (General Agreement on Tariffs and Trade) which came into force in 1981. Its general objective was to eliminate non-tariff barriers between signatory countries, creating an environment of *transparency* and *non-discrimination*[5] between national and foreign suppliers for governmental purchases, effectively forbidding practices and procedures which could be considered as restrictive to trade.

In 1994, as part of the Uruguay Round negotiations, the Government Procurement Agreement (GPA) was proposed, supported by some (but not all) of the member states of the WTO (World Trade Organization). This multilateral agreement sought to guarantee transparent and non-discriminatory treatment in governmental acquisitions of products and services and in the contracting of infrastructure projects. The underlying aim was to extend the liberalization of markets and strengthen international trade.

Brazil was not among the signatories of the GPA, and was wary about opening governmental purchases to international competition. When the agreement was revised in 2011, Brazil adopted the position that the country should 'maintain its ability to adopt public policies that can stimulate development'. As a result it continued to privilege governmental purchases from domestic suppliers or Mercosul (Common Market of the South) countries (Moreira, 2011).

The GPA raises a series of questions related to food sovereignty and the right of each nation state to define its own agricultural and food policy and to protect and regulate its domestic agricultural production and trade.[6] Brazil was recently questioned on the WTO Agricultural Committee by the United States and Canada about public funds invested in the PAA and the PNAE for the purchase and distribution of food in social programmes, which they view as an indirect form of subsidy to agriculture and rural producers, and hence in violation of international rules (Chade, 2013). Episodes of this type are indicative of tensions within the global agri-food system, an environment in which transnational food and agricultural corporations have enormous power and where there are intense disputes over trade rules and the control of productive resources.

The debate about governmental procurement also came to the fore in the OECD's (Organization for Economic Cooperation and Development) deliberations in the 1990s and 2000s. An OECD publication entitled *Public Procurement for Sustainable and Inclusive Growth: enabling reform through evidence and peer reviews* (OECD 2012), drew attention to the fact that 'public procurement is big business', estimating governmental expenditure on products, services, and infrastructure to be on average 13 per cent of the GDP of its member countries, although with significant variations among them. According to the OECD, a significant part of this value (69 per cent) is spent by provincial and local governments (OECD 2012).

From the 1990s onwards, both the OECD and the European Union assumed favourable positions towards the incorporation of principles of sustainability in governmental purchases. In 2002 the OECD approved a specific recommendation aimed at improving the environmental performance of governmental acquisitions (Johnstone and Erdlenbruch 2003) and has since published various other documents on this theme. Public purchases have come to be seen as an important tool for strengthening synergies between innovation, markets and environmental protection. Yet at the same time the OECD remains committed to the removal of commercial barriers and ensuring that governmental expenditure represents value for money. In a recent publication the OECD presented a set of indicators about the strategic use of government procurement (OECD 2013). According to this publication, by 2011, 25 of the OECD's 33 member states had adopted policies and actions for green public procurement – mostly guided by environmental criteria; 23 countries had implemented measures aimed at incorporating small and medium sized companies in institutional markets, while 16 of them used governmental purchases as a support instrument for innovative products and services. In OECD discourses the growing valorization of these innovations has advanced in parallel with other objectives, such as emphasizing value for money in public expenditure and minimizing waste and corruption.

Within the European Union (EU) there has also been debate about incorporating the principles of sustainability in public procurement. In the past decade these debates have moved from an initial reference to green public procurement (GPP) to an idea of sustainable public procurement (SPP), which seeks to embrace the economic, social, and environmental aspects of sustainable development (Morgan and Sonnino 2010, Steurer *et al.*, 2007).

In 2007, a study carried out by the High Level Group on Corporate Social Responsibility, identified 103 SPP initiatives within the Union (Steurer *et al.*, 2007). The authors noted a predominance of 'smoother' instruments (from a regulatory point of view) and relatively few enforced implementations of SPP. They also observed that it was often difficult to incorporate social aspects within SPP.

It has frequently been argued that technical specifications related to the environment can be more readily incorporated within the norms and rules that govern public procurement than ethical or social specifications linked to sustainable development. Morgan (2008) claims that governments and large corporations perceive the environmental dimension as less problematic than the other two. Environmental variables are more easily managed than economic and social aspects, which raise questions about social justice and economic democracy, potentially challenging the status quo.

This echoes McCrudden's (2004) observation that there are many disconnections between the institutional strategies associated with GPP and the incorporation of social considerations in governmental purchases. McCrudden's research demonstrates that state contracting of goods and services has been used since (at least) the nineteenth century as a mechanism for social regulation, preventing unemployment and reinforcing desired patterns of labour relations. This process expanded during the twentieth century, especially in Europe and the United States, with the advent of the welfare state. Governments have also used social criteria in their procurement policies in order to promote social justice and overcome various forms of inequality and discrimination (McCrudden 2007).

This brief overview shows that governmental purchases have long been the subject of debate and controversy. They are the subject of global disputes, yet are seen as a way of solving problems that challenge longstanding institutional-ized power relationships and are a focus for emergent social dynamics. Multi-lateral agencies, such as the WTO, view the procurement of products, services, and infrastructural works by government as a market that should be internation-alized and regulated through voluntarily directives or international treaties. Pro-ponents of a green economy see government procurement policies as an instrument capable of encouraging the production and consumption of environ-mentally sustainable services. Finally for the social movements engaged with defending food sovereignty, they are a mechanism that mobilizes the purchasing power of the state so that it can ensure rights, redistribute resources and promote sustainable ways of life.

Several research projects have explored the connections between public pur-chases of food and the transformation of the agri-food system (Morgan and Sonnino 2010, Izumi *et al.* 2010, Triches and Schneider 2010, Allen and Guthman 2006). Many of these studies emphasize that government procurement has the potential to reconnect agriculture and food with their social and environ-mental surrounds, creating institutional links between sustainable food produc-tion and the public plate.[7]

This literature has produced some interesting debates and controversies. Several authors see the defence of the local as a privileged (and at times romanti-cized) space for the exercise of new food-related values as being problematic (Winter 2003, Goodman *et al.* 2012, Morgan and Sonnino 2010). Political and institutional arrangements to facilitate the acquisition of organic or local food in the United States school system and the public-private partnerships established to implement them have been criticized for having a neoliberal bias (Allen and Guthman 2006). Morgan and Sonnino (2010) have done detailed case studies (in New York, Rome, London and Ghana) examining the political and institutional complexity that characterizes 'the byzantine world of governmental procure-ment'. They highlight the numerous challenges involved in the transition to a sustainable system of school meals that incorporates environmental dimensions together with social justice and economic democracy.

These various initiatives, which seek to reconfigure the role of government procurement, can play a key role in contributing to the sustainability of existing agri-food systems. Yet they also involve establishing a labyrinth of regulations. The following section explores the complexity of these in Brazil.

Regulatory mechanisms for government procurement in Brazil

In Brazil, legal mechanisms aimed at regulating the purchase of goods and ser-vices by public administrations have been in place since the beginning of the twentieth century. But it was only with the 1988 Constitution that governmental purchases came to be systemically regulated. Under Article 37 of the Federal Constitution the guiding principles of public administration are defined as: legal-ity, impersonality, morality, publicity and efficiency. These parameters are intended to regulate governmental contracts. Law 8666/1993 regulated Article

37 of the Constitution, consolidating a wide range of norms which now govern public bidding and contracts entered into by public administration. In the 1990s, and later in the 2000s, the Public Bidding Law was amended a number of times through a series of regulations and bureaucratic procedures which sought to overcome restrictions to family farmers accessing institutional markets.

An in-depth examination of this legal device is outside the scope of this chapter. It is, nonetheless, worth highlighting some aspects of the law, which can help to contextualize the initiatives that emerged in an attempt to introduce new selection criteria for governmental procurement of goods and services. Law 8666/1993 established different types of bidding, taking into account the price offered and/or the technical specifications for the product or service in question (Brasil 2010). It also allows for different bidding processes: direct competition, price-setting, public contests, invitations and auctions. Exemption from[8] bidding can be permitted in specific circumstances stipulated by law. Originally, these Brazilian legislation processes did not establish any fiscal, labour, commercial, legal, or other form of differentiation between Brazilian and foreign companies (Moreira and Morais 2002), a criteria that was recently altered by Law 12.349/2010.[9]

Law 8666/1993 establishes a system which stipulates a sequence of procedures which require contracting parties to make significant time and resource investments in order to meet these legislative demands. Historically these rules acted as an entry barrier to family farmers and their organizations, (although for very small volumes of produce these requirements were simplified). As the procurement requirements were primarily focused on regulating the agricultural product market, they used one purchase system for agri-businesses and family farming, which historically prevented the large majority of family producers from selling their produce to the government.

Law 12.349, approved in 2010, altered Article 3 of the Public Bidding Law, introducing the promotion of sustainable national development as a selection criteria for government procurement. A later decree[10] defined the following criteria for sustainability: (a) less impact on natural resources, such as flora, fauna, air, soil and water; (b) a preference for materials, technologies and raw materials with a local origin; (c) greater efficiency in the use of natural resources, such as water and energy; (d) the generation of more jobs, preferentially employing local labour; (e) longer working life and lower maintenance cost of the items purchased; (f) the use of innovations which reduce pressure on natural resources, and (g) acceptable environmental origin of the natural resources used in goods, services and works. This new criteria have only very recently been implemented so it is too early to properly evaluate the decree's effect. It does however reflect an ambition to move beyond solely environmental aspects of sustainability.

Data from the Brazilian Ministry of Planning, Budgeting and Administration (*Ministério do Planejamento, Orçamento e Gestão* – MPOG) shows that, in 2012, sustainable purchases only accounted for 0.1 per cent of the total governmental spend (including those made by agencies and foundations) of R$72.6 billion (approximately US$31.5 billion). No separate figures are available for food purchases, whether or not from the family farming sector.[11]

In Brazil the new perspectives about the criteria used in procuring goods, services and infrastructure works seem to have been propelled by two distinct visions of institutional purchases.[12] On the one hand it's possible to identify in recent years, the implementation, at the federal level, of a series of measures aimed at stimulating sustainable public procurement (SPP). This effort seems to be grounded in the international debate about SPP and the role of the State in promoting sustainable development. In the Guide to Sustainable Purchases for the Federal Administration (Brasil, undated),[13] sustainable procurement is described as an approach which seeks to 'integrate environmental and social considerations in all phases of governmental purchase and contracting processes, aiming at reducing impacts on human health, the environment, and human rights'. According to the same manual 'the practice of SPP allows the specific needs of final consumers to be met through the purchase of the product which offers the greatest number of benefits for the environment and society' (Brasil undated, p. 9). SPP has created a large market for businesses with an ethos of sustainability and stimulated competiveness and innovation. It is important to note that, at the federal level, most sustainable purchases are industrial products, and the largest purchasers are the Ministries of Justice, Education, and Defence, which were jointly responsible for 70 per cent of sustainable contracting in 2012.[14]

Food purchases from the family farming sector that are exempt from competitive bidding has been practiced in Brazil since 2003, but its implementation cannot solely be explained by the institutionalization dynamics of SPP. The two central objectives of the Food Acquisition Programme are: to provide access to food for people suffering from food insecurity and to promote social and economic inclusion in the countryside, through strengthening family farming.[15] The objectives of other main food acquisition programme, the PNAE[16] include: (i) the adoption of a healthy and adequate diet, composed of healthy and safe foods, respecting culture, traditions and promoting healthy eating habits among students; (ii) support for sustainable development, with incentives for the acquisition of a diverse range of foodstuffs produced at the local level, preferentially by family farmers and rural family entrepreneurs, prioritizing traditional indigenous communities and the remnants of *quilombos*,[17] and; (iii) universal provision to students registered in the public education network.

It is worth noting that the priority attributed by the Lula (2003–2006 and 2007–2010) and Dilma Roussef administrations (2011 to the present) to the fight against hunger and the reduction of poverty and social inequalities strongly influenced the establishment of the PAA and the reformulation of the PNAE. These policy objectives had broader developmental aspects: seeking to promote economic stability, the provision of social services and benefits to the bottom half of the income spectrum (fostering market inclusion) and the expansion of the domestic market. Consumer access to credit (above all for housing), wage growth and cash transfer policies were other important accompanying instruments of state intervention (Singer 2012, Alves 2013, Arbix and Martin 2010)[18]

The use of the state's purchasing power as a tool for promoting growth and social inclusion is part of this political agenda. However, as we explain later, exemptions for the family farming sector from bidding for sales to social distribution programmes can only be explained by taking into account the historic struggle of family farmers for differentiated recognition in public policies, and the lobbying of Brazilian CSOs who put FNS centre stage in public policy.

The Food Acquisition Programme and the National School Feeding Programme: weaving new connections between food policy, family farming and institutional markets

Brazil's experience in structuring an institutional framework to organize food acquisitions from family farmers to supply school meals and social assistance programmes is part of a broader movement that links the (socially constructed) category of family farmers to the process of formulating and implementing FNS policies. Organized civil society groups are strongly involved in this process.

Since 2003 the fight against hunger and the eradication of poverty has (once again) become a priority for the Brazilian State. Hunger emerged as a public issue as far back as the 1940s and 1950s, and re-emerged after the re-democratization of the country in the 1980s. At the beginning of the 1990s, following the defeat of Lula in the presidential elections, a 'parallel government' – a shadow cabinet was organized by the *Partido dos Trabalhadores*. Against the context of widespread market liberalization and spending cuts designed to cut the budgetary deficit this shadow cabinet proposed a National Food Security Policy (Leão and Maluf 2012). In 1993, when there was much social pressure to impeach President Collor, a group of CSOs launched a campaign called *Ação da Cidadania contra a Fome, a Miséria e Pela Vida* (Action of Citizenship against Hunger and Misery and for Life). Citizen committees, organized by churches, labour unions and other CSOs, were established across the country to take emergency grassroots actions to counter the hunger that was widespread at the time. The campaign also sought to foster public debate around structural issues, such as employment and agrarian reform. In 1993, under the Presidency of Itamar Franco, the National Food and Nutrition Security Council (*Conselho Nacional de Segurança Alimentar e Nutricional – CONSEA*) was created. This led to the organization, in 1994, of the First National Food and Nutrition Security Conference, in which CSOs played a major role.

Two years later, in 1995, the newly elected President, Fernando Henrique Cardoso, closed down CONSEA and established a new strategy for social programmes with a focus on decentralizing anti-poverty measures. This effectively narrowed the scope of the FNS measures for reducing hunger and malnutrition, targeting them towards specific segments of the population (Valente 2004: 397). FNS only reoccupied a central place in the government's agenda in 2003, following the election of Lula as President and the launching of the *Fome Zero* (Zero Hunger) Strategy.

Fome Zero initially estimated that its target population included 44 million people, 45.5 per cent of whom lived in rural areas (Instituto Cidadania 2001). It recognized that the main cause of hunger was not an inadequate supply of food, but limited purchasing power among low income groups. The programme included both people excluded from the labour market and those on low incomes. It aimed to: (i) expand demand for food among the socially vulnerable; (ii) encourage the supply of foodstuffs by family farming and production aimed at self-consumption, (through a set of agricultural policies that included FNS as a strategic objective), and (iii) implement an emergency programme aimed at those excluded from the labour market (Instituto Cidadania 2001). This document identified institutional markets as a potential instrument for strengthening family farming. The *Fome Zero* was incorporated in the Federal Government's 2004–2007 Plan and was strongly supported by CSOs.

This created the possibility for creating differentiated or nested markets,[19] whose governance structures and forms of coordination depended strongly on the state's legal framework and institutional apparatus – but which also had important links with different social networks. A fundamental aspect of this was the recognition of family farmers as a specific and distinct category of producers.

This recognition was the culmination of a 50-year struggle by rural workers (peasants, family farmers and wage labourers) that had created an agenda that called for access to health care and social security, agrarian reform and land rights and an agricultural policy that recognized the role of family farmers. While this movement was harshly repressed during the military governments of the 1960s and 1970s, it re-emerged in the 1980s following the re-democratization of the country.

The 1988 Federal Constitution, reinforced by other legal mechanisms, contributed to the recognition of the social rights of farmers and agricultural wage labourers working in family-based economic structures. From 1995, the Federal Government responded – at least partially – to the demands of rural CSOs, and established specific regulations and payment rules to allocate credits to family farmers. This new line of credit, known as PRONAF (*Programa Nacional de Fortalecimento da Agricultura Familiar* – the National Programme for Strengthening Family Farming), marked a small change in the ways in which credit was targeted at small-scale agricultural producers.

PRONAF was subsequently improved by the creation of new loan categories and rebate criteria which established a financing system more suited to the needs of family farming. A range of other policy instruments was also created, including agricultural insurance tailored for family farming, the National Rural Technical Assistance and Extension Policy, the National Programme of Sustainable Development for Rural Territories and the Food Acquisition Programme.

The definition of family farming adopted by PRONAF has been the subject of numerous controversies among academics and family farming organizations. Originally dating from the 1990s, the definition has been redrafted a number of times, and was later consolidated by Law 11.326/2006, which established

The Directives for the Formulation of the National Family Farming and Rural Family Enterprises Policy. This law established four criteria for defining family farming: (i) the land should not exceed four fiscal modules;[20] (ii) the farm should mainly rely on family labour; (iii) a minimum percentage of family income must be derived from the agricultural establishment or enterprise;[21] (iv) the farm has to be administered/managed by the farmer and his or her family. The social construction of family farming as a political category[22] played an important role in influencing the form of government procurement programmes such as the PAA and the PNAE.

The PAA was created in 2003 as one of the central pillars of the *Fome Zero* strategy. It was conceived during the preparation of the 2003–2004 Family Farming Harvest Plan, with the strong involvement of CONSEA. One of its innovative characteristics was that its institutional design created an inter-sectoral connection that linked agricultural policies with FNS policies and poverty reduction strategies. Foodstuffs produced by family farmers are acquired by the Federal Government through a simplified purchase mechanism and are used to build up public stocks, which are then distributed to people suffering from food insecurity, supplied to different food assistance programmes (through popular restaurants, food banks, community kitchens, and others), or to supplement the PNAE.

The PAA utilizes a diverse set of purchase mechanisms which means it can be applied in different situations.[23] The programmes' resources can only be used to purchase products from family farming (a key difference with the PNAE).

Brazil has had a national school meals programme since the 1950s. During this time the programme has undergone various reformulations, including becoming universal and changing its name to the National School Meals Programme (*Programa Nacional de Alimentação Escolar* – PNAE) in 1979. Unlike the PAA, which since its creation has been aimed at strengthening family farming, it was only in 2009, following approval by the National Congress of Law 11.947/2009, that the PNAE allowed preferential acquisition procedures for the produce of family farming. The new law stipulated that a minimum of 30 per cent of total funds allocated to state and municipal governments and federal schools have to be used to acquire foodstuffs directly from family farmers or their organizations, with priority being given to settlements established under agrarian reform programs, traditional indigenous communities, and *quilombola* communities. These regulations significantly expanded family farmers' opportunities to gain access to public food procurement. Previously they had only indirectly or occasionally participated in this market. Furthermore, this market offers a reliable demand for high volumes of produce, as the programme is implemented across all of Brazil's municipalities. As well as creating a market for local products it also validates and strengthens local food cultures among students.

Both the PAA and the PNAE use the legal definition of family farming in defining those who qualify for preferential access to institutional markets. In order to qualify, farmers must hold a Declaration of Aptitude to PRONAF

(DAP), a certificate issued to family farmers by institutions and organizations accredited by the Ministry of Agrarian Development. As such, the DAP acts as an entry point (or barrier) depending on the whether farmers are able to access these different institutions.

In Morgan and Sonnino's exploration (2010) of the acquisition of local products for school meals in developing countries they observed that the process does not simply involve directing institutional purchases to a new type of supplier or product, but rather *'fashion(ing) a supply side from scratch'* (Morgan and Sonnino 2010: 154). This involves constructing the conditions under which farmers can actually participate in this market. What is important in the acquisition of family farmed products is the political decision to strengthen family farming as a specific way of practicing agriculture and organizing agricultural activities, producing positive connections between agricultural policies and the provision of care for vulnerable social groups.

Both the PAA and the PNAE directly purchase from family farmers or through bodies which are formally recognized as family farming organizations (associations or cooperatives). This is a very significant achievement, and was the subject of numerous controversies at critical moments, such as the reformulation of the School Meals Law. Both programmes stipulate an annual limit in the amount sold per year by each family farm. In the PNAE this is currently R\$20,000 (approximately US\$8,500), while in the case of the PAA these values vary between R\$5,500 (approximately US\$2,826) and R\$8,000 per year (approximately US\$3,400). The aim here is to avoid an excessive concentration of supply from a limited number of producers. In certain circumstances a farmer can participate in more than one programme or purchase scheme simultaneously, expanding his or her share in the institutional market.

The funds provided by the Ministry of Social Development and the Fight Against Hunger (*Ministério do Desenvolvimento Social e Combate à Fome* – MDS) and the Ministry of Agrarian Development (*Ministério do Desenvolvimento Agrário* – MDA) involve two distinct system of implementation. In one the funds are given to the National Provisioning Company (*Companhia Nacional de Abastecimento* – CONAB)[24] and then passed on to a wide range of family farming organizations. In the other, state and municipal governments who have signed up to the Terms of Adhesion[25] use covenants to operationalize the programme. These different decentralization mechanisms give the programme some flexibility, allowing the PAA to be able to acquire an extremely diverse range of products to meet different food demands. At the national level the programme is deliberatively administered by a group which includes representatives from six different ministries. Control over the social aspects of the programme is exercised by the Councils of Food and Nutrition Security (CONSEA).

The PNAE is a nationwide programme involving federal, provincial and municipal levels of government. Linking this long-established programme to supporting family farming involved redesigning its established regulatory frameworks and operationalization schemes; a process of transformation that is still under way. The management of the programme is coordinated by the National

Development Fund for Education (*Fundo Nacional de Desenvolvimento da Edu-cação* – FNDE). There is a decentralized management structure which involves public authorities at three levels (municipalities, states and federal).

The modifications introduced by the new School Meals Law, passed in 2009, significantly expanded the scope of the programme which now covers pupils in infant and secondary schools as well as young people and adults in education. The management of the programme at the state and municipal levels is overseen by the School Meals Councils (*Conselhos de Alimentação Escolar* – CAEs).

The local administrators of the PNAE publish public notifications of the food it wishes to acquire from the family farming sector, specifying the prices and quantities of products required for school meals from local producers (which take into account the characteristics of local agriculture).

Both the PAA and the PNAE offer a premium of up to 30 per cent for organic or agroecological products. The PNAE also gives priority to local and organic or agroecological foodstuffs if there are competing tenders. Sustainability, season-ality and the diversification of agricultural products in the region are other factors that are included in the directives for the preparation of the menus offered in schools. There is a strong emphasis on acquiring basic foodstuffs, with restric-tions on the purchase of processed foods, such as tinned food, cold meats/ sausages or semi-prepared products and a ban on the acquisition of drinks with low nutritional value (such as soft drinks). With the PNAE, nutritionists oversee the nutritional adequacy of the meal service provided by its outlets.

While there are differences between the two programmes (described above), there are important complementarities between them too, as they are part of the same institutional innovation regarding governmental purchases. Various reports (IPC-IG, 2013, Maluf 2009) have highlighted how the creation of the PAA set a benchmark for other programmes (such as the PNAE) to establish protected markets to support family farmers. The PAA demonstrated the feasibility of this approach to other social programmes. Also, as more programmes become involved in such purchasing arrangements, public administrators and farmer organizations have become more adept at managing these transactions.

Final considerations

The Brazilian experience in constructing new market circuits for governmental procurement as an instrument for strengthening family farming is currently being consolidated. Above all, it represents an exercise in food sovereignty, the ability of each country to define its agricultural policy and development strategies. The pro-grammes analysed have led to the creation of differentiated markets, which are designed to strengthen family farming and which also incorporate incentives to encourage organic and ecological agriculture. It is important to note that this has occurred in a country in which 85 per cent of farming establishments qualify as family farms (4.3 million agricultural establishments), but which only occupy 25 per cent of the total agricultural land area (IBGE 2009) and where the commercial farming sector receives a far greater share of public funds than family farming

Since its establishment the PAA was designed to function as a bridge between agricultural policies and social protection policies. The aim was to significantly strengthen the productive and commercial potential of family farming activities. The programme provides important support for a wide range of regional initiatives, reinforcing the identity, autonomy and self-esteem of communities marginalized by traditional agricultural policies.[26]

A recent study by IPC-IG (2013) of the PNAE showed that 48 per cent of municipalities and states that had submitted their accounts to FNDE, purchased food from the family farming sector (independent of the percentage) in 2010, and by 2012, this figure had risen to 67 per cent. According to data collected by the same authors, in 2012, 45 per cent of PNAE implementation agencies were already using 30 per cent or more of the funds received to purchase products from the family farming sector and 29 per cent of the total funds allocated by FNDE for the implementation of PNAE was being used in these acquisitions, albeit with strong disparities between the regions.

Without a doubt the implementation of these two programmes has made a substantial contribution to increasing the volume of family farmed produce purchased by the Brazilian government and as a result has strengthened the resilience of this farming sector. Nevertheless, in implementing these policies some important constraints and obstacles have been encountered.

First, differential treatment in public policy requires the use of objective criteria. In these programmes two main forms have been used. The first, which is social, is proof of belonging to the family farming sector through possession of a family farming certificate (DAP). However women, young people, indigenous peoples, and traditional peoples and communities often experience great difficulties in obtaining such a certificate, thus effectively excluding these groups from participation in these newly created markets. The second criterion is the economic cut-off established by the annual sales limit. There has been some pressure to expand this limit, based on the argument that this would expand economic opportunities for participating families. Yet this would run the risk of undermining the ethos of the programmes by reproducing conventional market dynamics through the concentration of purchases from a reduced number of families with a higher individual volume of production.

It should also be highlighted that the PAA and PNAE have employed different research methods to arrive at their price setting, which often means that they offer different prices for similar produce, even within the same region. Equally with high inflation rates affecting food prices, the cost of maintaining these programmes is constantly increasing. Finally, it is worth emphasizing that the purchase of organic or agroecological products does not attract extra funding for the programme operators, sometimes leaving them facing the dilemma of whether to expand the quantity they purchase or give priority to quality.

Notes

1 The *Fome Zero* programme was launched in 2003 at the beginning of the first Lula administration and had four central themes: (i) expanding access to foodstuffs; (ii) strengthening family farming; (iii) income generation; (iv) social linking, mobilization and control (Brasil 2003, Leão and Maluf 2012).

2 About two-thirds of the members (the board?) of CONSEA are civil society representatives, the other third being government officials.

3 The idea of social justice draws on a series of questions involving the equality of rights, access to resources and capacities, the liberty and autonomy of individuals and groups and different understandings of what a 'good life' means. Important steps towards the construction of a reflexive vision of justice have been developed by Goodman, DuPuis and Goodman (2012). Their concept moves away from a pre-established vision of justice and emphasizes the processes and relations (which operate at different levels) through which justice is constructed.

4 Agroecology, as a field of knowledge, is taken to refer to the study of the sustainability of agricultural systems and the agri-food system as a whole. See: Gliessman (1997) and Francis *et al.* (2004).

5 The terms in italics are those used in the official text of the WTO – GPA agreement. Retrieved from: www.wto.org/english/docs_e/legal_e/tokyo_gpr_e.pdf. (27 November 2013).

6 It's important to note that food sovereignty is an expression that has multiple meanings that allow for different conceptual and contextual associations. An interesting discussion on the topic can be found in the proceedings of the 'Agrarian Conference on Food Sovereignty – A Critical Dialogue' which was held in September, 2013 and sponsored by the Programme in Agrarian Studies at Yale University and the Journal of Peasant Studies. See: www.yale.edu/agrarianstudies/foodsovereignty/ (15 December 2013).

7 Here we borrow the expression used by Morgan and Sonnino (2010) and Morgan (2008).

8 Exemption from bidding is permissible by law in times of war, public order disturbances, calamities and when the Federal government has to intervene economically to regulate prices and normalize supply.

9 Law 12.349/2010 established the promotion of Brazilian sustainable development as an objective for public administration, opening space for the definition of margins of preference for nationally manufactured/provided goods and services in public bidding. As Monteiro (2011) notes, this involves a substantive alteration in the role of public purchases in the promotion of the internal market in Brazil. (2013, December 2012). Retrieved from: www.planalto.gov.br/ccivil_03/_Ato20072010/2010/Lei/L12349.htm (15 December 2013).

10 Decree 7.746/2012. Retrieved from: www.planalto.gov.br/ccivil_03/_Ato2011–2014/2012/Decreto/D7 746.htm. (15 December 2013).

11 See: BRASIL. Ministério do Planejamento, Orçamento e Gestão. (2012). Retrieved from: www.comprasnet.gov.br/ajuda/Estatisticas/2013/01_A_08_INFORMATIVO_COMPRASNET_Compras_Sustentaveis_2013.pdf (12 December 2013).

12 It is too early to ask whether or not these perspectives are contradictory, considering the different ways in which SPP and governmental purchases from the family farm sector equate social and environmental criteria. As we describe below, the PAA and the PNAE also consider quality, allowing the acquisition of organic or agroecological products with a price incentive of up to 30 per cent.

13 The guide (Guia de Compras Públicas Sustentáveis para Administração Federal) was published by the MPOG (in full please) in partnership with the ICLEI – Local Governments for Sustainability, a global association of cities and local governments for sustainable development.

14 Retrieved from: www.planejamento.gov.br/conteudo.asp?p=noticia&ler=9387 (15 December 2013).
15 BRASIL, Ministério do Desenvolvimento Social e Combate à Fome. Retrieved from: www.mds.gov.br/segurancaalimentar/decom/paa (15 December 2013).
16 See: Law 11.947/2009. Retrieved from: www.planalto.gov.br/ccivil_03/_ato2007–2010/2009/lei/l11947.htm (17 December 2013).
17 In Brazil the remnants of *quilombo* communities are defined according to the law as 'the ethnic-racial groups, according to self-attributed criteria, with their own historic trajectory and with specific territorial relations, with the presumption of a black ancestry related to resistance to the historic oppression suffered.' Decree no. 4887/2003. Retrieved from: www.planalto.gov.br/ccivil_03/decreto/2003/d4887.htm (15 December 2013).
18 The emergence of a new post-neoliberal developmentalism in Brazil has been the subject of numerous debates and controversies. Authors such as Singer (2012) and Alves (2013) interpret the neo-developmentalism that has characterized the Lula and Dilma Roussef administrations who led the Partido dos Trabalhadores (Workers' Party), as 'weak reformism', marked by the implementation of a series of social programmes with important redistributive effects, but equally by strong public incentives to strengthen large private economic groups; state support for business agriculture and the export of commodities and strong state investments in large infrastructure projects, often through public-private partnerships. According to Ban (2012) successive recent Brazilian governments have crafted a hybrid paradigm preserving some of the policy content of the Washington Consensus, while incorporating neo-developmentalist goals and policy instruments.
19 The concept of nested markets can be viewed as a heuristic way of describing arrangements that are located in a frontier zone between markets and hierarchical forms of governance (Polman *et al.*, 2010). They involve hybrid structures of governance anchored in a series of dynamic relations that involve institutions, networks and places. This permits new market circuits to emerge that are relatively independent of global market networks (van der Ploeg 2011).
20 The fiscal module is an agrarian measurement unit representing the minimum area for rural properties to be considered economically viable. A fiscal module can vary between 5 and 110 hectares, depending on the region. (Landau *et al.* 2012).
21 Originally the percentage was 80 per cent of the total family income. The recognition of pluriactivity as a contemporary feature of rural families has led to this being reduced.
22 Positive discrimination towards family farming is justified because of the role it plays in food supply, job creation and the eradication of poverty in rural areas.
23 The PAA currently has the following mechanisms: (i) Purchase with simultaneous donation, which allows the acquisition of products at a local level for donation; (ii) Direct purchase for stock formation by CONAB; (iii) Stock formation by family farmers' organizations for future selling; (iv) Milk production and consumption incentives, centred on the acquisition of milk in the north-eastern region, and; (v) Institutional purchase, which allows states, municipalities, and other public bodies to acquire food with their own resources with exemption from the public bidding process for prisons, barracks, universities, etc.
24 Since 2003, the National Provisioning Company (CONAB) has carried out activities related to family farming via the PAA.
25 The Term of Adhesion is a renewable form of agreement that allows the Federal Government to allocate financial resources to state and municipal governments to support the implementation of the PAA, according to an established work plan.
26 For an overview of the widespread literature about PAA, including various case studies, see Grisa *et al.* (2009).

References

Allen, P. and Guthman, J. (2006) 'From old-school to farm-to-school. Neoliberalization from the ground up', *Agriculture and Human Values* 23: 401–415.

Alves, G. (2013) '*Neodesenvolvimentismo e precarização do trabalho no Brasil – Parte II*', Blog da Boitempo, August 19, 2013. Retrieved from: http://blogdaboitempo.com. br/category/colunasgiovanni-alves/ (17 December 2013).

Arbix, G. and Martin, S. B. (2010) 'Beyond developmentalism and market fundamentalism in Brazil: inclusionary State activism without statism', paper presented at Workshop on States, Development and Global Governance, Madison, US: Global Legal Studies Center and the Center for World Affairs and the Global Economy (WAGE) – University of Wisconsin-Madison.

Ban, C. (2013) 'Brazil's liberal neo-developmentalism: new paradigm or edited orthodoxy?', *Review of International Political Economy* 20: 298–331.

Brasil, 4a Conferência Nacional de Segurança Alimentar e Nutricional (2011) *Declaração pelo Direito Humano à Alimentação Adequada e Saudável*, Salvador-BA: 4a CNSAN.

Brasil, Grupo Gestor do Programa de Aquisição de Alimentos (2010a) *Balanço de Avaliação da Execução do Grupo Gestor do Programa de Aquisição de Alimentos – PAA*, Brasília-DF: Grupo Gestor do PAA.

Brasil, Ministério do Planejamento, Orçamento e Gestão and ICLEI (n.d) *Guia de Compras Públicas Sustentáveis para Administração Federal*, Brasília-DF: MPOG/ ICLEI. Retrieved from: http://archive.iclei.org/index.php?id=7172 (12 December 2013).

Brasil, Ministério Extraordinário de Segurança Alimentar e Combate à Fome (2003) *Política de Segurança Alimentar para o Brasil. Fome Zero: o Brasil que come ajudando o Brasil que tem fome*, Brasília-DF: MESA.

Brasil, Tribunal de Contas da União (2010b) *Licitações & Contratos. Orientações e Jurisprudência do TCU* (4A ed.), Brasília-DF: TCU, Secretaria Geral da Presidência, Senado Federal, Secretaria Especial de Editoração e Publicações.

Chade, J. (2013) 'EUA questionam isenções e ações de programas sociais brasileiros' *O Estado de São Paulo*. Retrieved from: www.estadao.com.br/noticias/impresso, eua-questionam-isencoes-e-acoes-de-programas-sociaisbrasileiros-,1079321,0.htm (15 December 2013).

Da Silva, M. (ed.) (2001) *O Comunidade Solidária: o não-enfrentamento da pobreza no Brasil*, São Paulo: Cortez.

Francis, C., Lieblein, G., Gliessman, S., Breland, T. A., Creamer, N., Harwood, R., Salomonsson, L., Helenius, J., Rickerl, D., Salvador, R., Wiedenhoeft, M., Simmons, S., Allen, P., Altieri, M., Flora, C. and Poincelot, R. (2003) 'Agroecology: the ecology of food systems', *Journal of Sustainable Agriculture* 22: 99–118.

Gliessman, S. (1997) *Agroecology: ecological processes in sustainable agriculture*, Chelsea-Michigan: Ann Arbor Press.

Goodman, D., Dupuis, M. and Goodman, M. (2012) *Alternative food networks: knowledge, practice and politics*, Oxon-UK: Routledge.

Grisa, C., Schmitt, C., Mattei, L., Maluf, R. and Leite, S. P. (2011) 'O Programa de Aquisição de Alimentos (PAA) em perspectiva: apontamentos e questões para o debate', in J. Romano and R. Heringer (eds) *A política vivida: olhar crítico sobre monitoramento de políticas públicas*, Rio de Janeiro-RJ: ActionAid-Brasil/Ford Foundation.

IBGE (2009), *Censo Agropecuário 2006 – Agricultura Familiar. Primeiros Resultados: Brasil, Grandes Regiões e Unidades da Federação*, Rio de Janeiro-RJ: IBGE.

Instituto Cidadania (2001), *Projeto Fome Zero: uma proposta de política de segurança alimentar para o Brasil*, Ipiranta-SP: Instituto da Cidadania.

Izumi, B., Wright, D. and Hamm, M. (2010) 'Farm to school programs: exploring the role of regionally-based food distributors in alternative food networks', *Agriculture and Human Values* 27: 335–350.

IPC-IG (2013) *Structured demand and small holder farmers in Brazil: the case of PAA and PNAE*. Brasília: International Policy Centre for Inclusive Growth and WFP Centre of Excellence against Hunger.

Johnstone, N. and Erdlenbruch, K. (2003) 'Introduction' in OECD. *The Environmental Performance of Public Procurement. Issues of policy coherence*. Paris: OECD.

Landau, E., Da Cruz, R., Hirsch, A., Pimenta, F. and Guimarães, D. (2012) *Variação geográfica do tamanho dos módulos fiscais no Brasil*. Sete Lagoas-MG: Embrapa Milho e Sorgo, Documentos 146. Retrieved from: http://ainfo.cnptia.embrapa.br/digital/bitstream/item/77505/1/doc-146.pdf. (10 December 2013).

Leão, M. and Maluf, R. (2012) *Effective public policies and active citizenship: Brazil's experience of building a Food and Nutrition Security System*, Brasília: ABRANDH/OXFAM.

Maluf, R. (2009) 'Alimentação, escola e agricultura familiar', *Boletim do Observatório de Políticas Públicas para a Agricultura*, 26. Retrieved from: http://oppa.net.br/artigos/portugues/artigo_OPPA_br_026–05_2009-renato_maluf.pdf (10 December 2013).

McCrudden, C. (2004) 'Using public procurement to achieve social outcomes', *Natural Resources Forum* 28:257–267.

McCrudden, C. (2007) *Buying social justice. Equality, Government Procurement & Legal Change*, Oxford/New York: Oxford University Press.

Monteiro, V. (2011) 'A Lei nº 12.349/2010 e a promoção do desenvolvimento sustentável nas licitações públicas', Jus Navigandi, 16 (3085). Retrieved from: http://jus.com.br/artigos/20620/a-lei-no-12–349–2010-e-a-promocao-do-desenvolvimento-sustentavel-nas-licitacoes-publicas (8 December 2013).

Moreira, H. and de Morais, J. (2002) *Compras governamentais: políticas e procedimentos na Organização Mundial de Comércio, NAFTA, Estados Unidos e Brasil*. Texto para Discussão n. 930, Brasília: IPEA. Retrieved from: www.ipea.gov.br/portal/index.php?option=com_content&view=article&id=4174 (8 December 2013).

Moreira, A. (2011a) '*OMC revisa acordo de compra governamental. Brasil prefere não aderir', Valor Econômico (*Retrieved from: https://conteu doclippingmp.planejamento.gov.br/cadastros/noticias/2011/12/16/omc-revisa-acordode-compra-governamental-brasil-prefere-nao-aderir/. (8 December, 2013)).

Moreitra, A. (2011) *OMC revisa acordo de compra governamental; Brasil prefere não aderir. Valor Econômico*. Retrieved from: www.valor.com.br/internacional/1141028/omc-revisa-acordo-de-compra-governamental-brasil-prefere-nao-aderir (retrieved 15 December 2013).

Morgan, K. (2008) 'Greening the real. Sustainable food chains and the public plate', *Regional Studies* 42 (9): 1237–1250.

Morgan, K. and Sonnino, R. (2010) *The school food revolution: public food and the challenge of sustainable development*, London/Washington, DC: Earthscan.

OCDE (2012) *Public procurement for sustainable and inclusive growth: enabling reform through evidence and peer reviews*, Paris: OECD. Retrieved from: www.oecd.org/gov/ethics/PublicProcurementRev9.pdf. (8 December, 2013).

OCDE (2013) *Government at a glance 2013*, Paris: OECD. Retrieved from: www.oecd-ilibrary.org/governance/government-at-a-glance-2013_gov_glance-2013-en (28 November 2013).

Polman, N., Poppe, K. J., Schans, J. W. and van der, Ploeg, J. D. (2010) 'Nested markets with common pool resources in multifunctional agriculture', *Rivista di Economia Agraria* 65: 295–318.

Singer, A. (2012) *Os sentidos do lulismo: reforma gradual e pacto conservador.* São Paulo: Companhia das Letras.

Steurer, R., Berger, G., Konrad, A. and Martinuzzi, A. (2007) *Sustainable Public Procurement in EU Member States: Overview of government initiatives and selected cases* Final Report to the EU High-Level Group on CSR. Vienna: RIMAS, Vienna University of Economics and Business Administration. Retrieved from: http://www.sustainability.eu/pdf/csr/policies/Sustainable%20Public%20Procurement%20in%20EU%20Member%20States_Final%20Report.pdf (5 December 2013).

Triches, R. and Schneider, S. (2010) 'Alimentação escolar e agricultura familiar: reconectando o consumo à produção', *Saúde e Sociedade* 19: 933–945.

Valente, F. (2004) A política de insegurança alimentar e nutricional' in D. Rocha and M. Bernardo (eds), *A era FHC e o Governo Lula: transição?* Brasília: INESC.

van der Ploeg, J. D. (2011) *Newly emerging, nested markets: a theoretical introduction into their strengths and relevance*, paper presented at III Colóquio Agricultura Familiar e Desenvolvimento Rural, Porto Alegre-RS: PGDR/PPGS/IFCH/UFRGS.

Winter, M. (2003) 'Embeddedness, the new food economy and defensive localism', *Journal of Rural Studies* 19: 23–32.

5 Participatory systems of certification and alternative marketing networks

The case of the Ecovida Agroecology Network in South Brazil

Guilherme Radomsky, Paulo Niederle and Sergio Schneider

Introduction

While Brazil's southern region is best known for its 'modern agriculture', it also happens to be the cradle of an innovative and promising experience in the production of organic food, fibre and raw materials. This region (which consists of the states of Paraná, Santa Catarina and Rio Grande do Sul) is home to the Ecovida Agroecology Network, which was established[1] in 1998. This was the result of the confluence of social organization, resistance and political struggle by small farmers seeking not only to adopt new production practices and techniques, but also to establish 'another way of doing farming': a shared manner and lifestyle that reflects and embodies a set of common values and beliefs and the sharing of knowledge (Radomsky 2010b).

Ecovida Agroecology Network brings together groups of family farmers who follow agroecological principles. These groups are organized territorially, generally within a single municipality, although sometimes the groups span various municipalities. This territorial rootedness engenders the grassroots nature of each organization, which is fundamental for sharing information and technical knowledge and for gaining access to marketing channels to sell the produce. These groups are connected to each other through a coordinating body, which can be a cooperative, an association, or an NGO. This entity takes on the role of linking farmers, farm technicians and consumers within the region or municipality where it operates (Rover 2011, Radomsky 2013).

The network currently has 28 regional centres, which serve groups in around 170 municipalities in the three states of southern Brazil. There are 3,500 farmers involved, belonging to some 300 groups. These groups in turn are associated to 35 organizations and 8 consumer cooperatives (Ecovida 2012). The farmers' groups play an important role: it is here that the farmers make decisions and plan local activities, such as meetings, field work, the assignation of labels, set priorities for farm inspection visits and register farmers with the relevant authorities. These groups are linked via regional centres which also oversee labelling requirements and standards. They offer technical support, provide the structure needed to meet farmers' requirements and coordinate and strengthen the network. These centres can adapt the labelling process to local contexts, as long as the standards remain within the criteria established by the Ecovida Network and national standards on participatory systems of guarantee (Isaguirre-Torres 2012, Perez-Cassarino 2012, Radomsky 2010b, Niederle *et al.* 2013).

This chapter examines the innovative practices adopted by these ecological farmers in southern Brazil to create markets for organic products, through marketing strategies that emphasize both their high quality attributes and those related to their socio-cultural and regional embeddedness. Participatory eco-labelling systems play a central role here, helping to create nested markets and promote new pathways for rural development. The chapter draws on several research projects, conducted by the authors with the various regional centres of the Ecovida Agroecology Network. These centres operate as learning spaces that help to promote development in the region.

The Ecovida Network exhibits many of the features of nested markets. Van der Ploeg's analysis (Chapter 2 in this volume) of lamb meat production in Texel (the Netherlands) states that a nested market differs from other forms or types of markets in its distinction, and in the mobilization of local and regional resources and infrastructure, and also in the generation of a common pool of resources. Distinction, he argues, can be generated at three levels: through the social construction of quality with differentiated prices; through building trust between producers and consumers; and by means of symbolic exchanges. Van der Ploeg defines infrastructure 'as the set of specific artefacts and rules that are used to channel flows of goods and services between places and people'. In turn, common resources emerge from the infrastructure and the distinction of these nested markets, insofar as they allow participants to share their knowledge and build collective values that are locally embedded and shared by larger groups through trust and reputation. This explains why, despite being strongly rooted in a locality or territory, nested markets can reach distant consumers and other agents who share the same values.

Ecovida also plays a major role in 'creating the infrastructure' that allows producers to connect with consumers. The participative certification process is a mechanism for building bridges that connect ecological producers – who prize and protect the natural and organic bases of their products (that define their distinction and brand) – and consumers – who seek not only a commodity but a food product with a guarantee of origin, quality and compliance with ecological production standards.

To achieve this, Ecovida has built a socio-technical network that enables farmers to overcome entry barriers to markets and marketing channels. So, besides providing infrastructure, represented by the trucks and other vehicles to transport agroecological produce to street markets or other outlets, the Ecovida network established a further, and most important, mechanism – the participatory certification (ecolabeling) system. Participatory certification is a mechanism of 'socio-material infrastructure [that] can be defined as the set of specific artefacts and rules that are used to channel flows of goods and services between places and people' (van der Ploeg, Chapter 2 in this volume).

In this chapter we analyse the challenges involved in constructing these organic and agroecological markets. Besides this introduction and the closing remarks, the chapter is divided into three sections. The first section describes the Ecovida Agroecology Network and discusses how the participatory certification process acts as a mechanism that guarantees the quality of the products and has helped develop bonds of belonging and identity among the actors within the socio-technical network. The second section relates this experience to broader ongoing processes and the institutional environment in Brazil that together are leading to shifts in the rules that influence initiatives of this kind. We explore how Brazil's organic food markets have opened a space for the emergence of a distinct market logic, one that is not dominated by supply and demand mechanisms or solely regulated by the relative prices of products, goods and services. The third section analyses the processes of social interactions that underpin these distinct markets and the social networks required for these to flourish. Once these markets have been created, they require an infrastructure to ensure their continued operation, which is maintained by sales channels and intermediary agents. In our final remarks, we highlight some of the challenges facing the Ecovida Network and other similar initiatives and reflect on how it has changed participants' and other stakeholders' perceptions of markets.

The Participatory Certification System of Ecovida Agroecology Network

There are three different ways in which products can be certified as organic in Brazil. The first, the most commonly used internationally, is the third-party certification system, in which certification is provided by an independent organization. In this system, seals are issued following an independent review and assessment of the farm or food processor by an outside organization. Trust in the system is based on this division and is supported by documentary responsibility and objectivity.[2]

The second model covers participatory systems of organic certification which, in Brazil, are backed by administrative acts, norms and laws.[3] The participatory guarantee system is 'a set of activities performed within a given organization governed by principles, as well as organizational and operational rules (...)', which aims to 'assure that a product (including product, process, and service) meets the technical regulations and standards of organic farming, and went through a participatory assessment of conformity to such standards' (Fonseca 2007: 10). In this system, both the evaluators and applicants are stakeholders, and the guarantees stem from the collective accountability and participatory inspection by those who are directly involved and by their social partners (such as consumers, political and/or technical agents).

The third model allows ecological farmers to sell their products directly to consumers *without* certification. This is possible for those organized either into cooperatives or into groups and associations registered with the Ministry of Agriculture, Livestock and Food Supply as Social Control Organizations (SCO).

In this case, farmers can sell products with the inscription: 'Organic produce for direct selling by organized family farmers, not subject to certification in accordance with Law no. 10,831 of December 23, 2003.' This system is still little known and barely used by farmers, even though it can be used to sell produce in the institutional markets created by government procurement programmes, such as the Food Purchase Programme (Programa de Aquisicão de Alimentos – PAA) and the National School Feeding Programme (Programa Nacional de Alimentação Escolar – PNAE) (Schmitt and Grisa 2013, Grisa 2012, Schmitt *et al.* in this volume).

This participatory system allows for various methods and forms of social organization (within certain set parameters defined by law and other government acts regulating the market). While every organization must comply with some general principles, there is also room for flexibility.

The Ecovida Agroecology Network uses the participatory guarantee system. According to Radomsky (2010b) Ecovida's system of certification is guided by the principles of co-responsibility, active participation and involvement and a specific farming lifestyle based on co-production between nature and society. This implies that members of the network share more than just relations of exchange and flows of technical or even pricing information. Rather it creates a relationship marked by partnership and an adherence to certain values that are reflected and actualized in a set of practices, discourses and procedures. These, in turn, make up the cultural repertoire of the social group as a whole and become the source or locus of the social identity that distinguishes the Ecovida Network.

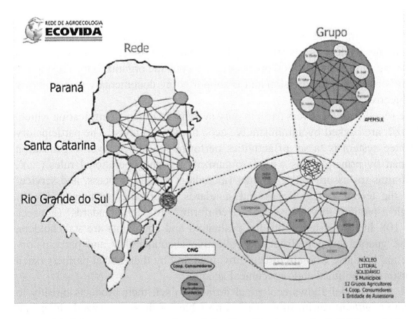

Figure 5.1 Schematic representation of the Ecovida Agroecological Network (source: Ecovida (2007: 16) and Perez-Cassarino (2012: 191)).

To be certified by Ecovida, applicants must meet several criteria to obtain the seal. First, family farmers who wish 'to convert' must attend local group meetings for one or two years, while their farm goes through the transition process towards meeting Ecovida's standards. They must provide a map of their property and complete a registration form. After that, an agronomist from the local agricultural extension service will visit the farm and prepare an assessment report. This report then goes to the ethics committee of the local group, which will also visit the farm after they have examined the report. A subsequent 'external review' ('olhar externo') is then carried out by members of other groups and technical assistants from the Ecovida Network. This forms the basis of an evaluation that is referred to the regional coordination committee.[4] If the reports demonstrate that Ecovida's standards are being met, the regional coordination committee will give its endorsement and the family farmer will be granted Ecovida's seal.

A farm may have just a part of its area certified, but only when the family farmer is committed to expanding the certified area to cover the whole farm. Certification involves very few expenses for the farmer, just a small annual fee for issuing and printing labels. Nonetheless, participation in the scheme does entail other costs, as members are obliged to take part in external reviews for conformity assessment, and the time that they devote to the network's activities is an opportunity cost, in terms of the time lost working on their own farm. This system of certification relies greatly on the knowledge that the members of the network have of each others' farms, and on regular visits by each farmer to their peers' farms. The ethics committee, particularly, is involved in regular farm visits.

While this scheme may seem to be very formalized, it is less schematic in practice and can be adapted to different local conditions. The seal is granted to growers insofar as they begin to participate in the meetings, open their farms to inspection by others and adopt agroecological farming as a lifestyle choice.

Figure 5.2 Ecovida Agroecology Network Seal (source: www.ecovida.org.br).

There is a (variable) conversion period (usually not less than one year) before a farmer can obtain the right to use the seal.

Ecovida participants claim that regular peer monitoring of farms is crucial to this process. They contrast this procedure to third-party certification, which usually involves an annual assessment and does not provide the support needed to guide a farmer through the gradual learning processes involved in the transition towards being agroecological). While the monitoring process cannot provide a complete guarantee that growers are behaving honestly, it does develop relationships of mutual trust. In this sense, Ecovida has redefined the concept of control, turning it from a formal and bureaucratic procedure into one led by informal monitoring.

What is the outcome of this collective mechanism? Ecovida's seal implies two opposing, though complementary, principles. On the one hand, it takes the farmers' 'word' about meeting standards, that is to say, their earnestness in ensuring that production is done without the use of agrochemicals. Yet it also establishes local ethics committees (composed of farmers, technicians and consumers) to ensure compliance with the guiding principles, and carries out inspections. Hence, the system applies a double criterion – it is based on mutual trust among participant farmers upon meeting the standards, and also on an evaluation process that grants a seal that endorses the goods, which per se could suffice. However, the agents involved in the process recognize that getting a seal may not be so difficult for someone willing to cheat the system. Therefore, they never waive the element of trust in the farmer's *modus operandi* (based on the assumption by both consumers and the other farmers that his/her farming is organic). This double criterion is constitutive of the Network and the continuous monitoring of peers' practices by participant farmers and technicians (during meetings at street markets, events, gatherings and visits to farms) reinforces the certification, while substantiating the intrinsic distinction between this model and that of third-party certification.

Participating farms are monitored throughout the year. Every one or two months, meetings are arranged at a different participating farm. The programme is quite flexible: there is an opportunity for informal discussions at the start of the meeting while the group members are arriving. There is then a formal structured meeting to discuss the group's activities. This is then followed by a group farm tour, visiting the crops and livestock of the host. Guests have the chance to observe the farm, exchange ideas and information with each other, ask the host about his/her practices and provide feedback. The tour usually takes about one hour, although it can take longer depending on the number of people and the geography of the land.

The group then returns to the meeting site and begins an evaluation of the host farm, raising questions, sharing impressions and giving advice. There is no fixed pattern of dialogue, since the subjects overlap and new issues appear, some not necessarily linked to the practices observed at the host farm. These discussions are usually harmonious and try to develop farmers' understanding of their farming methods: but sometimes they can be contentious, and dissenting views can be raised. The last part of the group meeting focuses on the problems and challenges facing the group and the network. Sometimes there are discussions about whether or not group members are showing sufficient commitment to agroecological farming.

Each meeting is more than just an opportunity to talk about agriculture. It becomes an opportunity for evaluation that ensures the continuance of certification for family farmers. Equally important, it is a way to create and maintain group cohesion and to meet the standards agreed upon within the Ecovida Network (Radomsky 2013). Since most groups are very localized, this monitoring is more connected to daily coexistence and knowledge exchange between farmers as part of their day-to-day activities, rather than just being confined to these meetings.

This participatory certification system plays an important role in the construction of nested markets. It means that participants are involved in a set of practices and experiences that extend far beyond guaranteeing the intrinsic qualities of their produce. It also involves the construction and sharing of social values that characterize a particular way of farming (Radomsky 2010b). In this sense the certification process is related to the formation of new marketplaces that create opportunities for collective learning and social action. In these new markets, producers and consumers engage in practices and discourses that seek to confer new meanings not only upon food, but also upon eating as a cultural and political practice.

Several scholars have shown that seals are a very important tool for giving consumers confidence in the authenticity, typicality and originality of food products (Ilbery and Maye 2007, Ilbery *et al.* 2005, Cruz and Schneider 2010). In this sense, certification is more than just an artifice for reducing information asymmetries between economic agents (reducing fraud and opportunism), or even a mechanism for reproducing the power of the market. It is, in fact, a means for enabling connections between distinct attributes linking processes, products, places and people. This is a crucial aspect of the certification process, since consumers who are concerned about food purity and quality have demanded certified products (Renard 2005). Therefore, on the one hand, certification is a mechanism that provides broader information on products and, at the same time, is a tool of power and control that bears contention (between certifying agents and accreditation entities). On the other hand, it is guided by the ideals of reconnection (Dupuis and Goodman 2005, Renting *et al.* 2003) and can establish relationships between social and symbolic values, which promote the appreciation of regional specialties (Niederle 2013, Bowen and Valenzuela Zapata 2009, Pratt 2007).

However, one should note that there are some inconsistencies between the organic farming daily practices and the formal certification procedures set by the agencies. Brazil has seen the emergence of a wide range of accredited certification agencies, largely as result of the strengthening of rules and legal provisions (both nationally and internationally). This process paved the way for other forms of equally legitimate certification that do not rely on third parties.

There is an emerging debate on how these different certification methods relate to the growth and recognition of 'new' food markets, particularly the alternative circuits of production and consumption, in which the definitions of quality as a set of inherent product attributes are not the only guiding principle (Lancaster 1966). Viewing quality as a socially shared value opens up new perspectives about the merits of different certification processes. Allaire (2004) shows that by considering the holistic nature of quality with a particular focus on immaterial aspects, it becomes clear that products are valued for representing symbolic values that are shared within the social networks within which they circulate.

Natural, social, cultural and economic attributes, which are provided by socially constructed images, can give food a recognizable identity. This involves more than just controlling farming techniques, but also the manipulation of cultural signs (Lash and Urry 1994). When a product leaves the market it also loses its 'condition as merchandise' and acquires a different meaning in the other spaces that it crosses during its social trajectory. Thus, when organic food circulates within different markets, its qualities are redefined. This means that the same product can have different attributes if sold in a street market, a supermarket, or through a government procurement programme.

Participatory guarantee systems attempt to validate these aspects, insofar as they seek, by means of solidarity and reciprocity, to integrate the dimensions of craftsmanship, tradition, know-how and locality within agroecological farming systems. Even so, there are limits as to how far this whole range of values can be represented by a seal. That is the reason why some agroecological movements place such a high value on direct markets, such as farmers' street markets. The social spaces that these markets provide create cultural interfaces that promote a re-enchantment of the relations around food consumption. In such settings, quality is based on values created through the relationships between producers and consumers. This at least partially replaces institutional symbols, such as seals and brands, with the trust and reciprocity that emerge from the recurrence of economic transactions and shared social values (Niederle and Radomsky 2008).

Emerging markets for organic food and the place of family farmers

The rapid growth of the Ecovida Network has occurred against a background of increasing production and consumption of organic food in Brazil in recent years. This growth has been followed by a deep institutional restructuring of the different markets in which these products are traded (Schultz 2007, Boström and Klintman 2008, Blanc and Kledal 2012). This is a multifaceted process, whose roots and implications can be interpreted in different ways. In general it is a reflection of three major changes: (i) the recognition by the state of ecological production systems, and the formulation of public policies designed to support this sector; (ii) the emergence of new actors at different stages of the production and marketing chains and in providing technical assistance and (iii) a substantial redesign of the regulatory framework, including new mechanisms of control and the increased involvement of certifying bodies (Niederle and Almeida 2013).

Such changes have prompted a rapid shift towards what Brandenburg *et al.* (2013) term the 'institutionalization of agroecology', which they define as the combination of increasing market penetration combined with the creation of a specific regulatory framework governing production. This process raises new challenges and opportunities for all of the actors involved in processes of agroecological transition, particularly for family farmers, the group that is the main supplier of organic foods in Brazil (Schmitt 2009, Sauer and Balestro 2009). According to the Brazilian Association of Organic Food, which represents growers, processors and certifying agencies, 80 per cent of organic food producers throughout the country are family farmers (Brasilbio 2012). Data from the Ministry of Agriculture, Livestock and Supply indicate that there are about 15,000 farmers producing certified organic food on an area of 1.7 million hectares (Brasil 2012).

This clearly brings some benefits. There has been a huge increase in market demand in recent years, which has encouraged other farmers to convert to organic farming and to form groups and social organizations. The creation and consolidation of new groups, associations and networks reflect these changes and have increased agroecological farmers' ability to connect with other actors. This is well illustrated by the creation of the National Alliance of Agroecology (Articulação Nacional de Agroecologia – ANA), a nationwide network of organizations dedicated to developing the production and marketing of agroecological products.

On the other hand, the requirements for entering markets have become increasingly stringent. It is not easy to gain access to the large retail chains, processing enterprises or export markets, and dealing with the institutional markets also poses significant challenges. Organic marketing channels are becoming increasingly diversified and segmented, with each one imposing a more or less specific set of requirements on producers, such as production scale, product diversification, frequency of delivery, quality standards etc. The implementation of such systems involves complex social engineering. The operation of each market clearly bears the imprint of the 'visible hands' of actors, who connect networks and the institutional arrangements needed to enable effective economic transactions. These arrangements include an array of different certification systems.

The institutionalization of distinct mechanisms for conformity assessment reflects the heterogeneity of organic food production and sales systems in Brazil. The coexistence of the three mechanisms discussed earlier in this chapter reflects the struggles of various organized social movements that have historically opposed agricultural modernization, developing innovative agroecological practices, and sought state recognition of the legitimacy of these approaches. These practices filled some of the voids left by the modernizing model, generating diverse local production systems, which have been able to reproduce themselves despite the lack of supportive public policies. Thus, they have given rise not only to multiple and varied ecological 'styles of farming' (van der Ploeg, 2008), but also to different markets, particularly alternative networks of production and consumption, which are strongly embedded in rural areas. Despite the pressures exerted by food empires, the street markets, growers' associations, small retailers, producers for home consumption and food bartering have survived and, in some regions, began to foster new models of endogenous rural development (Schneider and Niederle 2010).

From the mid-1990s onwards, official recognition of family farming has boosted these alternative systems, which are now no longer perceived as a remnant of traditional agriculture, but as examples of the most innovative practices of the contemporary food system (Schneider, Shiki and Belik 2010). Therefore, although the main policies towards family farms have maintained a focus on the production of agricultural commodities, they have also encouraged some initiatives related to organic production, either directly, by financing production and processing, or indirectly, by strengthening social organizations and encouraging the consumption of organic and agroecological food (Petersen 2013, Altieri *et al.* 2012).

It is also true that it took a long time for the issue of the environment to appear on the agenda of most rural social movements. Despite this, the activities of such movements have been crucial for the development of agroecology. The role that these movements have played in advocating ecological family farming and participatory certification undoubtedly contributed to the current regulatory framework for organic production and the institutional architecture of this market (Brandenburg 2008).

Moreover, these transformations in production have converged with equally important changes in the urban environment, especially within a segment of '*consommacteurs*' keen not only on organic foods but also on some kind of political engagement in the context of the new societal paradigm of sustainability (Stassart 2010, 2012). Hence, the institutionalization of agroecology has also been supported by the emergence of movements and consumer organizations that began to demand practices and policies to encourage the consumption of healthy foods, produced without the use of pesticides and GMOs. This has been a crucial aspect in the trajectory of the Ecovida Network, especially in southern Brazil, since the network is also supported by regular consumers of organic food, who have helped to build a community that brings consumers and producers closer together (Rover 2011).

As a result the cities have regained street markets (*feiras livre*), which were once seen as an outdated model of market relations, whose extinction was only a matter of time, depending upon the pace of expansion of large retail chains.[5] At the same time there has also been a significant growth in dedicated organic and natural products stores. These are outlets that, although not providing a direct link between producer and consumer, shorten the marketing chain and add value to local products, sometimes identifying the farmers by name as a marketing strategy. Nowadays, the newest frontier of organic consumption is the internet:

among the online organic stores there are also producers who are creating home delivery systems, and organic baskets are now included on group buying sites. Ecovida and its member groups make use of all these new marketplaces (Silveira 2013).

These phenomena indicate the rich diversity of new marketplaces, which is a clear reflection of the complexity of the social construction of organic markets in Brazil over the last two decades. Some of these markets are fully embedded in local relations, while others are attempting to interact at a distance, as Ecovida is doing. Both cases involve a process of social change that reinforces and strengthens local nested markets, extending their reach through the expansion of the network. Theoretically, this might be understood as a way in which the social material infrastructure unfolds at new and wider levels without losing its connection or embeddedness with the place of its production and its values (Massey 2005). This is what van der Ploeg (Chapter 2, this volume) means by 'building bridges', or 'by-passes' that allow people to overcome the 'structural holes' of conventional, globally controlled, networks and commercial exchange.[6] These new paths for accessing organic products also seem to reflect how actors are dealing with the significant shifts in Brazilian society as a whole, that are related to changing values towards food and its quality, purity and freshness together with new ways to build individual distinctiveness and common public goods.

Another key feature that has recently emerged is the involvement of the State in increasing demand for organic products. Public procurement is being used to create institutional markets[7] that aim to promote adequate nutrition through building channels for distributing and selling food produce. Both the Food Purchase Programme (Programa de Aquisição de Alimentos – PAA) and the National School Feeding Programme (Programa Nacional de Alimentação Escolar – PNAE) now play a key role in creating demand for local foods and provide a strong incentive for agroecological production systems (Schmitt *et al.* Chapter 4 in this volume, Grisa *et al.* 2011, Schmitt and Grisa 2013).

The social construction of markets and further developments

New challenges are posed for participatory guarantee systems in Brazil by the growing demand for organic food, the economies of scale achieved by some organic production experiences and the access of these products to institutional markets. Such challenges include the need to maintain and improve the mechanisms that guarantee the distinction of organic products. An organic seal has two roles: it distinguishes an organic farmer/product from a conventional one but it also provides a gateway to certain markets. One can only gain access to some markets by being certified. Carneiro (2007) emphasizes that certification is needed to expand markets. Brazilian law recognizes third party and participatory certification and a farmer, or group of farmers, may legally make simultaneous use of the two systems of certification. The existence of different certification options allows organic producers to expand their marketing channels beyond the local market, to build larger markets and reach new consumers. But it also raises challenges, which Meirelles (2002) has discussed in regard to the Ecovida Network. There is the implicit risk that meeting the demand from new markets will become the main motivation of the network, displacing the farmers' 'agroecological project'. Radomsky (2010b: 100) also noted the dilemma between the 'risk of decharacterization' and the preservation of the lifestyle of the members of Ecovida Network. He claims that belonging to the network involves sharing a set of values and beliefs, which recognize the practice of agroecology as a 'lifestyle choice', whose central aim is not "making too much money" (ibid.).

These paradoxes need not necessarily restrict the expansion of the network and its development in terms of production and sales volume. The question is not whether or not to enter new markets or expand sales volume, but how to conduct this process and how to maintain the autonomy of farmers' groups and even the network as a whole, in terms of decision making and control. The risk, therefore, does not lie in larger markets and higher revenues per se, but in whether or not involvement in them will erode the behaviour, values and ethics that sustain the network. The moral obligations that bound the members of Ecovida network allow them to adopt either one or both types of certification – participatory and/or third-party certification.

Farmers who choose to sell their products to food processors, exporters or large retailers are required not only to hold a third-party certification but also to meet additional requirements such as, for example, exclusive supply agreements, thus restricting their capacity to expand alternative markets. Such requirements expose social struggles within these markets and challenges to the legitimacy of the certification systems.

These different market segments are based on distinct standards, rules and values, which determine the different attributes of goods that flow through the networks. In a street market, for example, the market space is defined by a network of proximity. Producers and consumers interact through exchanging products whose value is highly related to the artisanship involved in their production. By contrast, in institutional markets, the government is a central actor in the network, and the social origin of the product (family farming) is the fundamental distinctive value. Large retail networks (and the certification systems that they adopt) in turn use industrial and commercial mechanisms for sustaining the standards that demonstrate the quality and safety of the produce. Family farming produce and participatory certification as well face barriers to enter this market segment.

However, many farmers wish to supply different markets and do adopt more than one certification system. Besides raising costs, this brings out some challenges for farmers, which are manifest in the dissenting logics that guide each system. The desire to link to more than one market is a question of autonomy. This is part of a broader struggle to create space for manoeuvre, to avoid 'marginal' exchanges at the local marketplaces and becoming completely overshadowed by a system of exchange governed by more or less 'free' interplay of price, supply and demand (Shanin 1973).

Institutional markets driven by public procurement policies (the PAA and the PNAE) have the potential to provide a major spur in shaping the structure of markets for organic foods and stimulating the participation of family farmers. However, there are still organizational and productive barriers to entering this market, which limit the proportion of organic produce sold in these markets to very small figures – about 2 per cent of the total food purchased from family farmers in Brazil. Nevertheless, family farming organizations are very optimistic about the potential expansion of their members' participation in these markets.

Grisa *et al.* (2010) and Grisa (2012) have studied these programmes and observed that there are both synergistic and competing dynamics between institutional markets and the other marketing channels used by family farmers. In some municipalities of Rio Grande do Sul, the demand for family farming products from institutional markets seems to have strengthened other existing markets, or even led to the creation of new ones. In other cases, the option of supplying institutional markets may have contributed to the breakdown of some traditional marketing spaces, such as street fairs. This has been the result of limited supply (and competing demand) but also of the work involved (in terms of sales and transportation) to supply both markets simultaneously.

These changes are already having a visible impact on the operation of family farming social organizations, including the Ecovida Network. A recent study by Perez-Cassarino (2012) makes clear that the network's technical assistants have increasingly focused on participation in government food procurement programmes, and somewhat neglected training and social organization, which are essential in order to build farmers' skills and knowledge and ensure their transition to ecological farming practices.[8] It is notable that farmers involved in the Ecovida Network generally make use of more marketing channels than conventional producers. This is not only because they have more opportunities to find alternative outlets, but also because creating alternative markets (either individually or collectively) is a conscious strategy among network members.

Ecovida has been involved in bringing together consumers, state bureaucrats and local politicians in order to establish booths for its farmers at public markets, to set up street fairs in new locations and to supply food to budget restaurants. As Medard *et al.* (Chapter 10 in this volume) note, such strategies can be characterized as having a *counter-development* dynamic, in the sense that these 'strategies and attempts of the local actors (e.g. farmers, traders, consumers, collectives) [to] actively respond to "failures" of the global markets they are confronted with'.

The construction and maintenance of these marketing channels raise questions and challenges. The main challenge concerns the maintenance of street fairs as favoured spaces for selling the produce and interacting with consumers so that to build trust and awareness. These farmers' fairs have resulted from the advocacy initiatives of farmers sometimes supported by consumer groups and a number of other intermediary agents. Recent developments in the organization of such fairs point to the relevant role of advocates, such as university professors familiar with agroecology, members of social movements and technical assistants (from both NGOs and government and at municipal and state levels). Street fairs also require substantial involvement from the municipalities that organize the spaces and oversee the marketing activities.

Some fairs are attended by both conventional and ecological farmers. The ecological farmers often attempt to distinguish themselves as organic and members of the Ecovida network, by wearing Ecovida T-shirts or hanging agroecology banners or posters promoting their farms on the booths or handing out small booklets on ecological food to differentiate themselves – always highlighting their link to the network and their status as organic farmers. The farmers' fairs allow direct interactions with consumers, often building bonds of trust and empathy between the two. Some booths become a favourite with consumers and the social ties built from repeated visits are another way of strengthening nested markets

Yet these farmers' fairs are more than just a market for selling food. They are the social and symbolic nodes within a network that emerges from the acts of buying and selling. Regular interactions lead many consumers to establish a commitment to organic farming and empathy for the stallholder farmers they visit. In this way, the act of purchasing connects people through a relational dimension that goes beyond a particular event (as in impersonal markets) and is reinforced over time, creating a shared sympathy. Thus, for some consumers, purchasing ecological food involves acquiring goods that contain social, moral and symbolic values.

Although these proximity relations are important, the seals and signs that distinguish certified ecological farmers are also necessary at farmers' fairs. Both Ecovida and the individual farmers make clear and constant efforts to ensure their products are known and marked as being certified as organic. While there are a number of loyal organic customers at these fairs, many other shoppers do not distinguish between agroecological and conventional products. Many others primarily shop on the basis of price. This problem can be overcome when municipalities hold farmers' fairs that are exclusively agroecological or organic, but attracting new customers to these fairs is not always easy.

In view of this, farmers' fairs are also spaces of contention. There is much discussion about which seals (third party or participatory certification) have the most credibility among consumers and the value of and conflicts involved in using more than one seal. Another issue is that conventional farmers sometimes hitch a free ride on the organic fairs, raising their prices closer to organic ones.

Among direct sales markets, street fairs are one of the most complexes regarding both its structure and its operation. This is not just about the strenuous work required from farmers, especially from those who work at several street fairs along the same week. It is also about the high risk of losses it involves, because of the huge variation of sales, which result from a number of factors. Among these latter, there are seasonal factors such as school holidays, when the number of customers decreases, despite this often being the period of highest supply. Often it is also difficult for a market to acquire enough 'critical mass' to attract sufficient customers on a regular basis to make it worthwhile attending. Many street markets have not succeeded as they have been located in inaccessible places or were in competition with other more established markets.

Future prospects for the Ecovida Network

The largest challenge currently facing the Ecovida Network and other organizations supporting agroecology in Brazil is the risk of 'conventionalization' exerted by the pressures that stem from the rapid expansion of the organic market. Conventionalization implies the appropriation of agroecological values and practices, reducing them to mere procedures for handling agroecosystems that closely resemble the patterns found in conventional agriculture (Niederle and Almeida 2013). This process largely occurs through specialization, intensification, scaling-up and input substitution (Buck *et al.* 1997; Guthman 2004; Lockie and Halpin 2005). This process of conventionalization does not only occur within production (with the increasing participation of large-scale enterprises), but also in the proliferation of new certification bodies, the repositioning of political mediators (driven by the emergence of new advocates of a 'green economy') and perhaps most of all through the increasing participation of large retailers in the distribution of organic food, previously restricted to local and regional short circuits.

It is worth noting that, in Brazil, the prevalence of family farming in the organic sector results from various historical and cultural factors, although until recently it has also been related to a lack of interest from the business sector in organic production (van der Ploeg *et al.* 2012). This lack of interest can be attributed to either the perception of a lack of demand, the lack of appropriate technologies for large-scale organic farming and, perhaps most of all, the lack of an institutional framework to ensure a stable market dynamic. All these factors have changed over recent years and though no detailed data is available there is much evidence that new actors are now exploring the potential of this market.

The introduction of new agents and new values into the Ecovida Network also raises several other questions. As previously mentioned, the network provides a mechanism for connecting local farmers and organizations, which means it is highly heterogeneous. There are striking differences between farmers from metropolitan areas, such as Curitiba/Paraná, and the family farmers located in the rural western region of Santa Catarina. These differences make it difficult to produce a clear profile of the production units that constitute the network. In some regions, farmers have been strongly embedded in ecological movements for quite some time, whereas in other regions there is an increasing number of entrant farmers who are motivated by the potential gains from increased demand.

These new agroecological entrepreneurs have responded to the changing markets with increased scale of production, specialization and aggressive marketing strategies. These farmers often remain at the first stage of the agroecological transition, essentially just avoiding the use of chemical and industrial inputs.

Yet they also bring new skills to the network – they show an impressive networking ability, combining participation in innovative circuits (e-commerce, basket deliveries, speciality stores, etc.) with participation in the conventional large retail segment.

For some of these new 'family entrepreneurs', their main reason for joining the Ecovida Network is the high cost of third-party certification. This has led many of them to migrate to the participatory system, provided that they don't lose access to the larger markets. This is possible now since the major retail chains are slowly beginning to recognize and accept participatory certification, whereas, until recently, they would only accept third-party certified products. Dissent and contention begin to arise within the network, stirred up by the admittance of these new entrepreneur farmers, the emergence of new intermediaries (including ex-farmers who have begun to buy and process food and are often perceived as middle men who are appropriating the value added) and the entry of these agroecological products in large supermarkets. The admittance of new values within Ecovida – profit, efficiency, scale, productivity – which are typical of the business and industrial worlds, is leading to the creation of distinct 'styles of ecological farming' inside the organization. This is provoking a serious debate within the network about its values and legitimacy, what Ecovida represents and which actors should represent the network.

In the light of this it is worth asking how these organic production networks will develop in the future and what contribution they will make to rural development in a broader sense. An outstanding consequence is that this experience is producing a real turning point in the most purist and orthodox conceptions about the role and characteristics of the markets. It is worth emphasizing this point. Until quite recently sociological debate over markets in Brazil tended to view them as 'satanic' (to recall Abramovay's (2004) insightful turn of phrase) something that can never provide a solution within a capitalist system. This view has now lost much strength as a result of both empirical research and theoretical developments and has given way to a more complex and nuanced view of markets (in the plural), whose value, especially when they are embedded, nested and perceived as socio-cultural constructions, are now seen in a different light. Markets are no longer a taboo and now attract interest from farmers, policy makers and public administrators.

A final issue to bear in mind is the challenges facing Brazilian organizations involved in developing agroecological and organic food markets, particularly that of preventing these spaces from being captured by outside, hegemonic, actors. While there is some evidence that these markets are, in places, being appropriated by new entrants, the future development of organic and agroecological markets is likely to involve an extension of their heterogeneity which should protect them from 'outside capture'. Instead of an unidirectional process of conventionalization, the emergence of short marketing circuits, especially the street markets, supported by agroecological producers and engaged consumers, suggests a kind of Polanyi's 'double movement' (Schneider and Escher 2011), in which the markets themselves are converted into arenas for socio-political struggles.

Notes

1 The network was officially founded on 28 April 1999 at a ceremony held in the Legislative Assembly of Santa Catarina. For further information, see: www.ecovida.org.br.
2 In Brazil, there are both domestic and foreign companies operating in this segment. The Brazilian certifiers include: Instituto de Tecnologia do Paraná – TECPAR; Ecocert Brasil Certificadora Ltda; IBD Certificações Ltda; IMO Control do Brasil Ltda; Instituto Nacional de Tecnologia (INT); Instituto Chão Vivo de Avaliação da Conformidade.
3 Three key documents regulate the production of organic food and the systems for certification and guarantee: Law no. 10,831 of 2003, Decree no. 6,323 of 2007, and Normative Instruction no. 64 of 2008, from the Ministry of Agriculture, Livestock and Food Supply.
4 The 'olhar externo' is a process of peer review and surveillance provided by other farmers and technical bodies involved in the participatory certification methodology.
5 Curitiba and Porto Alegre, the two largest cities of the South, have more than a hundred open air markets between them, two dozen of them exclusively for selling organic products.
6 In the same vein van der Ploeg points out that 'nested markets reconstitute, as it were, local and regional markets through short-cutting past the obligatory passage points of the general commodity markets. In this respect, they represent new and contrasting modes of governance. They are nested in new networks and distinctive qualities and are sustained by new socio-material infrastructures' (Chapter 2 in this volume).
7 Although, in essence, all markets can be defined as institutional, this term has acquired a particular meaning in Brazil. It has been widely used to define a specific market design, in which the networks of exchange are defined by norms and conventions negotiated between actors and institutions, with the state playing a central role through its public procurement activities.
8 This diversion of technicians' work priorities is hindering the agroecological transition process: the development of knowledge, practices and technologies that further agroecological production. This could mean that some farmers do not progress much beyond the stage of input substitution and do not make more substantial changes in the way their production systems are organized. This is also due to inadequate rural extension and research for devising creative agroecological production systems.

References

Abramovay, R. (2004) 'Entre deus e o diabo: mercados e interação humana em Ciências Sociais', *Tempo Social* 16: 35–64.
Allaire, G. (2004) 'Quality in economics: a cognitive perspective' in: M. Harvey, A. McMeekin and A. Ward (eds) *Qualities of Food*, Manchester: Manchester University Press.
Altieri, M., Funes-Monzotte, F. and Petersen, P. (2012) Agroecologically efficient agricultural systems for smallholder farmers: contributions to food sovereignty', *Agronomy for Sustainable Development* 32: 1–13.
Blanc, J. and Kledal, P. (2012) 'The Brazilian organic food sector: prospects and constraints of facilitating the inclusion of smallholders', *Journal of Rural Studies* 28: 142–154.
Boström, M.; Klintman, M. (2008) *Eco-Standards, Product Labelling and Green Consumerism*, Hampshire: Palgrave Macmillan.
Bowen, S. and Valenzuela Zapata, A. (2009) 'Geographical indications, terroir, and socioeconomic and ecological sustainability: the case of tequila', *Journal of Rural Studies* 25: 108–119.

Brandenburg, A., Lamine, C. and Darolt, M. (2013) 'Institucionalização do movimento ecológico na agricultura: Mercado e reorganização dos atores sociais', *Estudos Sociedade e Agricultura* 21: 222–247.

Brandenburg, A. (2008) 'Mouvement agroécologique au Brésil: trajectoire, contradictions et perspectives', *Natures Sciences Société* 16: 142–147.

Brasilbio (2012) 'Agricultura orgânica', Available at: www.brasilbio.com.br. Visited on Aug 13, 2012.

Brasil (2012) *Produto orgânico: melhor para a vida de todos e do planeta.* Brasília: MAPA, 2012.

Buck D., Getz, C. and Guthman, J. (1997) 'From farm to table: the organic vegetable commodity chain of northern California', *Sociologia Ruralis* 37: 3–20.

Carneiro, M. S. (2007) 'A construção social do mercado de madeiras certificadas na Amazônia brasileira', *Sociedade e Estado* 22: 681–713.

Cruz, F. T. da; Schneider, S. (2010) 'Qualidade dos alimentos, escalas de produção e valorização de produtos tradicionais', *Revista Brasileira de Agroecologia*, 2: 22–38.

Dupuis, E. and Goodman, D. (2005) 'Should we go "home" to eat? Toward a reflexive politics of localism', *Journal of Rural Studies* 21: 359–371.

Ecovida, Rede de agroecologia. (2012) *Cultivando Sonhos, dando eco à vida. Relatório do 8° Encontro Ampliado da Rede Ecovida*, Florianópolis, 28 a 30 maio 2012.

Ecovida, Rede de agroecologia (2007) Uma identidade que se constrói em rede. *Caderno de Formação* I, Florianópolis.

Fonseca, M. (2007) 'Desafios e perspectivas dos sistemas participativos de garantia', *Revista Brasileira de Agroecologia* 2: 1784–1799.

Grisa, C. (2012) *Políticas públicas para a agricultura familiar no Brasil*: produção e institucionalização das ideias. Unpublished PhD Thesis Social Sciences Graduate Program – Development, Agriculture and Society, Rio de Janeiro: UFPR.

Grisa, C., C. Schmitt, L. Mattei, R. Maluf and S. Leite (2011) 'Brazil's PAA: policy-driven food systems', *Farming Matters (LEISA)* 27: 34–36.

Grisa, C., C. Schmitt, L. Mattei, R. Maluf, and S. Leite (2010) 'O Programa de Aquisição de Alimentos (PAA) em perspectiva: apontamentos e questões para o debate', *Retratos de assentamentos* 13: 137–170.

Guthman J. (2004) 'The trouble with 'organic lite' in California: a rejoinder to the 'conventionalisation' debate', *Sociologia Ruralis* 44: 301–316.

Ilbery, B. and Maye, D. (2007) 'Marketing sustainable food production in Europe: case study evidence from two Dutch labelling schemes', *Tijdschrift voor Economische en Sociale Geografie* 98: 507–518.

Ilbery, B., Morris, C., Buller, H., Maye D., and Kneafsey, M. (2005) 'Product, process and place: an examination of food marketing and labelling schemes in Europe and North America', *European Urban and Regional Studies* 12: 116–132.

Isaguirre-Torres, K. (2012) *Os sistemas participativos de garantia: os sujeitos da ruralidade e seus sujeitos na sustentabilidade socioambiental.* Unpublished PhD thesis, Environment and Development Graduate Program. UFPR.

Lancaster, K. (1966) 'A new approach to consumer theory', *Journal of Political Economy* 74: 132–157.

Lash, S. and Urry, J. (1994) *Economies of signs and space.* London: Sage.

Lockie, S. and Halpin, D. (2005) 'The "conventionalisation" thesis reconsidered: structural and ideological transformation of Australian organic agriculture', *Sociologia Ruralis* 45: 284–307.

Niederle, P. (ed.) (2013) *Indicações Geográficas: qualidade e origem nos mercados alimentares*, Porto Alegre: UFRGS.

Niederle, P. and Almeida, L. (2013) 'A nova arquitetura dos mercados para produtos orgânicos: o debate da convencionalização' in: P. Niederle, L. Almeida and F. Vezzani (orgs.) *Agroecologia: práticas, mercados e políticas para uma nova agricultura*, Curitiba: Kayrós.

Niederle, P., Almeida, L. and Vezzani, F. (eds) (2013) *Agroecologia: práticas, mercados e políticas para uma nova agricultura*. 1. ed. Curitiba: Kayrós, UFPR.

Niederle, P. and Radomsky, G. (2008) 'Social actors, markets and reciprocity: convergences between the New Economic Sociology and the Paradigm of the Gift', *Teoria & Sociedade* 4: 1–26.

Massey, D. (2005) *For Space*, London: Sage.

Meirelles, L. (2002) *Agricultura Ecológica e Agricultura Familiar*. Dom Pedro de Alcântara, June 2002. Available at: www.centroecologico.org.br.

Perez-Cassarino, J. (2012) *A construção social de mecanismos alternativos de mercado no âmbito da Rede Ecovida de Agroecologia*. Unpublished PhD Thesis Environment and Development Graduate Program. Curitiba: UFPR.

Petersen, P. (2013) 'Agroecologia e a superação do paradigma da modernização' in: P. Niederle, L. Almeida and F. Vezzani (ed.) *Agroecologia: práticas, mercados e políticas para uma nova agricultura*, Curitiba: Kayrós.

Pratt, J. (2007) 'Food values: the local and the authentic', *Critique of Anthropology*, 27: 285–300.

Radomsky, G. (2013) 'Conocimientos situados y biodiversidad: tensiones entre prácticas de pequeños agricultores ecológicos del sur del Brasil y el régimen internacional de propiedad intelectual', *Anthropologica* 31: 149–169.

Radomsky, G. (2010a) 'Propriedade intelectual e certificação de produtos da agricultura ecológica' in O. Leal and R. Souza (eds) *Do regime de propriedade intelectual: estudos antropológicos*. Porto Alegre: Tomo Editorial.

Radomsky, G. (2010b) *Certificação participativa regimes de propriedade intelectual*. Unpublished PhD thesis Anthropology Graduate Program, Porto Alegre: UFRGS.

Renard, M. (2005) 'Quality certification, regulation and power in fair trade' *Journal of Rural Studies* 21: 419–431.

Renting, H., Marsden, T. and Banks, J. (2003) 'Understanding alternative food networks: exploring the role of short food supply chains in rural development', *Environment and Planning A* 35: 393–411.

Rover, O. (2011) 'Agroecologia, mercado e inovação social: o caso da Rede Ecovida de Agroecologia', *Ciências Sociais Unisinos* 47: 56–63.

Sauer, S. and Balestro, M. (eds) (2009) *Agroecologia: os desafios da transição agroecológica*. São Paulo: Expressão Popular.

Schmitt, C. (2009) 'Transição agroecológica e desenvolvimento rural: um olhar a partir da experiência brasileira' in S. Sauer and M. Balestro (orgs.) *Agroecologia e os desafios da transição ecológica*, São Paulo: Expressão Popular.

Schmitt, C. and Grisa, C. (2013) 'Agroecologia, mercados e políticas públicas: uma análise a partir dos instrumentos de ação governamental' in P. Niederle, L. Almeida and F. Vezzani (eds) *Agroecologia: práticas, mercados e políticas para uma nova agricultura*. Curitiba: Kayrós.

Schneider, S. and Niederle, P. (2010) 'Resistance strategies and diversification of rural livelihoods: the construction of autonomy among Brazilian family farmers', *The Journal of Peasant Studies* 37: 379–405.

Schneider, S., Shiki, S. and Belik, V. (2010) 'Rural development in Brazil: overcoming inequalities and building new markets', *Rivista di economia agraria* 65: 225–259.

Schneider, S. and Escher, F. (2011) 'A contribuição de Karl Polanyi para a sociologia do desenvolvimento rural', *Sociologias* 13: 180–219.

Schultz, G. (2007) *Relações com o mercado e (re)construção das identidades socioprofissionais na agricultura orgânica.* Unpublished PhD thesis Agribusiness Graduate Program. Porto Alegre: UFRGS.

Shanin, T. (1973) 'The nature and logic of the peasant economy 1: a generalisation', *Journal of Peasant Studies* 1: 63–80.

Silveira, S. (2013) 'Rede Ecovida de Agroecologia: uma inovação estratégica para o desenvolvimento territorial sustentável na zona costeira catarinense', *Revista Interdisciplinar Interthesis* 10: 181–213.

Stassart, P. (2010) 'Le rôle des "consommateurs" dans la construction d'un accord entre agriculteurs et environnementalistes' *Anais do Encontro da Rede de Estudos Rurais, 4. Curitiba: UFPR.*

Stassart, P. and Jamal, D. (2012) 'Agriculture biologique et verrouillage des systèmes de connaissances', *Desenvolvimento e Meio Ambiente* 25: 117–131.

van der Ploeg, J.D (2008) *The New Peasantries: struggles for autonomy and sustainability in an era of empire and globalization*, London: Earthscan.

van der Ploeg, J.D, Jingzhong, Y. and Schneider, S. (2012) 'Rural development through the construction of new, nested, markets: comparative perspectives from China, Brazil and the European Union', *Journal of Peasant Studies* 39: 133–173.

6 The construction of new nested markets and rural development in China

Huifang Wu, Baoyin Ding and Jingzhong Ye

Introduction

Since the reforms at the end of the 1970s, especially the introduction of the Household Responsibility System which restored land to individual peasant households, China has experienced an accelerated and sometimes contradictory process of development. The change of production system has promoted not only a rapid increase in food production, but also greatly reduced the number of poor peasants through generating ongoing increases in their incomes. However, the urban–rural duality, which is both economically and socially persistent, has become a main bottleneck for rural development since the late 1990s. In the first part of this period, the agricultural tax burden was still unreasonably high for peasants, and the cost of agricultural production kept increasing while benefits were stagnating. The migration of rural labourers towards cities and industrial centres continued to accelerate. This created the real threat of the countryside being hollowed out, with an increase in the feminization, and an aging, of agricultural labour. The lack of dynamism is a real threat to the development of the countryside in China, as is evident in the sharply growing differences in income between rural and urban populations (Ye *et al.* 2010). In response to these challenges the Chinese government started, in 2004, to formulate more comprehensive rural policies and increased its financial support for agriculture.

At the same time new and changing social needs are offering new opportunities to Chinese agriculture. As the sheer size of the cities, the overcrowding, traffic jams and environmental problems continue to grow, the longing for nature is becoming increasingly strong among urban inhabitants. The countryside is becoming a major destination for holidays, weekends and short trips. At first, this ran counter to the dominant pattern of agricultural development in China, which gave exclusive priority to production and productivity. Extensive application of chemical fertilizers and pesticides, herbicides (usually more than necessary) have also created serious pollution in the countryside. While urban people started looking for beautiful nature and clear air in the countryside, they frequently encountered a polluted environment and this triggered a search for new solutions. At the same time, there was an increase in the frequency of food safety problems which promoted public demand for safe food and have enhanced consumers' awareness about food safety and quality. Most Chinese people's concerns have moved beyond having enough food and towards enjoying good and healthy food. There is a widespread feeling that the current agricultural marketing system cannot ensure the safety of produce.

The Chinese government established a number of policies to address these problems. Basically, the focus of policy shifted from agricultural growth to integrated rural development. This translated into significant increases in government investment in the countryside and a greater emphasis on increasing peasants' incomes through a new combination of agricultural and rural development (Research team of the Ministry of Agriculture of China 2005: 65). A set of supportive policies on agricultural and rural development was launched under the guideline of 'giving more, taking less and deregulating'.[1] Another important change is that policy makers and society at large are paying more attention to the (potential) multifunctionality of agriculture. The policy for the 'Construction of a New Socialist Countryside',[2] which is now central in state–countryside relations, identifies five development goals for the countryside, 'advanced production, improved livelihoods, a civilized atmosphere, clean and tidy villages and democratic management'. This context has allowed the beginnings of development for new markets for things such as agro-tourism and organic food.

These new markets are specific segments of the far wider, general markets for food, agricultural products and services. They are embedded in these wider, general markets by particular institutional arrangements and they are supported by particular infrastructures. This allows them to have dynamics that differ from those of the general markets.

This chapter explores two examples of the development of such new markets. One case regards agro-tourism and focuses on the role of government in stimulating and extending this new market. It is a story of peasant initiatives that became integrated in government schemes that work at higher levels of aggregation. It also shows how the government has accommodated a market that was initiated by peasants within its rural development policies. The second case is about the marketing of glass noodles, in which peasants have built on their social networks to create a new market for a local speciality food. While there is no government involvement in this market, this case study demonstrates the crucial importance of external actors.

Agro-tourism: from the 'happy peasant home' (nongjiale) to the landscape

Since 2000 scholars and government agencies have come to pay more attention to what are known as the '*Three Nong*' issues. This concept describes the many interdependencies that exist between agricultural production, the quality of rural areas and peasants' income and wellbeing. '*Three Nong*' implies that none of them can be improved without improving the others. The concept has made people aware that rural areas are not only a means for agricultural production; they are also there to support the development of rural society as a whole, including the beauty of its landscapes, its natural values, biodiversity, the quality of its resources, and, last but not least, the wellbeing of peasants (Ye *et al.* 2010). From then on, the new rural development model has gained considerable ground. This has resulted in the emergence of a wide range of organic products, green food, markets for pollution-free products, ecological agriculture, agriculture with the characteristics of 'one village, one product', several forms of community supported agriculture and a large increase in agro-tourism.

Agro-tourism is a form of tourist activity that greatly depends on the scenic beauty of the landscape that has evolved from farming, the healthiness of the agroecological environment, the nature of agricultural production activities, the specificity and quality of food products and the traditional folk customs preserved in the villages. Together such features constitute *rurality*. These features all contribute to the attractiveness of a rural area. Tourists visiting attractive rural areas can enjoy these qualities through sightseeing, eating, learning, participating, walking in the fields or shopping whilst on vacation. Agro-tourism allows tourists to meet, and interact, with living nature, and especially with those who interacting with living nature on a daily basis. The supply of and demand for agro-tourist services constitute a specific market, strongly bound to a specific place carrying a specific form of rurality. Through developing a specific market the elements that compose this rurality can be sustained and enhanced and those supplying these services can earn good incomes from it (Wang, 1999).

Agro-tourism germinated in China in the late 1980s, more or less simultaneously in several different places. One of these was Shenzhen, the first Special Economic Zone in China, where all kinds of economic experiments were possible and encouraged. One village/town organized a 'Lychee Feast' (comparable to an Italian *Sagre*: festivals that put the spotlight on a high quality food product). This aimed to attract business men and it turned out to be highly successful. Another initiative was born in Sichuan province (in 1986) after local peasants started to produce flowers and ornamental plants in order to sell the seedlings in the urban markets. This resulted in attractive, blossoming fields around the village that in turn attracted many visiting businessmen. One local peasant, Mr. Xu, thought that he might try to offer accommodation and food to those businessmen and, after discussing this at length with his family, he started doing so. This resulted in the first '*nongjiale*', which translates as the 'happy peasant home' (*nong* is peasant, *jia* is house and *le* is happiness). Thus visitors may find 'happiness in the peasant house' (this is another possible translation). These first examples were quickly followed elsewhere and many turned out to be successful (as was Mr. Xu's business). Mr. Xu later received a visit of the then-Vice President Hu Jintao of China in 2001 (an important recognition) and is now owner of a chain of 'peasant restaurants' that have traditional architecture (including the kitchen) and which serve delicious peasant meals.

Agro-tourism developed through three stages. The first can be characterized as the *nongjiale* period (before 1994). Here local peasant initiatives were central; they were limited, however, to the level of the single farm and household. Next followed a period that mostly can mostly be characterized as the one of folklore tourism (1995–2000) in which the scale of operations moved to village level. During this stage the architecture of a village as a whole, its rituals, festivals and/or culinary traditions were put centre stage. This stage critically required some government support in terms of planning, coordination and financial contributions. Finally, after 2001 attention moved to yet another scale of the landscape as a whole, embracing several villages at the same time (Zou 2005). Scenic beauty, nice roads, walking paths, panoramic viewpoints, archeological monuments and/or natural parks become the new, overarching points of reference. They embrace and support the 'lower' levels, i.e. the folklore villages and the 'happy peasant homes'. At this third level of aggregation, state interventions were decisive.

Thus, a progressively process of evolution can be detected. Agro-tourism was initiated in response to growing demand from urban dwellers to experience the countryside livelihood, and the initial rural entrepreneurs tended to rely on local attractions to attract city tourists. At this stage there was no governmental support. However, the government gradually realized the potential impact of developing agro-tourism in terms of increasing peasants' incomes and making the countryside more attractive. As such their attitude to agro-tourism slowly transformed from indifference to acquiescence and active support.

In 1998 China National Tourism Administration launched the '*Huaxia* (the ancient name of China) Urban-Rural Tourism Programme'. This sought to promote 'eating in peasants' families, living in peasants' residences, working on the farms, and enjoying rural sceneries and the happiness of rural families'. In 2006, the same organization launched the 'Countryside Tourism Programme', which related closely to state's programme for the 'Construction of a New Socialist Countryside'. The slogan of this programme was 'new countryside, new tourism, new experience and new fashion'. In 2007, a new programme of 'Harmonious Urban-Rural Tourism' was established under the heading of 'charming countryside, vigorous cities and harmonious China'.

At present, there are four types of agro-tourism in China. The first type is '*nongjiale*' which has been already discussed. Eating the peasants' food, staying in the peasants' residences, experiencing the traditional folklore, picking fruits, vegetables and fishing are the main features of this type of tourism. The second type involves more hi-tech sightseeing farms which combine the functions of technology demonstration, tourism, science education and recreation within one farm. The third agro-tourism type aims to conserve and restore old villages by demonstrating the architectural layout, style and cultural landscape of picturesque historical villages. The fourth agro-tourism type involves special agricultural landscape areas, such as terraces in hilly areas, etc. An example of this latter type is located in Qianjiadian Township in Yanqing County, about 100 kilometres north-west of Beijing. Agro-tourism here is closely connected to the city of Beijing: the county is actually part of the greater municipality of Beijing and is explicitly included in the spatial planning strategy as it is part of the ecological protection zone surrounding Beijing. Most of the county has an elevation of more than 500 metres, giving it a climate that, while cold in the winter, is cool in the summer, leading it to gaining the reputation of Beijing's 'summer capital'. Yanqing County gives special emphasis to environmental and ecological protection, which it regards as crucial for its economic development. Thus it is also known as 'the back garden of the capital and its green oxygen bar'. Yanqing County emphasizes the development of eco-friendly industries and urban eco-agriculture. In this context, agro-tourism has gained key support from the government. By 2011, 27 municipal folklore tourism villages have been developed in the county. There were 1,520 peasant households engaged in folklore tourism and the agro-tourism revenues reached 180 million Yuan[3] (equals to about 22 million euro) in that year.

The county has rich cultural resources including the 'Baili Gallery' (100 miles of valley with a beautiful mountainous landscape), the National Geo-park of Petrified Wood (showing the remnants of million-year-old woods) and other national scenic areas. Qianjiadian Township alone has seven villages open for tourists, three recognized folklore villages and 108[4] *nongjiale* households. Two of these villages are discussed here in more detail.

Xinshanzi Village

Xinshanzi Village is located in the vicinity of National Geo-park of Petrified Wood which borders the Baili Gallery. The village began to develop agro-tourism in 1998: as the first village in this township to develop agro-tourism, it is known as 'the first village of petrified wood'. The development of agro-tourism in Xinshanzi Village would have been impossible without multi-faceted support from the government. The village cadres proposed the idea of agro-tourism when they saw the rapid development of agro-tourism in other places around Beijing and realized that the village was well placed to develop its agro-tourism (a few individual single peasant households were already involved in agro-tourism activities). But any further development required interventions at higher levels, which began to occur in the year 2000 when the first of a series of complementary interventions and policies was put in place. The first policy was to return farmland to forests. This mostly involved returning hillside farmland into forested land through planting apricots, plums, peaches and other fruit trees. This policy changed peasants' livelihoods and greatly improved the local ecology and environment, increasing the scenic beauty and biodiversity. Second, the government invested considerably in rural infrastructure: village roads were repaired, street lights installed, containers for garbage disposal were constructed and sanitation was greatly improved. Improving the roads made it easier to travel between the city of Beijing and the village, while the other changes significantly improved the living and sanitation conditions in the village. Third, a small village factory that generated a lot of sewage was closed down, village livestock breeding was re-planned with all the activities for livestock and poultry breeding being re-located far from peasants' residences in order to avoid bad smells in the village. Fourth, when the individual village households needed funds to develop agro-tourism initiatives, the village committee provided help for the villagers to get loans from local banks. These loans were mainly used for (re-)building toilet systems and for improving and/or enlarging houses so they could accommodate (more) guests.

With this multi-level policy support, agro-tourism in Xinshanzi Village developed rapidly. In 2006, around 2/3 of the village's peasant households were actively involved in agro-tourism activities and their incomes increased significantly. The annual income from agro-tourism in the village reached several million yuan; a well-functioning *nongjiale* household can earn around 200,000 yuan (equal to about 25,000 euro) every year. After deducting costs, the net income is several times higher than the income that can be obtained through labour migration. The development of agro-tourism has also promoted the emergence of new small industries and service providers. In 2009, for instance, a cutlery cleaning factory was established in Xinshanzi Village. This factory has cleaning and disinfection equipment and offers this service to households that provide agro-touristic facilities. The development of agro-tourism has also led to the development of raising free-range chickens on the hillside, which provides tourists with fresh eggs and chicken meat.

Gujia Village

Gujia Village is also located close to the National Geo-park of Petrified Wood. It has a charming environment and a pleasant climate. The current village is actually quite recent and was a result of relocating three villages all previously located in lower lying, small valleys and very prone to landslides and other geological disasters. To protect the villagers, the municipal government provided funds to relocate the residences of the three villages to their new location (part of the campaign aiming at 'the construction of a new socialist countryside'). Building the new residences near the petrified wood park facilitated the development of agro-tourism and improved the livelihoods of local villagers.

As in Xinshanzi Village, the development of agro-tourism in Gujia Village also involved joint efforts. Initially, 20 peasant households expressed their interest to the government in engaging in folklore tourism. These peasants invested considerable money in decorating their houses and equipping them with solar water heaters, air conditioners and other facilities to provide visitors with a comfortable living environment. These peasants generally grow vegetables and fruits in their own yards for tourists' consumption or picking, seldom using any chemical fertilizers or pesticides. The village committee also played an active role in the development of agro-tourism. In the process of resettlement, the village committee planned a uniform style of the new houses so as to ensure a beautiful and balanced appearance. When the new village residences were completed, the village committee employed eight villagers, aged between 40 and 50 years old, to take charge of public cleaning. This kept the village clean and tidy and it also provided these villagers with some earnings. Government support was not only concerned with the 'hardware' (residences, infrastructure, etc.) but also 'software'. Courses and trainings on cooking, health, services and etiquette were provided; households certified; sanitary licenses issued; and competitions among different agro-touristic households were organized, judged by high school teachers. This provided the peasants with free opportunities to learn and exchange experiences. Random hygiene checks ensure the level of service provided by agro-tourism peasant households is maintained.

Agro-tourism and common pool resources

The development of agro-tourism in Yanqing County is based on unique natural resources, largely the petrified wood and the beautiful Baili Gallery. Coupled with the comfortable accommodations and hospitable folk customs, more and more tourists are being attracted to visit this area. This new model of rural development not only increases the income levels of local peasants, but also stimulates the development of other related industries. In the process of agro-tourism development, the value of *rurality* is re-discovered and recognized and attains some importance as it is recognized as carrying a new market that generates considerable employment and income.

The resources on which agro-tourism builds, such as beautiful natural landscapes, historical interests, rural lifestyle and simple and honest folk-customs, are not the property of any one single peasant household. They are the common pool resources (CPR) of the local community (van der Ploeg *et al.* 2012) and the economy of peasant households is increasingly based on these CPR. The peasants provide the services that make CPR accessible to, and enjoyable for, tourists. Without CPR the additional income flows and associated benefits (as the generation of additional enterprises) would quickly disappear and the progress made would quickly be reversed. It is the CPR that attracts the tourists, guarantee the high quality of tourism 'products' and generate the basis for the development of agro-tourism. These CPR include both tangible material resources and intangible social resources as outlined in Table 6.1.

By clearly defining the ways in which the common pool resources are used, they are translated into the social-material basis that allows for the development of agro-tourism that provides consumers with high-quality rural experiences. Enjoying *rurality* not only includes sightseeing in beautiful natural scenery, but also consuming fresh local agricultural products and experiencing the comfortable rural lifestyle. Conversely, the development of agro-tourism contributes to the maintenance of common pool resources. The development of agro-tourism encourages governments and the villagers to recognize the social and economic value of these unique resources. Thus, they actively maintain the local natural landscapes, traditional agricultural cropping patterns and lifestyle, etc. All these contribute to the formation of a unique pattern of rural development. When, however, a major upgrading of the resources that make up the attractive *rurality* is needed, state intervention, in the form of funding, planning and coordination, becomes indispensable, as demonstrated by the two case studies above. These stories also demonstrate that state interventions do not have to undermine the CPR nature of *rurality* but can strengthen it.

Table 6.1 The different constituent common pool resource elements

Common pool resources for agro-tourism		
Tangible resources	Fresh and healthy vegetables and fruits	The peasants do not use chemical pesticides and fertilizers; instead, they use organic fertilizer to ensure the safety of the products. Consumers can pick and taste the products during their stay.
	Rural landscape	Differentiated from urban landscape, there is lush vegetation in the mountains, the picturesque natural scenery of the Baili Gallery, the traditional farmland and historical village residences.
	Natural heritage	The petrified wood and other natural historical resources in the National Geo-park have a hundred million year history.
Intangible resources	Rural livelihood	Compared to urban livelihoods, the rural livelihood is slow, comfortable and in harmony with nature.
	Simple and honest folk-customs	Harmonious human relationships and hospitable villagers.
	Agro-tourism brand and reputation	Generating the unique brand of Baili Gallery Landscape Residences and building a reputation among tourists.

Multiple actors

The rapid development of agro-tourism in the two villages is also associated with the specific social context and is the result of the *joint actions of multiple actors*. National, regional and local governments,[5] village committees (considered officially as 'self-governing organizations'), peasant households and urban consumers all help to (co-)shape the current forms of agro-tourism. They do so through interactions at different levels with each actor operating according to his or her own interests and prospects.

From the perspective of central government, the development of agro-tourism is an effective way of fighting the multiple crisis faced by agriculture. Agro-tourism can improve peasants' incomes as well as ameliorating food safety and quality. Government agencies understand that promoting the development of agro-tourism is a manifestation of the policy that 'industry fosters agriculture and urban areas promote rural areas'. Support for agro-tourism not only reinforces the multi-functionality of agriculture, but also meets the needs of urban consumers for a good natural environment and healthy food and establishes a new urban-rural relationship. Central government's support for the development of agro-tourism has a number of aspects. First, central government is investing in rural areas, which gradually improves the infrastructure such as roads, residences, water and electricity, thereby making it easier for urban tourists to travel to rural areas and increasing the degree of comfort of living in rural areas. Second, central government carries out various activities to promote agro-tourism activities and publicizes it extensively to consumers. Third, central government implements ecological protection policies, such as returning farmland to forests, which reduces the pressure between population growth and natural environment and creates an attractive natural landscape.

Local government (usually a close cooperation between the county and township levels) also has an interest in developing agro-tourism. As an ecological protection zone of Beijing, Yanqing County cannot develop industries that pollute the environment, it therefore faces the dilemma of protecting the natural environment while also stimulating economic development and raising residents' incomes. Developing agro-tourism provides a solution to this, in which local government has played an essential role. Through a series of concrete actions, local government has aligned national-level rural development policies with local conditions, possibilities and initiatives and made full use of the locally available resources for development. The County government provides also multiple forms of support to peasant families involved in agro-tourism, including funds, capacity and awareness building and advocacy.

The role of village committee is especially important when it comes to implementation. On one level, the village committee may well encourage villagers to develop agro-tourism (for example in Xinshanzi Village, the village cadre initiated the idea of developing and promoting agro-tourism). On another level it is the village committee that safeguards the common pool resources through implementing a range of measures, such as organizing people to maintain the village sanitation or making the village more attractive for tourists.

Peasant households involved in agro-tourism are the direct providers to urban tourists (consumers). It is the peasant households that play the primary role in producing and maintaining the products and services that make *rurality* accessible, attractive and enjoyable. Thus the willingness of the peasants to improve their living conditions and increase their income levels is the fundamental driving force for developing agro-tourism.

As the peasants' efforts are in line with the objectives of governmental policies, they have received recognition and support from the government. Thus, the two sides, the state and peasants, achieve multiple targets: protecting the ecology and environment and increasing peasants' incomes. The role of tourists in this process should not be neglected. Tourists have a unique understanding of the products provided by agro-tourism. They are clear that their aims in coming to the village are to enjoy the fresh air, a quiet environment, healthy food and a different pace of life from that in the city. They are willing to pay good money for agro-touristic facilities that offer access to these values. The flow of income from these tourists encourages and facilitates peasant households to maintain (and perhaps improve) these common pool resources.

Glass noodles: a nested market based on tradition and social network

Whereas state apparatuses played a key role in the previous case study, they are more or less absent in the construction of a nested market for hand-made glass noodles, although external actors' have played a strategic role. Another difference between the two cases resides in the contrasting nature of the two, nested markets. Whereas the new market for agro-tourism is strongly grounded in, and delineated by, space and the *rurality* contained in it, the nested market for glass noodles is defined by the distinctive quality of the glass noodles – a quality that is rooted in tradition, craft and local resources. And, where the market for agro-tourism is sustained by state interventions, the market for glass noodles is sustained by social networks.

Sanggang Village, located in Yixian County within Hebei Province, is well-known for its glass noodles, made from sweet potatoes using traditional processing techniques. Every winter, local peasants process the locally grown sweet potatoes into glass noodles. Before the Spring Festival, consumers from the nearby townships, county towns and, even from Beijing, will come to the village to acquire glass noodles, which have a unique and attractive taste. Most of the visitors are usually friends and relatives of the villagers, or friends of friends. Based on this social network, a small market was created and this market has subsequently been extended to include other local products such as pork, chicken, free-range eggs and persimmons.

The distinctiveness of the product, processing techniques and producers

Glass noodles are a favorite food in the northern part of China. Traditionally, they are processed from sweet potatoes through a complex process that embraces some ten different steps. However, glass noodles are also produced by industrialized lines in food factories. These industrial processing systems use various chemical ingredients to improve the look of the noodles for marketing purposes. Starch derived from beans and maize is mixed with agar and then added to the starch from the sweet potato. This increases the whiteness of glass noodles so that they look beautiful, but diminishes the quality of the taste. Chemical thickener is also widely used in factories for glass noodles. Some producers even use sulphur to fumigate glass noodles, or put chemical gelatine in the ingredients to make the noodles lucent and to improve their texture. Thus, industrial glass noodles not only lack the special taste and flavour of traditional ones – there is also a potential food-safety problem. The deterioration of industrially processed glass noodles provides the background against which traditional glass noodles from Sanggang, produced in an artisanal (i.e. non-industrial) way have (re-)obtained their distinction. The demand for these good and safe glass noodles has revitalized traditional processing and helped to construct a new, nested market.

The traditional production process of glass noodles is strongly intertwined with local agriculture. The local cropping system, culture, knowledge, techniques and social networks render a quality that is different from all other types of glass noodles available in the market. Sanggang Village is located in the mountainous area of northern China: farming land is scarce and scattered in a myriad of small plots at the foot of the mountain slopes. The soil and climate are favourable to producing sweet potatoes and there is a long history of growing this crop here. Local peasants always spread their different crops across different parcels of land so that their families could have more types of food (part of their strategy of increasing family food security) (Ye and An 2009). Consequently, large scale cultivation of sweet potatoes was never developed. For years, it was simply part of the staple food for local peasants, and also used as feed for pigs. In the 1950s, local village cadres invited some peasants from another province to train local peasants in the processing techniques that convert sweet potatoes into glass noodles. From then on, glass noodles were produced for domestic consumption and for the local market.

It takes a group of five to six male labourers to successfully manage the process of transforming the sweet potatoes into glass noodles. The potatoes need to have high starch levels and the work needs to be done when the temperature is around zero centigrade. The processing is very labour intensive and needs to be constantly refined and adjusted in order to obtain the best possible final product (it cannot be standardized). Making glass noodles is a craft: it requires well-developed skills and considerable context specific knowledge. This has several implications. In the first place it is difficult, if not impossible, to extend the scale of production. Second, it implies that it cannot be 'taken over' or relocated in industry (for if this occurs, the quality declines sharply, as noted above). Thus, the 'resistance' of this local practice, and the associated quality product, reside in the 'materiality of things' (van der Ploeg *et al.* 2012). The temperature requirement implies another limit (and another line of defence): there is only a brief time span available for the processing work. Taken together, this means that the production of high quality glass noodles is tied to both the locality and the small-scale artisanal processing.

Autonomy is also an important feature. In Sanggang, the production of glass noodles is based on local resources and is mainly, though far from exclusively, for the local market. The sweet potatoes are locally produced; the labour is local; the tools for producing and drying the noodles are local. The residuals from noodle processing are locally used for pig feeding. By taking full advantage of local resources, the glass noodles become a very distinctive local product.

Over time there local peasants developed a custom of sending noodles as a special gift to their friends and relatives elsewhere. In 1950s, 1960s and 1970s, when the market economy was not developed in China, some businessmen from the southern part of Beijing Municipality[6] came to this area to buy glass noodles and sell them in their local market, but this market consumed a very small part of the production. When the children of some local peasants moved to cities, they still bought glass noodles with them or were sent noodles as gifts from this village. These consumers were very familiar with the quality and characteristics of the noodles and appreciated these characteristics as an expression of the special *rurality* of their home village. Since the product was not closely connected with or dependent on external resources or markets, the producers could gain good incomes from it.

From the late 1980s onwards, labour, especially young males, started to migrate to cities for employment and a shortage of labour led to a decrease of glass noodle production. Glass noodle production is both a labour-intensive job and a highly skilled task (Bray, 1986). Even when male labourers were available, they might not be skilled enough to complete the whole process. As a consequence, the production of glass noodles shrank a lot, and even the local peasants started to buy the manufactured ones. Many years later, though, the situation changed again when food safety problems become serious in China.

The development of a new, nested market for glass noodles

While labour migration provoked labour shortages that were detrimental for glass noodle processing, it ironically also had a positive, although unpredicted, effect. As migrant labourers traveled from Sanggang, the glass noodles from the village also travelled to many other places throughout the country. It is a tradition to return home for the Spring Festival and to bring back gifts for relatives or bosses in the city with you when you return. Glass noodles and free-range eggs are the traditionally very welcome gifts. Thus, in this way the glass noodles became known far beyond the local area. Their distribution was closely interwoven with the social networks of the migrant workers – and definitely limited by and to these networks.

At the end of 2010, The College of Humanities and Development Studies (COHD) of China Agricultural University (CAU) in Beijing designed a project for poverty alleviation through the promotion ofdirect agro-product marketing. The project aimed to reduce poverty in the village of Sanggang through encouraging the establishment and development of direct connections between the peasants (as producers) and consumers who might share a common frame of reference about food quality. The project builds on the notion that the networks through which glass noodles circulate could be expanded by including 'conscious consumers', looking for high quality safe food products. Against the background of growing numbers of food scandals, it was thought that their number would be growing, An initial meeting between the producers from Sanggang and a group of interested consumers from Beijing was established by using an internet website and personal contacts. This first encounter proved to be very promising, and led to the establishment of an infrastructure for ordering through the internet and for the villagers to deliver the orders to Beijing. A wide range of produce can be ordered in this way, although glass noodles are, by far, the most popular item in the range and have become the flagship and logo for this newly created nested market. It is a market that is nested in a mutual understanding between producers and consumers; it is nested, in a longing for, and capacity to produce and consume quality, safety and distinctiveness. This mutual understanding has been strengthened further through organized excursions to the village. This has led the village to establish a new organization and a new set of protocols in order to make sure that sufficient produce of good quality is available and can be delivered on time. This has involved the organizing committee in the village equipping themselves with computers, digital cameras and internet access.

This new way of marketing has allowed for considerable increases in farm gate prices, even though consumers only pay about the same price as they would in Beijing's markets. One *mu*[7] of land can produce 3,000 yuan (equal to about 365 euro) of income by producing sweet potatoes. But, when it is processed into glass noodles, another 3,000 yuan can be created for peasants, with a fluctuated price from 16 to 20 yuan/kg for glass noodles in the local market. Currently, under the new marketing regime the price has increased to up to 30 yuan/kg, increasing the income available by 35–50 per cent and allowing a peasant to realize 4,000 to 5,000 yuan more income for per *mu* of sweet potatoes.

The new market has now been functioning for almost three years. It has developed well and villagers have increasingly taken over the organizational and logistical tasks that were initially done by staff and students of COHD. The scheme has now been extended to a wide range of local agricultural products. Moreover, the economic opportunities created by the project have encouraged some labour migrants to return to the village and re-engage in farming.

Although there are quite a few evident dissimilarities between the previous market structure (which critically depended on migrant workers) and the one that has recently been created, there are also some striking similarities. First, in both models there is a distinct absence of any middlemen. They are both about direct relations between producers and consumers. This makes trust an important vehicle for transactions. The producers know who will buy their produce, while the consumers know about the producers and how they produce, process and distribute their products. The previous pattern was based on locally created social networks between friends and relatives (networks that often extended over large distances), while the new market might be seen as a reconstruction and extension of such networks. Second, producers and consumers share a common definition of the quality and value of the products. It is a social definition that avoids 'getting trapped in various labels' (Patel, 2008) and that is built on a common recognition of quality and a shared value system for food, agriculture and *rurality*. For example, the traditional glass noodles may not be as standard in terms of their length and colour as industrialized glass noodles and they often look dark without shiny packaging. However, consumers recognize and appreciate their natural colour, safety and taste, so green food or organic labels are not necessary. Third, the new type of marketing increases the value added by agriculture. In the new market, the price for glass noodles is often double the local price. The prices for other agricultural produce are also higher (to a different extent) than in the local market. This is an important driving force for peasants that strongly stimulates them to continue (or return to) farming.

Constructing new markets: some final observations

There are many differences between the two cases of market development discussed in this chapter. They reflect the multiplicity of current rural development processes in China. Yet they are both responses to poverty and the squeeze on rural incomes and the growing urban discontent with on polluted landscapes and unsafe food.

Both cases also show that the *starting point* of new nested markets might well initially be hidden in hardly recognized new practices (perceived by many as uncomfortable deviations from the rule) and/or in traditional practices such as bringing gifts from the village to the towns – that is: in peasant initiatives and peasant practices. However, the *further unfolding* of new markets critically requires either state interventions (as in the case of agro-tourism) or active coalition with urban partners (such as the COHD of CAU in the case of glass noodles). Only after a certain period of *consolidation* (when the new market becomes increasingly institutionalized) do the peasants come to play a more active and decisive role in the management of the new market.

All this shows that time is important, and, consequently, that *sequencing* or *timing* (getting things done at the right moment) is crucial in the construction of new markets. The time dimension is also crucial when it comes to *nesting*. New markets are not nested through just one activity at one moment. Nesting takes time, it is an iterative process that is gradually extended. Agro-tourism was first nested in *nongjiale*, the 'happiness offered by the peasants' home'. Then it was further nested in the attractiveness of the village ('the folklore village') as a whole and finally the process of nesting embraced the landscape, and the entailed *rurality*, as a whole. The same goes for the glass noodle case. This market was gradually extended from being nested in personal networks to being nested in the search for food safety and quality and then wider social networks that build on, and reproduce, trust. Shared notions of *rurality* contributed greatly to the subsequent phases of nesting.

Both cases demonstrate that state interventions (or interventions by urban institutions or actors) become especially important when the need arises to include higher levels of aggregation (that go beyond the single farm).

It is important that the state (or urban partner) offers a general *framework* that allows for different possibilities and for different forms of support. Such a general framework allows peasants (and other local partners) to articulate their *specific interests*. Then, at the *interface* of the general framework and the particular local interests new solutions, new projects and new initiatives can be wrought (and negotiated) which combine the general and the specific and start to sustain the construction of new realities. These include the new, nested markets that fulfil a crucial role in rural development (Ye *et al.* 2010). Thus, interaction and negotiations at the different interfaces are far more effective mechanisms than working from a blueprint of a fully designed and highly detailed rural development policy and/or a perfect local project. It is the meeting of relatively 'open' policies and relatively 'unfinished' local projects that is decisive in the construction of new nested markets. Constructing new markets is an ongoing task and should be dealt with in an iterative fashion. Rivers are crossed by feeling the stones as you make your way across – whichever bank of the river you depart from.

Notes

1 During the national video and telephone conference on reducing the peasants' burden in September 2002, a guideline of 'giving more, taking less and deregulating' was put forward. The No. 1 Document in both 2004 and 2005 attached particular emphasis to this point. 'Giving more' means increasing the financial input to agriculture and countryside, hastening the construction of infrastructure, enhancing development-oriented poverty reduction, scaling up conversion of cultivated land to forest and directly increasing peasants' income. 'Taking less' means further promoting the reforms of rural taxes and fees and alleviating peasants' economic burden. 'Deregulating' means pushing forward rural reforms, effectively implementing various policies in countryside, motivating peasants' activeness and creation and broadening the ways of rural employment through developing rural economy.
2 In 2005, in the Fifth Plenum of the 16th National Congress of Communist Party of China, the proposal for the 11th Five Year (2006–2010) Guidelines for National Economic and Social Development was discussed. In the conference, the central government proposed the momentous historical task of Constructing the New Socialist Countryside. The concept itself is far from new: it was discussed 50 years ago. However, the contents, objectives and requirements have changed considerably. Today, the Construction of a New Socialist Countryside is driven in the context of coordinating rural and urban economic and social development.
3 Source: The website of Yanqing County Government, www.bjyq.gov.cn/sy/yqgk/yqgk/, accessed on 15 July 2013.
4 Source: The website of Yanqing County Government, www.yqtour.gov.cn/xcly/xclyt-syt/319011.htm, accessed on 15 July 2013.
5 In China this involves the following hierarchy: national state, provinces, prefectures, counties and townships.
6 Sanggang Village is about 150 km away from the southern part of Beijing Municipality.
7 A Mu is the Chinese unit for measuring the area of land. 1 ha. = 15 mu.

References

Bray, F. (1986) *The Rice Economies: Technology and Development in Asian Societies*, Oxford: Blackwell.
Patel, R. (2008) *Stuffed and Starved: The hidden battle for the world food system*, London: Portobello Books.
Research team of the Ministry of Agriculture (2005) Strategic research on coordinating rural and urban socio-economic development, In *Rural Development Strategy of New Era*, Bejing: China Agricultural Press.
van der Ploeg, J.D., Ye, J.Z. and Schneider, S. (2012) Rural development through the construction of new, nested, markets: comparative perspectives from China, Brazil and the European Union, *Journal of Peasant Studies*, 39: 133–173.
Wang, B. (1999) Viewing the prospect of China's agro-tourism by contrasting agro-tourism in foreign countries with that in our country, *Tourism Tribune*, 2: 38–42.

Ye, J.Z. and An, M. (2009) Sociological analysis of agricultural production and food security, *Issues in Agricultural Economy*, 6: 9–14.

Ye, J.Z. and Wang, W. (2011) The rise of nested markets: Resistance to infinite markets and modern agriculture, *Guizhou Social Science*, 2: 48–54.

Ye, J.Z., Rao, J. and Wu, H.F. (2010) Crossing the river by feeling the stones: rural development in China, *Rivista di Economia Agraria*, 65: 261–294.

Zou, T.X. (2005) On the development pattern of rural tourism in China: Comparative studies on the development between the happy-farmer in Chengdu and the folklore-hamlet in Beijing, *Tourism Tribune*, 20: 63–68.

7 Rural governance and the unfolding of nested markets in Europe

Henk Oostindie and Rudolf van Broekhuizen

Introduction

This contribution focuses on the growing trend towards *multi-level rural govern-ance* within Europe and, more specifically, on how this affects the unfolding of nested rural markets. The introduction looks at the ongoing transition towards multi-level governance in rural Europe, paying specific attention to the emergence and significance of new meso-level institutional arrangements. This is empirically illustrated by case study material, gleaned from a recent EU funded comparative research project, Assessing the Impacts of Rural Development Policies (incl. LEADER) (RUDI), from Sweden, Italy, Germany, Ireland and the Netherlands. This rich empirical material forms the basis for developing an analytical tool, the '*rural policy performance triangle*', which explains the effectiveness of rural policy as being dependent on three territory-specific mechanisms: (1) the role of Rural Development Programmes (RDPs) in wider rural governance processes; (2) the active construction of new institutional arrangements that facilitate place-based rural governance; and (3) the social capital available within territories. This analytical approach is then used to explore the underlying sets of mechanisms that influence the unfolding of nested rural markets. Here we draw on empirical evidence from the Laag-Holland region in the Netherlands. This section demonstrates how the creation of nested rural markets is closely interwoven with the three components of the rural policy performance triangle.

Rural development policy

European rural policy distinguishes four axes of rural development: (1) the competiveness of agriculture; (2) agri-environmental performance; (3) the widening of rural economies and (4) participatory systems for delivering rural policy and programmes (e.g. LEADER). This suggests a transition from a, primarily, sector-based agricultural policy into a broader *rural* policy approach. This transition is illustrated by the trends in CAP expenditure in recent decades. Figure 7.1 shows that export subsidies and other forms of market support are in decline, while the rural development pillar (Pillar 2) is gradually gaining in importance. This pillar

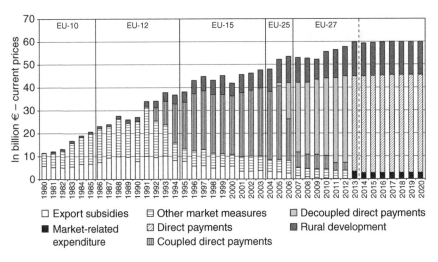

Figure 7.1 Trends in CAP expenditure since 1980 (source: DG Agriculture and Rural Development).

allows member states to adopt Rural Development Programmes (RDPs) – at the national or regional level – a set of measures designed to foster the development (or counter the under-development) of their rural areas, which must comply with the broad parameters set by the EU's rural development objectives.

Figure 7.1 shows that the lion's share of CAP expenditure still consists of income support to farmers. Since 2005 when direct payments were introduced, this has increasingly been decoupled from production volumes. These direct income support measures are designed to compensate farmers for the gradual decline of price subsidies and other market protection instruments. They continue to be subject of heated debate. Some argue the need to redirect much CAP expenditure to other policy domains, while others have questioned the efficiency and effectiveness of direct income support measures in meeting changing rural needs. There have also been calls for fundamental changes in the current allocation of direct income support budgets at farm, regional and member state (MS) level. Later, we discuss the ongoing 'greening' of CAP Pillar 1 support, as manifested in the recent EU-level decision to link 30 per cent of the direct payment system to environmentally friendly farming practices and how this may affect rural governance at lower scales as part of wider changes to Pillar 2 for the forthcoming RDP period (2014–2020). These include:

- a stabilization in terms of the percentage of the overall CAP budget (101.2 billion euro out of a total budget of 418.4 billion euro);
- extra measures to mitigate climatic change;
- the strengthening of risk management tools;
- more flexible interrelations with Pillar 1;

- increased flexibility in the RDP toolkit measures ('from 3 axes towards 6 themes');
- a strengthening of the LEADER approach across EU funds; and
- a reinforcement of support for joint action with regard to the provision of agri-environmental services (European Commission 2013).

New institutional arrangements

RDPs represent a new institutional arrangement for delivering rural policy, an arrangement that works at multiple levels. While the EU remains responsible for the distribution of the Pillar 2 budget among member states (MSs), the MSs have a great deal of discretion as to how to allocate their budget. Thus, a new set of institutional arrangements is emerging that (partly and under specific conditions) transfers responsibility for the design and delivery of rural policy to lower administrative levels. The relevance of new (or alternative) institutional arrangements for influencing rural development has long been recognized by social scientists. Ostrom *et al.* (1993) explored different institutional arrangements for providing rural infrastructure, distinguishing several different configurations for distributing responsibility between public and private actors. Institutional economists have also discussed how institutional arrangements affect policy efficiency and transaction costs (e.g. D'Haese *et al.* 2005; Huylenbroeck *et al.* 2009; Huylenbroeck and Mettepenningen 2011). The effect of new institutional arrangements on agri-environmental policy regulations (Renting and van der Ploeg 2001) and in influencing the potential for developing multifunctional agriculture (Oostindie and Renting 2005; Laurent 2005) has also been explored. Hodge (2001: 99) concludes that new institutional arrangements evolve in response to the changing demand for the products and services from rural areas, arguing that:

> (w)e are currently experiencing a significant change in the relative priorities attached to the alternative products of rural areas and in order to meet them, new institutional arrangements are becoming relevant. These are necessary to articulate the demands for countryside goods, to establish incentives for resource managers and to co-ordinate resource management across space. This indicates a new approach towards the governance of the rural environment.

Thus, many commentators on agricultural and rural development policy have stressed the relevance of new institutional arrangements. Yet, at the same time the notion of new institutional arrangements is often rather loosely defined. Here, we opt for a definition of new institutional arrangements which is rooted in innovation and development studies:

> different (in)formal regimes and coalitions for collective action and inter-agent coordination, ranging from public-private cooperation and contracting regimes, organizational to policy arrangements.
>
> (Geels 2004; Klijn and Teisman 2000)

Scholars in innovation and development studies recognize that this broad definition, which covers new forms of formal and informal collective action between public as well as private actors, also needs to take into account the fact that new institutional arrangements are often simultaneously shaped at the local, regional and (inter) national level and that these different levels often mutually influence each other within a framework of complex interlinkages and strategic feedback (Teisman and Klijn 2000). Knickel *et al.* (2008: 115) describe how these new institutional arrangements can foster rural development. They do so by:

> facilitating beneficial linkages and producing efficient connections between different activities and actors in (rural) regions and between the different levels in a multilevel governance system.

The authors further argue that the meso-level of institutional arrangements is of particular importance, as it is at this level that European regulations are interpreted. Innovation and boldness at this level can provide incentives for experimentation with new ideas and concepts at lower policy levels.

In the following section we present a range of different types of new institutional arrangements for rural policy design and delivery. In line with the theoretical considerations discussed above, our focus will be on the meso-level, although always taking into account the interactions between this level and the higher level institutional arrangements, such as CAP Pillar 2. The specific features, objectives and results of these newly emerging institutional arrangements provide the empirical basis for further theoretical reflection on how to better understand rural policy performances in multi-level policy settings, including their role in the governance of rural markets.

This analysis of new institutional arrangements is derived from the EU funded RUDI project. This project explored the processes and structures underlying the formulation, implementation and impacts of European rural development policies for the 2007–2013 programming period, with a particular focus on the new assessment methods for CAP Pillar 2 (see Dwyer *et al.* 2011; Mantino 2011; Schiller 2010). Without going into detail about the wider case-study objectives and methodology (see Oostindie and van Broekhuizen 2010a), we focus here on five RUDI cases that will highlight the challenges of coordination between different levels of rural governance. The study of the Swedish *Västerbotten* region especially deals with issues associated with devolving rural policy design and delivery (Hedstrom 2010). The case study of the *Mecklenburg-Vorpommern* region (Germany) highlights how new forms of territorially based cooperation have emerged in response to a broadly felt need to better integrate different EU policy frameworks (Huelemeyer and Schiller 2010). The *Grosseto* case study (Italy) focuses on the problematic issue of combining multiple policy frameworks that originate from different levels (Mantino *et al.* 2010). Our Irish case study, of *Local Development Companies*, deals with the benefits and disadvantages of integrating the European LEADER Programme with a national policy framework for social inclusion (Maye *et al.* 2010). Finally, the case study of *performance contracts* in the Netherlands explores how attempts to develop a more territorially-based rural policy needs to be matched by more flexible and performance-based accountability rules (Oostindie and Van Broekhuizen 2010b).

New institutional arrangements for rural policy design and delivery

Rural policy devolution in the Västerbotten region (Sweden)

Sweden has one national RDP. The search to increase efficiency, and the background of a move towards carrying out development initiatives at regional level led to the establishment of County Administrative Boards. These boards design county-level development strategies and establish partnerships between public, private and voluntary sector actors, who play strategic roles in implementing these 'regional' RDPs. A regional multi-stakeholder partnership (*samsynsgrupp*) was established to forge consensus on regional rural strengths and challenges. This devolution process was intended to lead to a RDP better aligned to regional conditions, which would also enhance the sense of responsibility at regional level. This public-private partnership assesses funding applications for regional/ rural development and has to guarantee that the programme is guided by priorities of the national RDP. The case study showed that, in general, the stakeholders agreed that the devolution process made a positive contribution to regional decision making power, led to the RDP being better aligned with regional conditions, led to a more efficient implementation of rural policies and to more coherence between existing rural and regional policies and programmes. Yet, it was also recognized that the RDP only had a modest impact, as the funding available was limited compared to other funding sources. Moreover, the complexity of RDP procedures and rules was thought to create a certain 'project fatigue' and to limit the number of interesting and innovative project proposals. It was also noted that the many institutions involved in the design and implementation of regional/rural policy support systems obscured the transparency of the overall policy processes. Overall the case study illustrated the complexity of multi-framework and multi-level regional/rural policy frameworks and the many challenges inherent in devolving rural policy design and delivery systems.

A joint authority in the Mecklenburg-Vorpommern region (Germany)

Mecklenburg-Vorpommern is a lagging German region struggling with a high unemployment rate and labour outmigration (especially of more qualified workers). Against this background in 2005 the regional government has established a joint strategy for utilizing EU structural funds (the European Regional Development Fund (ERDF), the European Social Fund (ESF) and the European Agricultural Fund for Rural Development (EAFRD)) in order to better support its policy objectives of ensuring sustainable economic growth and securing long-term jobs. The cross-fund strategy is reflected by a corresponding system of implementation aimed at efficiently administrating and monitoring EU support. This initiative builds on a joint strategy that was developed within the first RDP period (2000–2006) when there was one operational programme for ERDF, ESF and EAGGF (European Agricultural Guidance and Guarantee Fund). During this period a Joint Administrative Authority (*Gemeinsame Verwaltungsbehörde*) was established to manage EU structural funds. This authority harmonized the interests of the three different fund administrations and acted as a consulting body for issues related to EU law and the feasibility of proposed measures and coordinated with the monitoring committee. During the second RDP programming period (2007–2013) EAFRD was added to its responsibility making use of the opportunity established under (Council Regulation (EC) No 1083/2006) to appoint a single authority to manage several operational programmes. At the same time the Joint Administrative Authority was transferred from the Ministry of Economics to the State Chancellery in order to reduce any potential bias towards 'economic' programmes and avoid the problem of 'steering inertia'. This has increased the authority's competencies and it is now better placed to coordinate rural policy at the territorial level. It now acts as a single managing authority, coordinating all EU funds and different sources of co-financing, while the administration and implementation of funds remains the responsibility of different ministries and departments. The Joint Administrative Authority has played an important role in the design of the RDP, has maintained regular contact between the various agencies administering RDP funds and provides a forum where different participating ministries can learn from each other. The implementation of the programmes is indirectly influenced by the strategic approach adopted in the design of the programme. Importantly, the RDP was based on a coherent strategy based on the needs of the region, rather than allowing programme measures to be driven by funding opportunities. The continuity and coherence of the RDP have been ensured by intensive coordination by the Joint Administrative Authority.

Another actor that has contributed to the success of this innovative governance arrangement is the intensive involvement of Economic and Social Partners (ESP) in rural policy design and monitoring and evaluation activities. This has resulted in the programme receiving broad support and given the ESPs a growing self-confidence of their ability to effectively address issues that are of concern to them. It has also encouraged ESPs to engage in 'joined-up' thinking which in turn has increased the Joint Authority's appreciation of the ESPs' involvement.

Place-based rural policy coordination in Grosseto province (Italy)

The province of Grosseto (in Tuscany) was seriously affected by an economic crisis during 1990s and responded by developing an alternative, more endogenous, policy strategy. This case study explored how the provincial administration succeeded adopting an integrated and complex strategy, which reduced economic disparities with richer adjacent provinces. It shows that the construction of an integrated strategy for rural development involved a continuous and complex process, which involved the provincial administration establishing positive synergies between multiple policy frameworks. This involved a process of continuous 'learning by doing', adjusting policy strategies to the needs of local stakeholders and creating new relations and networks between institutions and private actors. The provinces' strategy was guided by a number of criteria: (1) maximizing the mobilization of external policy funds to compensate for the lack of its own financial resources; (2) actively responding to the needs of critical sectors and; (3) exploiting synergetic opportunities between locally available (natural and social) resources. The coordinated strategy for rural areas that emerged was the result of a number of factors: (1) the need to respond to the economic crisis and to simultaneously draw on funds provided by a range of key national and EU programmes; (2) the priority given by provincial administrative to making use of these available funds to develop a local development strategy; (3) the presence of an dedicated department responsible for local development that acted as a coordinator at the provincial level; (4) the relative political stability within the province; (5) good interactions between policy makers and technical staff; and, (6) a strong network of actors at local level, with a strong commitment to the province. Together this created a well-functioning and broad regional 'institutional filter', through which multiple rural policy programmes from different administrative levels, including the European (ESF, ERDF) and national (Territorial Pact, Agricultural Pact and the Programme Contract for the Agro-Food Industry) could be delivered. The ongoing decentralization of the design and delivery of the RDP (from the regional to the provincial administrative level) had a positive influence on the capacity of the province to coordinate rural development measures. In turn, this process of devolution fostered a gradual learning process among the provinces' administration and strengthened rural policy coordination at the meso-level. The case study also shows that the development of institutional expertise in designing more integrated rural development strategies required getting involved in and/or establishing new networks. These have been actively promoted and supported by public policies and a number of institutions, including the National Expertise Network for Rural Development, which provide training, technical assistance and ongoing support.

Local development companies in Ireland

Ireland has implemented LEADER since the programme was first established in 1991. LEADER's funding and functions changed significantly in the new 'mainstreamed' 2007–2013 European RDP. Its budget for this period was €425.4 million, almost three times the size of the budget for 2000–2006, with LEADER accounting for all of the Axis 3 expenditure within Ireland's RDP. The national mechanism for delivering the LEADER programme was also significantly changed, through the insertion of a clause by the Dept. of Community, Rural and Gaeltacht (Gaelic language) Affairs that all potential applicants should be in 'compliance with governance measures'. This means that the former Local Action Groups (LAGs) no longer exist as such. They have been replaced by

'Integrated Local Development Companies' (ILDCs), a 'cohesed' governance structure that combines LAGs and Local Development Partnerships and deliver a range of social inclusion programmes. ILDCs are thus responsible for administering LEADER. The case study focused on how these changes in rural governance structure and delivery, including a split in policy delivery at the macro-delivery level, have worked. The case study gives a picture of the merging ('cohesion') of (already existing) social inclusion companies and LAGs. In many instances, this has extended the geographical coverage of the social inclusion element, from relatively small urban areas to cover the whole area covered by the ILDCs. The case study also highlighted some emerging problems, including differences in institutional and organizational cultures and procedures, fears over budget cuts following the financial and economic crisis that emerged in 2008, and the general absence of a well-integrated rural development strategy. However, the employees of the first ILDCs also saw several benefits. They emphasized that the integration of the two programmes allows them to provide a 'one stop shop' for community support, a single point of contact for the public, which provides clearer information. It also means that social inclusion policies can now be delivered across the whole country to disadvantaged rural groups who are likely to be more dispersed than their urban counterparts. In this sense, rural development projects are now more able to address social inclusion issues than before. There are some managerial advantages, such as a better use of staff expertise, a reduction in administration and a better use of office space. Staff who specialize in rural development or social inclusion working more closely together, allowing for overlaps between social inclusion and rural development aspects, which facilitates the potential for positive synergies. This was part of the rationale for bringing the two programmes together:

> when working with unemployed people, staff can suggest that they apply to LEADER for funding in order to set up their own business; likewise, staff can progress people from one project to another.
>
> (Oostindie and van Broekhuizen 2010a: 27)

ILDC staff are hopeful that this kind of synergy will be achieved, but they also recognize that it takes time for the new integrated companies to gel and that it is still early to draw conclusions on whether these potential synergies are actually being realized. Within those companies that have genuinely integrated strategies for delivering a range of programmes, there are clear signs that synergies are possible and that this can enhance the development prospects of these areas.

Performance contracts in the Netherlands

The design and delivery of RDP in the Netherlands occurs in a context in which land is scarce, there are multiple claims on rural areas and a move towards policy devolution. This implies that RDP involves complex multi-stakeholder negotiation and an ongoing learning process. It is increasingly recognized that this requires effective (and well-integrated) rural policies and that this is a major challenge. Since 2006 the policy frameworks of different national ministries (including those for Agriculture, Spatial Planning and the Environment and Transport and Water) have been joined together in what are known as Investment Budget Rural Areas. These ministries have agreed to merge parts of their budgets and to introduce a new conditionally decentralized mechanism for rural policy delivery which is managed through 'performance contracts' between national and provincial administrations. Provincial administrations that sign up to these contracts commit themselves to achieving national goals, but have discretion in choosing how they do so. This implies a transfer of traditionally centralized and sector-based policy frameworks into a more place-based approach to rural policy.

One of the main findings of this case study was that rural policy makers and rural stakeholders, particularly those that succeeded in getting the privileged status of sub-contract partner, have quite high expectations of this new policy coordination mechanism. Having a sub-contractor status brings benefits, as it implies less transaction costs in accessing to rural policy funds, longer term relationships with public administrations and less dependency on short term project-based funding support. The seven-year contract periods coincide with RDP2 2007–2013 period in order to facilitate a good match with EU policy frameworks and different performance indicators for nature and landscape values, water management and rural leisure infrastructure. It is expected that these performance contracts will bring benefits in terms of more integrated and performance-oriented rural policies and less bureaucratic, more flexible and tailor-made rural policy delivery systems. However it is too early to draw any conclusions about whether these expectations will be fulfilled. Some stakeholders have expressed some doubts and concerns as to whether this will actually occur. Some point at the emergence of new types of 'exclusion mechanisms' that have excluded rural stakeholders with less opportunity to secure co-financing. Others expressed concern about the tendency among provincial administrations to reduce the influence of strongly embedded territorial multi-stakeholder platforms on the grounds that these platforms lack any/sufficient formal democratic legitimacy.

With a few minor exceptions the RDP policy instruments have mostly been incorporated into existing national or provincial policy instruments. This makes it hard to assess the impact of the RDP. One of the most visible impacts of the RDP has been to increase the level of trust-based relationships between rural policy makers at different administrative levels, who now need to work much more closely together in the design and delivery of the RDP. Thus, at best, the RDP might be seen as a catalyst that indirectly supports policy experiments with performance contracts.

The rural policy performance triangle

The empirical material from the RUDI Project highlights the need to approach European *rural* policy design and delivery as processes that work across multiple levels, involving multiple policy frameworks and multiple actors. The empirical material also shows that, within these highly complex rural *governance* settings, a wide variety of new institutional arrangements are emerging with the aim of making rural policy and its delivery more integrated, more consistent, more coherent, more accessible, more effective, more efficient and more flexible.

The empirical material also shows that these new institutional arrangements cover multiple aspects which include: (1) a redistribution of policy responsibilities between different administrative levels and institutions; (2) more place-based integration of multiple and multi-level policy frameworks; (3) the active involvement of (new) rural stakeholders in policy design and delivery; and, (4) more flexible and performance-based ways of policy accountability regulations.

The empirical material also shows significant differences in the interactions between RDPs and these newly emerging institutional arrangements. In some cases (notably those from Germany, Sweden and Ireland) the RDPs have functioned as a trigger or catalyst for institutional reform. This happened much less in the Dutch and Italian settings where RDPs were relatively small influences within a far wider set of interacting policy frameworks. While such frameworks may well provide welcome additional co-financing instruments to support rural development, it can also be difficult to align RDP regulations with ongoing experiments in developing novel, more territorially based forms of rural policy. Finally, the five case studies suggest that the territorial capacity to create such novel policy approaches is intrinsically interwoven with the available social capital.

Figure 7.2 presents the rural policy performance triangle. It aims to illustrate how territory-specific rural policy outcomes are the result of the mutual

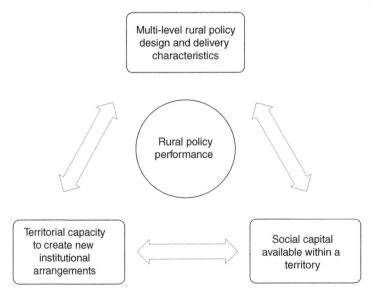

Figure 7.2 The rural policy performance triangle (source: Oostindie and van Broekhuizen (2010a)).

interactions between: (1) multi-level rural policy design and delivery characteristics; (2) the territorial capacity to create new institutional arrangements; and, (3) the availability of social capital within a territory. We discuss the relevance of these interrelations by returning to the individual case studies.

The County Board in Västerbotten (Sweden) is a new institutional arrangement set in a context of centralised rural policy design and delivery, with little active involvement from rural stakeholders. Although the *County Board* succeeds in contributing to policy and societal demands for more integrated and needs-driven rural policies, local stakeholders perceive policy delivery, and particularly the RDP, as being insufficiently transparent or accessible. Put differently, this new institutional arrangement has not (yet) succeeded in creating positive interactions between the different components of the performance triangle.

The Joint Administrative Authority in Mecklenburg-Vorpommern (Germany) is clearly more successful in activating rural stakeholders and getting local stakeholders engaged in the regional rural policy delivery system. This is probably partly due to its longer experience with territory-based policy coordination,

The Irish *Local Companies for Integrated Development* demonstrates how new institutional arrangements can emerge as specific responses to policy and broader societal concerns about social exclusion. Its attempt to re-allocate funds for the benefit of social vulnerable groups can be understood as a contribution to territory-based social capital building which is being achieved through the introduction of a new, more territorially-based institutional arrangement.

The Grossetto Province in Italy shows that it can take time to develop new institutional arrangements that build upon the available social capital within a territory. It also shows that informal networks and trust based relationships between public and private actors can be more effective than formal relationships. This case confirms the importance of mutual reinforcing interrelations between the three components of the rural policy performance triangle.

The experience with *performance contracts* in the Netherlands suggests that this new institutional arrangement may be making a positive contribution towards developing more integrated, tailor-made and coherent rural policies. It also shows that performance contracts can induce new types of exclusion mechanisms by giving resource-rich rural stakeholders a privileged position as sub-contract partners. From a short-term perspective this may be understandable, but in the longer term it will most probably have negative repercussions for territorially available social capital.

The rural policy performance triangle and the unfolding of nested rural markets

The rural policy performance triangle can also be used to analyse and understand the governance of rural markets. The different components of the triangle allow us to view the governance of rural markets from a multi-level perspective and explore the significance and potential of emerging new, more nested rural markets in Europe (see Oostindie *et al.* 2011 and Chapters 2 and 3 of this book). This builds on the burgeoning body of literature on alternative food networks (Renting *et al.* 2003; Goodman 2004), short food chains (Ilbery and May 2005; Tregear 2011) and changing balances between the public and private governance of food systems (see e.g. Lang and Heasman, 2004; Renting *et al.* 2013).

The empirical material presented thus far does not explicitly refer to the governance of *markets*. In this section we do so by drawing on empirical material from the Laag-Holland region of the Netherlands (a rural area directly north of Amsterdam). At the end of the 1970s the introduction of the Dutch nature preservation policy framework aroused considerable hostility among farmers in this region (as elsewhere). This policy framework envisaged a complete abandonment of agricultural activity in this area (characterized by man-made wet-land peat soil areas) in order to maintain its highly (and increasingly) appreciated nature and landscape values. Local farmers resisted this idea forcefully and this led to a new collective farmers' initiative; one of the Netherlands first agri-environmental cooperatives. This cooperative challenged the government's policy objective and sought a prominent role for farmers in regional nature and landscape management. Over time this farmers' initiative evolved into a professional organisation which acted as a mediator between individual farmers and national and regional policy actors in the formulation, implementation and realisation of agri-environmental policies. It also prepared the ground for the emergence of a wide variety of other, new, forms of territorially based cooperation, set out below.

1   A return to multifunctionality as guiding principle for sustainable agricultural and rural development.
2   The active exploration of newly emerging rural markets through establishing new institutional arrangements for: agricultural care-provision (www.landzijde.nl); agri- and rural tourism (www.boerenkamer.nl); short food chains (www.natuurvlees.nl, www.marqt.nl); and, green and food related educational activities for urban school children (www.klaszoektboerderij.nl).
3   New public-private partnerships, such as the Laag-Holland Regional Project Office, which includes public, private, rural and urban stakeholders and has the objective of improving the consistency and coherence of policy interventions in the area.
4   The establishment of a public fund (the Regional Land Bank) that enables the purchase of land that can be leased on a long term basis to local farmers interested in incorporating nature management in their farming strategies.
5   Active learning communities to strengthen of self-regulation capacity in relation to the provision and monitoring of agri-environmental services and green-care, re-localizing food production and consumption systems and recreating strong functional ties between the rural and the urban through the valorisation of available endogenous rural resources.

Taken together this set of activities and practices demonstrates how the territorial capacity to create more nested rural markets is closely related to the different components of the rural policy performance triangle. The available social capital within Laag-Holland (which was initially manifest in farmers' collective resistance against national agri-environmental policy but later, increasingly, through the sharing of between public and private, rural and urban stakeholders about the key role of agriculture in preserving nature and landscape values) has been a crucial driver for different types of new institutional arrangements. These have enabled the mediation and reshaping of conventional food market forces in a way that favours the valorisation of available endogenous resources and the preservation of rural distinctiveness.

This, in turn, has led to the establishment of a number of new multi-stakeholder institutional arrangements: the Agri-Environmental Cooperative for Water Land & Dykes, the Cooperative for the Provision of Green Care (Landzijde), the Regional Land Bank, the Laag-Holland Regional Project Office, and the Agritourism Foundation (Boerenkamer). Individually, but mostly through collaboration, these new institutional arrangements have contributed to an increasingly coherent, consistent and resilient system of rural market governance that encourages farmers to explore multiple income sources and to adopt multifunctional rural businesses models. Through these multifunctional rural businesses, models farmers in Laag-Holland have increasingly been able to; (1) reduce their dependency on conventional food markets; (2) generate significant and growing incomes from new rural development activities; (3) use their engagement in new rural development activities to further agricultural development; and, (4) have a growing sense of optimism about further business development opportunities (van Broekhuizen and Oostindie 2010).

At the same time it should be noted that territorially based rural market governance is often not easy to realize in multi-level governance settings, especially give the institutional voids that may exist within them. Hajer (2003: 175) defines institutional voids as:

> the absence of clear rules and norms according to which politics is to be conducted, policy measures are to be agreed upon and thus without generally accepted rules and norms.

The Laag-Holland case demonstrates that it can be difficult to align the collective provision of agri-environmental services (with performance-based delivery systems as a second crucial aspect of these self-governance initiatives) with national and European policy frameworks. The accountability rules associated with such frameworks can often frustrate the further exploration of agri-environmental self-governance potentials. Institutional voids also play a significant role in delineating the policy instruments that can be employed to mobilize extra public and private funding to support the expansion of agri-environmental services. Examples include constraints on longer contract periods, which provide more scope to better integrate agri-environmental services with overall farming strategies. So far these institutional voids have been addressed by 'back door solutions'. One example of this back door strategy is the National

Catalogue of Green and Blue Services. This catalogue provides extra, EU support-proof experimental space for such new policy instruments, although there are no opportunities here for RDP co-financing. Another, more far-reaching illustration concerns the current lack of transparency, uncertainty, confusion, tensions and conflicts that surround the 'greening' of the CAP Pillar 1 single payments. So far it remains highly uncertain whether this 'greening' will be accompanied by a reallocation of CAP Pillar 1 funding towards rural regions and individual farm enterprises that contribute most effectively to the preservation of nature and landscape amenities. The Water Land & Dykes Agri-Environmental Cooperative in Laag-Holland is one of the pilot partners that is currently exploring the practicalities, opportunities and limitations of more territorial and performance-based allocation systems within these greening proposals for Pillar 1. Because of relatively low average single payments per hectare (due to history and the continued presence of extensive animal production systems), overall outcome of necessary combined learning and negotiation processes in multi-level governance settings will have a major impact on the future preservation and strengthening of the boundaries and defence-lines that explain the emergence of nested rural markets in Laag-Holland.

Conclusions

Our initial analysis of the European transition from a primary agricultural policy framework towards a *rural governance approach* illustrated that RDPs are key symbols for effecting this change. The performance of RDPs is, in turn, closely influenced by: (1) the ability of a territory to create new institutional arrangements within increasingly complex multi-level governance settings and (2) the territorial availability of social capital. We have illustrated the relevance of these key components of the rural policy performance triangle and extended this analysis by examining its relevance to the emergence of new, more nested rural markets in Europe. Drawing on Dutch empirical material we have shown how territorially-based social capital may stimulate processes that result in a range of new institutional arrangements. The *combination* of these new institutional arrangements can provide robust and resilient defence-lines against hegemonic food market forces. Their mutually re-enforcing relationships, grounded on multifunctional rural resource use as broadly shared guiding principle of sustainability, can provide a successful alternative mode of rural market governance. The multi-level nature of such governance is partly reflected in shifting interrelations between Pillars 1 and 2 of CAP. The foreseen 'greening' of CAP support might be strengthened by a national re-allocation of CAP funding in line with Laag-Holland's' ability, willingness and commitment to provide rural amenities. Yet, so far such a re-allocation continues to be surrounded by controversies, sensitivities and institutional voids. In the shorter term there is more room for optimism about other opportunities provided by the proposed CAP Pillar 2 changes for the forthcoming 2014–2020 period. These reflect a growing acknowledgement from Europe of the relevance of the collective provision of agri-environmental services and enlarge the opportunities for supporting such collective approaches. This might open new chances and trajectories for further institutional redesign in Laag-Holland, which may facilitate and enhance the continuity of its increasingly nested rural markets.

References

Broekhuizen, R. van and H. Oostindie (2010) National landscape Laag-Holland; rural web dynamics in a metropolitan landscape. In: Milone, P. and F. Ventura (eds), *Networking the Rural; the future of green regions in Europe*, Assen, Royal Van Gorcum.

D'Haese, M, W. Verbeke, G. van Huylenbroeck, and L. D'Haese, (2005) New institutional arrangements for rural development, the case of local woolgrowers' associations in the Transkei Area, South Africa, *Journal of Development Studies*, 41: 1444–1466.

Dwyer, J. (2010) EU Rural Development Policy after 2013: What will be needed? *Agra-Europe* AE2414 Friday 28 May 2010.

European Commission (2013) *Political agreement on new direction for common agricultural policy*. Press Release, Brussels, 26 June.

Geels, F. (2004) From sectoral systems of innovation to socio-technical systems; insights about dynamics and change from sociology and institutional theory, *Research Policy*, 33: 897–920.

Goodman, D. (2004) Rural Europe redux: reflections on alternative agro-food networks and paradigm change, *Sociologia Ruralis*, 44: 3–16.

Hajer, M.A. (2003) Policy without polity? Policy analysis and the institutional void, *Policy Sciences*, 36: 175–195.

Hedstrom, M. (2010) *Devolution in the Swedish Rural Development Programme; the case of Västerbotten*. Rudi Deliverable D 8.1, www.rudi-europe.net.

Hodge, I. (2001) Beyond agri-environmental policy: towards an alternative model of rural environmental governance, *Land Use Policy*, 18: 99–111.

Huelemeyer, K. and S. Schiller (2010) *Coordination of rural policies in Mecklenburg-Vorpommern, Case-study on the Joint Administrative Authority*. Rudi Deliverable D 8.1, www.rudi-europe.net.

Huylenbroeck, G., A. Vuylsteke, and W. Verbeke (2009) Public good markets: the possible role of hybrid governance structures in institutions for sustainability, in: V. Beckmann and M. Padmanabhan (eds) *Institutions and Sustainability* 1, Dordrecht: Springer.

Huylenbroeck, G. and E. Mettepenningen (2011) The role of institutional arrangements in rural development, in: *Agrarian perspectives: proceedings of the 20th international scientific conference*, pp. 377–386, Czech University of Life Sciences Prague, Faculty of Economics and Management, http:/hdl.handle.net/1854/LU-1921568.

Ilbery, B. and D. Maye (2005). Alternative (shorter) food supply chains and specialist livestock products in the Scottish-English borders, *Environment and Planning A*, 37: 823–844.

Klijn, E. and G. Teisman (2000). Governing public-private partnerships, in: S. Osborne (eds) *Public private partnerships: theory and practice in international perspective*, London: Routledge.

Knickel, K., S. Schiller, S. von Münchhausen, H. Vihinen and A. Weber (2008). New institutional arrangements in rural development, in *Unfolding Webs, the dynamics of regional rural development*, in: van der Ploeg, J.D. and T. Marsden (eds), Assen: Royal Van Gorcum.

Lang, T. and M. Heasman (2004) *Food Wars: The Global Battle for Minds, Mouths and Markets*, London: Earthscan.

Laurent, C. (2005) *Multifunctionality of activities, plurality of identities and new institutional arrangements, MULTAGRI WP4 Summary report for France.* Paris, INRA SAD-APT.

Mantino, F. (2010) *The Reform of the EU Rural Development Policy and the Challenges ahead*, Notre Europe Policy Paper.

Mantino, F., S. Tarangiolo and L. Tudini (2010) *Horizontal and vertical rural policy coordination in the Italian Grosseto Province.* Rudi Deliverable D 8.1, www.rudi-europe.net.

Maye, M., J. Kirwan and S. Simpson (2010) *New modes of rural governance in Ireland.* Rudi Deliverable D 8.1, www.rudi-europe.net.

Oostindie, H. and H. Renting (2005) *Multifunctionality of activities, plurality of identities and new institutional arrangements. MULTAGRI WP4 Summary Report for the Netherlands*, Wageningen: Rural Sociology Group, Wageningen University.

Oostindie, H. and R. van Broekhuizen (2010a) *Case study synthesis report, assessing the import of rural development policies (incl. LEADER)*, RUDI Deliverable D 8.2.

Oostindie, H. and R. van Broekhuizen (2010b) *RDP and performance based rural policy delivery in the Netherlands*, Rudi Deliverable D 8.1, www.rudi-europe.net.

Oostindie, H., J.D. van der Ploeg, R. van Broekhuizen, F. Ventura and P. Milone (2011) Il ruolo centrale dei 'Nested Markets' nello sviluppo rurale in Europa, *Rivista di Economia Agraria*, 65: 191–224.

Ostrom, E., L. Schroeder, and S. Wynne (1993) Analysing alternative institutional arrangements for sustaining rural infrastructure in developing countries, *Journal of Public Administration Research and Theory*, 3: 11–45.

Renting, H. and J.D. van der Ploeg (2001) Reconnecting nature, farming and society: environmental cooperatives in the Netherlands as institutional arrangements for creating coherence. *Journal of Environmental Policy and Planning*, 3: 85–101.

Renting, H., T. Marsden and J. Banks (2003) Understanding alternative food networks: exploring the role of short food supply chains, *Environment and Planning*, 42: 12–31.

Renting, H., H. Oostindie, C. Laurent, G. Brunori, A. Rossi, M. Charollais, D. Barjolle, S. Prestegard, A. Jervell, L. Granberg and M. Heinonen (2005) *Multifunctionality of activities, plurality of identities and new institutional arrangements. MULTAGRI WP4, Synthesis Report*, Wageningen: Rural Sociology Group Wageningen University.

Renting, H., M. Schermer and A. Rossi (2013) Building Food Democracy: Exploring Civic Food Networks and Newly Emerging Forms of Food Citizenship, *Journal of Sociology of Agriculture and Food*, 19: 289–307.

Schiller, S. (2010) *Assessing the impacts of rural policies (including LEADER). Extended policy brief for the final conference*, www.rudi-europe.net.

Teisman, G. and E. Klijn (2000) Public-private partnerships in the European Union: officially suspect, embraced in daily practice, in: Osborne, S (ed.), *Public-Private Partnerships; Theory and practice in international perspective*, London, Routledge.

Tregear, A. (2011) Progressing knowledge in alternative and local food networks: critical reflections and a research agenda, *Journal of Rural Studies*, 27: 419–430.

8 Smallholder irrigators and fresh produce street traders in Thohoyandou, Limpopo Province, South Africa

Kgabo Manyelo, Wim Van Averbeke and Paul Hebinck

Introduction

South Africa desperately needs to increase employment. For more than a decade it has experienced an unemployment rate of about 25 per cent, and it is the youth who are most affected.[1] Both academics and policy makers consider agrarian development to be the main way in which employment can be generated in rural areas (National Planning Commission 2011; Van der Heijden and Vink 2013). Politically, this view was expressed and elaborated in the National Development Plan: Vision for 2030 (National Planning Commission 2011). This plan includes an agrarian development strategy which envisages the establishment of a vibrant smallholder farming sector, mainly on irrigated land. For farmers to make a living from small plots they need to participate in high value markets (Van der Heijden and Vink 2013). Fruit and vegetables are prime examples of high value crops that can be grown on smallholdings, especially where irrigation is available (Van Averbeke *et al.* 2011; Cousins 2012). Linking smallholders to fresh produce markets, on the other hand, has proven to be difficult (Louw *et al.* 2008a; Senyolo *et al.* 2009; Van der Heijden and Vink 2013). One of the underlying reasons is the ongoing trend towards vertical integration and consolidation that has occurred in the South African agro-food sector during the past two decades (Louw *et al.* 2008a; Madevu *et al.* 2009; Ramabulana 2011; Van der Heijden and Vink 2013). Supermarkets have been the principal drivers of this trend, which also applies to fresh produce (Madevu *et al.* 2009; Ramabulana 2011). Supermarkets have actively developed 'preferred supplier networks' to ensure reliable supplies of large quantities of fresh produce that meets their quality standards. These supplier networks are dominated by a select number of mainly large-scale farm enterprises. There is general agreement that, *ceteris paribus*, the scope for smallholders to become part of these networks is limited (D'Haese and Van Huylenbroeck 2005; Louw *et al.* 2007; Louw *et al.* 2008a; Ortmann and King 2010; Ramabulana 2011; Van der Heijden and Vink 2013). Moreover, as part of their expansion strategy, major supermarket chains in South Africa have been establishing branches in rural towns (D'Haese and Van Huylenbroeck 2005; Louw *et al.* 2008a; Crush and Fraine 2011). These rural town outlets are linked to the 'preferred supplier networks' through a national distribution system, which tends to disconnect the produce on the shelves of these supermarkets from production on the farms in their hinterlands (D'Haese and Van Huylenbroeck 2005; Du Toit and Neven 2007; Crush and Fraine 2011; Van der Heijden and Vink 2013).

Supermarkets are not the only retailers of fresh produce in South Africa. Greengrocers and informal street traders are also important (Louw *et al.* 2004; Madevu *et al.* 2009). They primarily source their fruit and vegetables from national fresh produce markets, which are found in all the major cities (Madevu *et al.* 2009). For smallholders these city markets are accessible, but the high implicit and explicit transaction costs of marketing relatively small quantities of produce depress margins (Senyolo *et al.* 2009; Ortmann and King 2010; Ramoroka 2012), and this probably goes a long way towards explaining the very limited smallholder participation in these markets. It follows that the outlook for effective participation of smallholders in the mainstream fresh produce markets is bleak. Without access to markets for high value crops, such as fresh produce, the policy aim of establishing a vibrant smallholder sector in South Africa will not be realized.

The prevailing view in research circles is that ways can and must be found to integrate smallholders into the mainstream agri-food systems (D'Haese and Van Huylenbroeck 2005; Louw *et al.* 2008b; Ortmann and King 2010). Recommendations to facilitate this development include implementation of the Broad Based Black Economic Empowerment for Agriculture (D'Haese and Van Huylenbroeck 2005); linking smallholders to agri-business and supermarkets; promoting collective action among smallholders by forming producer organizations and cooperatives aimed at creating economies of scale and raising quality; and equity share schemes (Louw *et al.* 2008b; Ortmann and King 2010). Ortmann and King (2010) also pointed out the potential for smallholders to become part of alternative food networks that not only bring food closer to consumers but also provide it in different forms or types than the supermarkets.

The case presented in this chapter documents an alternative food network that involves fresh produce. It differs from the mainstream South African fresh produce network in terms of the relationships between producers, traders and consumers, the quality control and price setting mechanisms, and, most importantly, the distribution of benefits. From a developmental perspective this alternative fresh produce network is significant because it generates high levels of local employment and gives people living in the locale broader access to fresh produce than supermarkets do. This broadened access is the result of improved distribution and low prices, which are brought about by competition among farmers and traders, and also at present, between the traders and the supermarkets. This fresh produce network was created by local people without external intervention. To an extent it involves 'unconventional' fresh produce, which forms part of the local food culture, explaining why some of this produce escaped the attention of supermarkets, at least initially. Considering the local embeddedness of this alternative food network and the various ways in which it differs structurally from the mainstream food network, it can be regarded as a 'nested market'. The development and expansion of this 'nested market' was made possible by a change in policy from one which was highly interventionist and regulatory to one which is almost totally 'laissez faire'.

Five fresh produce crops are important to the case described in this chapter: green maize (*Zea mays* L. var. *indentata*), white cabbage (*Brassica oleracea* L. var *capitata*), Chinese cabbage (*Brassica rapa* L. subsp. *chinensis*), nightshade (*Solanum retroflexum* Dun.) and pumpkin (*Cucurbita maxima* Duchesne). Smallholders in the Thohoyandou area have been producing green maize as a commodity for at least the past 35 years (BENSO & RAU 1979). They sell it to consumers as a ready-to-eat snack, which is prepared by boiling the maize cobs leaving the light-green inner leaves of the husk on and adding some salt for taste (Van Averbeke *et al.* 2013). Selling maize as green cobs is advantageous for farmers, because the income they receive for these cobs is about three times more than they would receive for leaving them to mature and selling the grain (Van Averbeke, 2008). Not all maize cobs can be sold green: cobs need to meet particular quality criteria. First, they should not show any visible damage, which can occur when birds shred the tip of the husks or when insects bore into the cobs to get at the developing grain. Second, the cobs should be large. Measurements at Dzindi showed that a cob covered by the inner leaves of the husk should be at least 31 cm long to be suitable for the green maize market (Van Averbeke *et al.* 2013).

Pumpkin, like maize, is a summer crop that can be grown for the harvest of mature fruit, but in the area of Thohoyandou it is mainly produced for the harvest of its leaves, flowers and young fruit (Jansen van Rensburg *et al.* 2007; Van Averbeke *et al.* 2012). These plant parts are boiled together to produce a side-dish that accompanies the stiff porridge made of white maize meal, which is the local staple food. Non-heading Chinese cabbage and night shade are traditional leafy vegetables, which are grown during winter. The leaves of these crops are used to prepare much appreciated relishes that add flavour and texture to the stiff maize porridge (Van Averbeke *et al.* 2007). Leaves of Swiss chard, which can be grown throughout the year in the area, are used for the same purpose, but are considered less tasty than the leaves of Chinese cabbage and nightshade.

The town of Thohoyandou and the Dzindi smallholder canal scheme also play an important role in the scheme. Thohoyandou was planned and constructed during the Venda homeland era (1970 to 1993) and is best described as a Central Business District without a resident population. The entire town consists of roads, parking areas and buildings used for administrative and trading purposes. The people who work in Thohoyandou live in townships around the town. During the past decade, several of the parking areas that were part of the original CBD have been converted to shopping malls, adding two new supermarkets to the one that already existed.

Dzindi Irrigation Scheme (23°01'S; 30°26'E) (Figure 7.1) is one of 27 smallholder irrigation schemes in Thulamela Municipality (Figure 7.1). Dzindi is located southwest of Thohoyandou, about 10 km away by road. The scheme forms part of Itsani village and has a command area of 135.6 ha, which

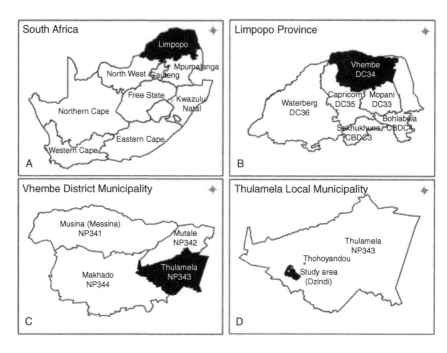

Map 8.1 Location of Dzindi Irrigation Scheme and Thoyandou.

is subdivided into 106 plots of 1.28 ha each. These plots are held by a total of 97 plot holders.[2] Dzindi consists of four hydraulic units, referred to as 'blocks', which are numbered from 1 to 4, with block 4 closest to the weir on the Dzindi River, which is the source of water for the scheme. A concrete-lined canal conveys water from the weir to the different blocks and concrete furrows bring it to the farmers' plots, which are divided into a varying number of border strips, depending on the slope of the land and the shape of the plot. These strips form the elementary units of production and are irrigated using the short-furrow method (Van Averbeke 2008).

Setting the scene

The marketing of fresh produce by farmers at Dzindi has a relatively long and varied history. Construction of the Dzindi Irrigation Scheme was completed in 1954 (Van Averbeke 2009). At that time, Dzindi was part of a 'Native Area' governed by a Native Commissioner (Van Averbeke 2008). Before the Scheme was constructed, the command area and about 450 ha of veld that surrounded it were detribalized and ownership was transferred to the Native Trust, making the area the property of the state. The settlement of farmers on the scheme was organized through applications, whereby people who had land rights prior to the construction of the scheme were given priority. A resident agricultural extension technician was appointed to teach plot holders how to irrigate (Manyelo 2011). In line with the trust tenure system[3] and the conditions for plot occupation that applied at the scheme, the extension technician instructed farmers what to grow on the main part (70 to 85 per cent) of their plots. Among the crops grown, cotton, pigeon peas, rice, wheat and tomatoes were the most important. Farmers delivered the harvests of these crops to the office of the extension technician, who sold them to mining companies or on the spot market at the town of Louis Trichardt. Cash payments were made to farmers. Farmers were allowed to grow what they wanted on three of the 10 to 20 strips that made up a plot. These strips were used to grow maize and vegetables, almost entirely for home consumption, but farmers occasionally bartered vegetables for maize with people residing in settlements surrounding the scheme (Manyelo 2011).

From about 1960 onwards a small number of farmers started to sell vegetables. This was done in neighbouring villages using door-to-door trading and on the fresh produce market at Khwevha in Tshisahulu, a few kilometres west of the scheme. The scale of these self-marketing initiatives remained limited until 1970, when the administration of the Native Areas was indigenized.[4] This political transformation lessened state interference with farming at Dzindi and farmers increasingly planted the crops they wanted to grow. Cropping patterns changed. Wheat, grown during winter, progressively made way for Chinese cabbage (*Brassica rapa* subsp. *chinensis*) and nightshade (*Solanum retroflexum* Dun.), two traditional leafy vegetables that are very popular among the local population. Maize and ground nuts became the two main summer crops and farmers began marketing more of their produce themselves. Farmers also started to access the more distant Khumbe fresh produce market, about 12 km west of the scheme. However, on these fresh produce markets they experienced fierce competition from the white farmers of the Levhubhu Irrigation Scheme. Dzindi farmers cited this competition as one of three main reasons why they increasingly abandoned self-marketing in favour of selling at farm gate to fresh produce traders, who had their own means to cart fresh produce from the farm to trading places. The second reason was that many Dzindi homesteads lacked the labour required to handle both the production and the retailing of fresh produce. The third was the banning of donkeys from the rangeland allocated to Dzindi plot holders. Farmers had previously used donkey carts to transport fresh produce from their plots to the various market places (Manyelo 2011).

Governmental intervention in the marketing of crops produced at Dzindi reappeared briefly around 1980. In an effort to commercialize smallholder agriculture, the Venda Department of Agriculture and its agricultural parastatal wing Agriven encouraged plot holders to collectively enter into production contracts with different buyers, including mines, retailers, and food-processing companies. Plot holders at Dzindi still recall this era as a dark period in the history of the scheme, because of broken promises and financial losses incurred by farmers. The last collective marketing initiative facilitated by government took place in 1986. Agriven encouraged farmers to grow tomatoes for delivery to a processing plant and provided farmers with production loans. Farmers recall that the greater part of the tomatoes they produced ended up rotting in the fields, because the processing company did not collect the produce. Farmers suffered considerable financial losses and Agriven took several farmers to court because they did not repay their loans in time. The collective distress emanating from this experience ran so deep within the farmer community of Dzindi, that they not only refused to participate in any subsequent state-initiated marketing initiatives proposed to them, but also refrained from planting tomatoes for more than 20 years. In recent years, the crop has made its re-appearance at the scheme, but is only grown by a few young farmers who were not around in 1986 (Manyelo 2011).

Also around 1980, following the building of the Thohoyandou CBD, a new kind of fresh produce trader appeared at Dzindi. They differed from existing traders in that they made use of public transportation instead of using their own means of transport to carry goods from farm to trading place. Their relative importance in the marketing of vegetables grew at Dzindi over the next two decades. In 2009, when the fieldwork for this study was done, they were by far the largest group of traders operating at Dzindi (Manyelo 2011).

Farmers and farming at Dzindi

In 2003, gross farm income contributed 30 per cent on average to the total home-stead income of Dzindi plot holders (Mohamed 2006; Van Averbeke 2008). Other sources of income included state transfers (social grants), salaries and wages from employment, informal trade and service provision and remittances. Thirty-six of the 97 plot holders obtained at least half of their income from social grants, 21 through being employed, 11 from informal sector activities (other than farming), and nine from a combination of these sources. There were also 20 plot holders (21 per cent) who generated at least half of their homestead income from farming. Fifteen of them were labelled 'market-oriented farmers', who generated more than half of their gross farm income through sales, whilst the other five were labelled 'subsistence farmers', as they allocated more than half of the value of their crops to self-consumption (Mohamed 2006; Van Averbeke 2008). Diversity in liveli-hood portfolios among plot holder homesteads at Dzindi was matched by diversity in the way farming was practised. Van Averbeke and Mohamed (2006) provide a detailed description of farming at Dzindi, identifying five different 'farming styles'. They labelled the majority of farmers as 'food farmers'. These 'food farmers' produced Chinese cabbage, nightshade, pumpkins and maize. They sold most of the leafy vegetables they grew and kept most of the maize for harvest as grain, satisfying their own staple food needs and selling the surplus. Cabbage pro-duction, lucrative but difficult in this sub-tropical climate, was almost exclusively the domain of a select group of 16 farmers referred to as 'profit makers' (ibid.).

Street traders linked to Dzindi

The population of street traders covered by this case study consisted of all people who purchased fresh produce from the farm gates of Dzindi plot holders to sell in 2009. We excluded people who purchased fresh produce for their own consumption, and the supermarket stores in Thohoyandou, which purchased fresh produce from selected plot holders. The population of street traders was further subdivided into four trader categories, namely, 'bakkie traders', 'central business district (CBD) traders', 'township pavement traders' and 'door-to-door traders'. Use of their own motorized transport (van), mobility (sedentary or mobile), and place of trade were the criteria for defining these groups.

Bakkie traders were mobile traders, who made use of small trucks (bakkies) to collect produce from Dzindi and transport it to their place of trade where they displayed it to the public for retail purposes. Bakkie traders did not only purchase from Dzindi. They mainly purchased cabbages from Dzindi and obtained other vegetables, such as tomatoes, butternuts and onions, from elsewhere. Their mobility enabled them to access fresh produce from different places, including large commercial farms and smallholder irrigation schemes. Central business district (CBD) traders were sedentary traders, whose place of trade was located within the boundaries of the business district of Thohoyandou. They made use of public transport to get fresh produce to their place of trade as, unlike bakkie traders, they did not own motorized transport. Township pavement traders were also sedentary traders but their place of trade was located along roadsides in townships and other sites with relatively heavy flows of potential customers, such as the Tshilidzini hospital in Tshifulanani. Door-to-door traders were mobile traders. They did not own motorized transport but hawked fresh produce in the settlements surrounding Dzindi, moving on foot from house to house, carrying a bag of fresh produce. In all a total of 101 street traders were purchasing fresh produce from farmers at Dzindi in June 2009 (a number that was almost identical to the number of farmers at the scheme). The categorization of the 101 street traders is shown in Table 8.1.

Table 8.1 shows that street traders consisted predominantly of rural women, with most being CBD traders. Men also participated in the street trade of fresh produce purchased at Dzindi but they were all bakkie traders. Generally, the low

Table 8.1 Number of street traders who purchased fresh produce from farmers at Dzindi by category (June 2009)

Street trader category	Number of traders		
	Male	*Female*	*Total*
Bakkie traders	15	2	17
CBD traders	0	54	54
Township pavement traders	0	12	12
Door-to-door traders	0	18	18
Total	15	86	101

Source: Manyelo (2011): 63.

Note
CBD = Central business district.

level of formal education of street traders limited their chances of finding work in the formal sector of the South African economy, especially against the backdrop of persistently high unemployment. Even though most women traders were married, their husbands were often not earning an income. As a result, all of the single women and several of the married female street traders were the 'breadwinners' in their households. The majority of them had entered the street trade after losing their previous livelihood as a result of retrenchment or lay-off, or when it had failed to deliver sufficient income to attain an acceptable standard of living (Manyelo, 2011).

Exchange between farmers and street traders

Differences existed between bakkie traders and the other three categories of street traders in terms of their exchange with farmers. As indicated, bakkie traders only purchased white cabbages from Dzindi farmers. They relied on telephone contact (cellular phones) with them to identify the availability of cabbages. The price of cabbage was usually negotiated over the phone. In 2009, the commonly charged price for cabbage was R5[5] per head. Bakkie traders harvested the cabbages themselves and only picked heads that met their quality requirements. Farmers assisted with loading and counted loudly as the cabbages were packed onto the van. Traders paid farmers in cash, once all the cabbages had been loaded.

CBD, township pavement and door-to-door traders purchased African leafy vegetables (Chinese cabbage, nightshade, pumpkin leaves and sporadically Swiss chard) and green maize from farmers at Dzindi. Scouting the fields was the main way in which they identified the availability of vegetables for sale. Occasionally, farmers would wait at the entrance gate of their irrigation block for the arrival of traders to inform them that fresh produce was obtainable from their plots. Farmers and traders also communicated using cellular phone, with traders calling farmers to enquire about availability of produce and farmers calling traders to notify them that produce was ready for sale. Scouring for stock required traders to walk up and down the paths separating the plots. When traders identified vegetables ready for harvest they would approach the plot holder and ask for permission to purchase.

Walking to the scheme and scouring the fields was usually done in groups of people who lived in the same village. Moving around as a group provided the women with a degree of protection against attack and robbery, which occurred sporadically, as explained by one of the traders:

> I live far away from the members of my group and I am the one who wakes them up, starting with the one closest to my house. A man once attacked me with a knife. I was with the others and it was early in the morning. I only felt his fist hitting me. He ran away because the others who were with me picked up stones and attacked him. Then we continued on our journey to the field and purchased produce. On our way to the field I started to realise that he had stabbed me three times with a knife.

Another benefit of working in groups was that members assisted each other with the identification of produce. This applied particularly to information gathered through telephonic contact between farmers and traders. Farmers would call one member of a group, counting on that person to inform the other members.

The different groups of traders, typically from different villages surrounding the scheme, competed with each other. They refused to disclose the location of available produce to members of other groups and did not hesitate to send other groups on a wild goose chase. The seriousness of the competition among groups of traders is evident from the following statements:

> If a trader from one group gets asked by a trader from another group where she got her produce, she will not hesitate to mislead that person, even if she knows that it will waste her time and money. We never tell each other the truth. You know, there are so many vegetables in the field and one trader cannot finish them all but still we do not tell each other the truth about where we get our supply. There is a lady I know who was informed that she should come and purchase green maize. She went to the field and bought cobs and then asked a member from another group to sell cooked maize for her. She took a bowl full of cooked maize to the trade place of that lady. That lady did not want to sell for her but the owner of the cooked maize insisted and left the dish with her. The lady who was asked to assist did not have green maize herself that day, because she was not informed of its availability. Whenever customers came to her to buy green maize, she told them that the green maize was not hers and that it was not fresh, because it was yesterday's leftovers. Not a single customer bought green maize and when the owner of the maize came to collect her money, she found her bowl still full. We once met that very same lady with one of her trader friends in a plot purchasing nightshade. We also wanted to get in and buy but the two of them told us that all the nightshade in the plot belonged to them. We had to move on and continue searching somewhere else, because even the owner of the plot did not say a word when they claimed that the nightshade was theirs. Later on I saw that same nightshade looking poorly, because it was not harvested in time. From that day onwards I never returned to that farmer to purchase produce. When I walk past his plot and I see there is something to buy I just keep walking.

Members of trader groups also acted collectively in discouraging newcomers from entering the fresh produce trade. When a new trader was noticed in the fields, groups of existing traders would ill-treat her and nobody would come to her defence, not even the farmers. A new trader recalled her experiences as follows:

> When I came to purchase vegetables for the first time, I went with my friend but she did not show me how to harvest the vegetables. At that time I had no idea but now I am a professor. I copied others and taught myself. Existing

traders used to call me names. I just kept quiet. Groups of traders were secretive about the places where they were going to purchase produce. Even my friend sometimes used to do that and I also started to be secretive, lying, saying that I was going to one place whereas I was going somewhere else.

Some newcomers, who withstood the ill-treatment meted out by existing traders, eventually became accepted, but others ended up quitting. When that happened, the mission of the existing traders had been accomplished. The following account illustrates how existing traders went about discouraging newcomers:

Yesterday one of the newcomers picked some Chinese cabbage leaves from the ground, thinking it was yesterday's, but the leaves belonged to another trader. When the owner of the bunch saw her, she shouted, 'The newcomer is stealing our vegetables!' The newcomer explained that it was all a misunderstanding but the others made it an issue. All of them joined in and said that the newcomer was a thief. Even today they were loudly telling others to be careful of the newcomer, because she was a thief. I told her to just keep quiet and today she did not respond to their allegations. When I started trading I was treated badly as well. You know, I did not know where to get supply and I used to follow existing traders. When they saw me following them, they would tell me that they do not have tails, meaning that I, the newcomer, should not be following them. I persisted and now they know me and I am no longer experiencing bad treatment from them. One of them once said that they hoped I would quit.

Some farmers and traders had developed relationships of trust, which made special arrangements possible. For example, farmers would allow particular traders to enter their plots and harvest produce in their absence. After harvesting, these traders would wait for the farmer to come and charge them. The advantage of being allowed to harvest produce in the absence of the plot holder was that produce could be secured before the arrival of other groups. Traders were particularly keen to obtain produce from farmers who planted earlier than others. To that effect they would enter into informal contracts with farmers, which involved the payment of deposits. Once the produce was ready, the farmers would inform the traders and arrange for the harvest. In the absence of binding agreements between farmers and traders, farmers sold on a first come first served basis. Conversely, traders also bought produce from any farmer who was selling, even when they had agreed to purchase from someone else, whom they had asked to reserve produce. In such cases they would phone the farmer and postpone the appointment. Once farmers had shown the part of the plot where vegetables could be harvested, traders entered the field and started picking, whilst farmers kept a watchful eye on the proceedings. During harvesting traders operated individually and picked only what they believed they could sell, applying their own quality criteria. Farmers competed for customers and did not mind attracting traders who were harvesting in the plot of a neighbour. Traders also did not hesitate to switch plots. Once traders had harvested what they wanted they would pay for the produce they had taken. Even if they switched from one farmer's plot to another, both farmers would get their money.

The price of Chinese cabbage, Swiss chard and pumpkin leaves was dependent on the size of harvested bunch, and was negotiated after traders had completed their harvests. Nightshade was usually priced per planted row length but when the stand was uneven, it was also priced per bunch. In 2009, farmers typically charged R30 per bunch of leaves, irrespective of the type of vegetable. If the bunch that was harvested was larger than what the farmer considered to be worth R30, the farmer would remove leaves, for which the trader would pay extra. If the bunch was smaller, more leaves were added until the right-sized bunch had been obtained. Negotiating the price of green maize was done before harvesting commenced. In 2009, the price for good-quality green maize was R2 per cob. This price was reduced if the ears were small or slightly damaged.

Members of trader groups collaborated with each other during price negotiations with farmers, in an attempt to bring down prices. An entire group of traders would walk away if they thought that the farmer was asking too much. After a while they would come back to find out whether the farmer had changed his mind. They particularly applied this tactic during times of abundance, knowing that farmers were desperate to sell. Occasionally, farmers also joined forces to counteract the tactics of the traders. For example, in September 2009, plot holders in Block 2 of Dzindi fixed the price of a bunch of nightshade, because the price had dropped too low.

Place of trade

Place of trade, i.e. the site where retailing occurred, was the primary asset of street traders, because it determined turn-over (Manyelo 2011). Generally, the daily turnover of CBD traders was greater than that of township pavement traders, who, in turn, had a greater turn-over than door-to-door traders. Inside the Thohoyandou CBD, certain places, such as the newly-built taxi ranks and the pavements and parking areas around the two recently built shopping malls were out of bounds for street traders. In the remainder of the CBD they were allowed to operate on pavements and parking areas. Outside the Thohoyandou CBD, street traders were allowed to set up their enterprises in any open space along roads and streets.

Choice of trading place depended on whether traders were mobile or sedentary. Door-to-door traders selected particular villages or parts of townships where no other fresh produce traders were operating. CBD traders and township pavement traders selected sites with heavy flows of potential customers, such as places close to taxi ranks, bus stops or shops, streets that were used by a lot of pedestrians, or roads with high traffic volumes. Bakkie traders operating in the CBD of Thohoyandou used parking spaces. Their claim to a specific parking bay was sometimes contested. For example, parking bays located in front of shops were claimed by the owners of these shops. One of the bakkie traders recalled his experience with shop owners as follows:

> I came and parked my bakkie here on this spot and started to trade. These 'Indians' (pointing to shops belonging to Asians that he and his fellow traders were parked in front of) reported me to the police, saying that I took their parking. The police came and instructed me to leave but I refused. I told them that the 'Indians' were working for their families and so was I. It used to be tough in the beginning but I persisted until the 'Indians' and the police gave up.

Once traders had established their claim to a particular trading site, they defended it vehemently. In collaboration with other established bakkie traders, they also actively discouraged newcomers from entering into competition with them. When asked if he would allow new traders to take up position close to where he was parked, a bakkie trader responded:

> No we do not want new traders here. We (he and other bakkie traders who traded from the area where he was parked) would not agree. If a new trader would force himself into a parking spot over here, we would put our cars in front of his and leave. He will not stay. New traders should go there (pointing at another parking lot). We know each other here. Even these Indians (referring to Asians who ran the shop he was parked in front of) know where we park and we know where they park too.

In 2009, trading places in the CBD had become so valuable, that even when traders quit, they often insisted on retaining their right to these places. They tried to secure that right by handing their spots to relatives or friends. If that failed, they would inform the newcomer, who took over their trading place, of their right to reclaim the spot. The result was that newcomers found it very difficult to enter the street trade in the CBD. One of the door-to-door traders who attempted to set herself up as a CBD trader gave the following account of her attempt to set herself up as a CBD trader:

> I really want to get a trading place in town but until now I have not succeeded. I once tried to establish myself in Thohoyandou. I went there in the morning and found a nice space to trade from but no one bought from me. Around 2 pm, a woman arrived. She immediately started shouting at me and I could see she had a fighting spirit. She shouted that the space I was trading from was hers. Whilst shouting at me, she took a broom and started to sweep the floor, where I was sitting. I did not want to fight with her. I just told her that she should have explained to me nicely that I was occupying her space. I explained to her that old people talked politely to each other. After that she cooled down and I left. That same day, I went back to my customers, trading door to door, and I sold all my vegetables.

Local government claimed to regulate and control the street trade in collaboration with street trader organizations. Whilst this did occur in the past, when control over licensing was still applied, the social order and standards of cleanliness and hygiene in the street trader market were essentially dependent on self-regulation and informal rule systems imposed by organizations, which interacted with particular groups of street traders. The local taxi associations and owners of shops in front of which street traders erected their stalls were of particular significance in this regard. Local government made positive contributions to the street trade in the CBD of Thohoyandou by providing a regular and reliable refuse removal service as well as access to potable water and washing facilities. Only the last service was charged for, as the others were free of charge.

Exchange between street traders and consumers

Street traders marketed their wares in various ways. The mobile door-to-door traders moved from house to house and verbally informed potential customers of what they were selling. Sedentary street traders advertised their wares mainly through display. Sometimes they called out to people who passed their stands but that kind of approach tended to be reserved for people they knew personally. Bakkie traders used their vehicle to exhibit fresh produce. They left the bulk of their merchandise covered with a tarpaulin to protect it from the sun and displayed only a few items under a sun umbrella. In the case of cabbages, bakkie traders removed the outer leaves from the head once it had been purchased. These outer leaves were disposed of in municipal trash bins at the end of the day. Township pavement traders often displayed their vegetables on the wheel barrows they used to transport produce from the scheme to their place of trade, whilst CBD and some township pavement traders used wooden tables. Not all produce was displayed at once. Some was left in the bag under the table or wheelbarrow to keep it cool, and was used to replenish the produce after some had been sold. Leafy vegetables on display were sprinkled regularly with fresh water to protect them against wilting. Leafy vegetables only stayed fresh for one day in summer but in winter it was sometimes possible to keep them overnight and sell them the next day.

The aim of every street trader was to establish a loyal customer base. Creating 'loyalty' was pursued by extending 'special treatment', which included giving extra produce free of charge, reducing the price of produce, allowing customers to buy on credit, and purchasing from other traders when items requested by a customer were out of stock. Some would provide a service, such as cutting up leafy vegetables, free of charge or do home-deliveries if they lived in the same village as the customer. Among consumers the 'special treatment' they received from a particular trader would generate a feeling of obligation towards that trader, as is evident from the following statement:

> Sometimes I go and buy from someone else but I make sure that she (the street trader he usually went to) does not see me doing that. If she does catch

me carrying vegetables that I bought from someone else, and asks me where I got them from, I lie to her. I say that I got them from a colleague at work.

The daily challenge for traders dealing in cooked maize and leafy vegetables was to sell their entire stock by end of day, because freshness was paramount.[6] This created stiff competition among neighbouring traders selling the same items. At times, competition caused friction, for example, when the merchandise of one was selling faster than that of others. When this happened, the others would vent their displeasure. Despite being in competition there was also collaboration among neighbouring traders. They protected each other's trading places against 'invaders', helped each other out with change, and took care of each other's business when one had to leave for a while. Daily they also agreed on the price of the various vegetables they were selling but they rarely adhered to their agreement. When warranted, they would secretly charge their customers less than the price they had jointly set earlier in the day.

Discussion and conclusion

The National Development Plan: Vision for 2030 envisions a process of re-agrarianization, particularly of black people, to drive rural economic development in South Africa. To that effect, it aims to establish 500,000 new smallholder irrigators, which would generate the same amount of additional employment opportunities through related activities (e.g. marketing) (National Planning Commission 2011). For this plan to have any chance of success, new (and existing) smallholder irrigators need to actively participate in markets of relatively high-value crops, because life in South Africa is highly monetized (Du Toit and Neves 2007). Yet, the structure of contemporary food value chains in South Africa militate against widespread smallholder participation in such markets (Van der Heijden and Vink 2013), particularly because of the 'supermarketization' of food value chains. In 2003, an estimated 55 per cent of the food consumed in South Africa was acquired from supermarkets (Weatherspoon and Reardon 2003). This market share has most likely increased, considering the expansion of supermarkets into rural areas during the last decade (Crush and Frayne 2011). Global and local evidence indicates that supermarket food value chains, which rely heavily on 'preferred supplier networks' in their procurement strategy, particularly in the case of fresh produce, limit the scope for smallholder participation (Ortmann and King 2010; Van der Heijden and Vink 2013). Political proposals aligned with Broad Based Black Economic Empowerment to intervene in the procurement strategies of supermarkets have been suggested (D'Haese and Van Huylenbroeck 2005), but thus far there is little evidence of impact (Van der Heijden and Vink 2013). Accessing one or more branches of the National Fresh Produce Market in major cities is another doubtful proposition, not only because its market share is in decline (Van der Heijden and Vink 2013) but also because the transaction costs associated with presenting small quantities of produce are prohibitive (Senyolo *et al.* 2009; Ortmann and King 2010; Ramoroka 2012).

Collective action to raise the economy of scale of smallholder production and reduce transaction costs has been proposed but there are few successful examples of such initiatives (Ortman and King 2010). Another option, which has received little attention, is ring-fencing government procurement for black smallholders. Allocating sole mandates to black smallholders to supply food, particularly fresh produce, to public institutions, such as schools and hospitals is an option that warrants serious consideration. Participation in alternative food networks is another option for smallholders to market their produce, which has thus far been largely ignored. The evidence from this chapter demonstrates the viability of this option and points out the significant impact that alternative food networks can have on local economic development, particularly in terms of employment generation through forward linkages in economic activity, represented by the street trade in fresh produce. Other important advantages of the alternative food network described in this chapter are that the benefits accrue almost entirely to the people involved. This is in sharp contrast to the direction of the flows of money used to buy food in many other rural areas of South Africa. This money, most of which is derived from sources external to the rural locale, is largely spent on purchasing food from supermarkets in the local town, and thus leaves the rural area before ever entering it (Du Toit and Neves 2007; Hebinck and Van Averbeke 2013). From a rural development perspective the central questions emanating from this chapter are 'what makes this particular 'alternative food network' or 'nested market' work?' and 'what is the scope for establishing similar "nested markets" elsewhere in the country?'

As pointed out by van der Ploeg in Chapter 2 of this book, 'nested markets' are shaped by different interacting components, and this also applied in this case. If one component had to be singled out for its significance, it would be the (latent) demand for leafy vegetables that existed in the area. Leafy vegetables are central elements in the culinary repertoire of the local population. They form part of what African Americans call 'soul food'. In the past, growth of leafy vegetables was seasonal and they were only sporadically available, because they were mostly harvested from the wild or from land planted with other crops where they were growing as weeds (Jansen van Rensburg *et al.* 2007). Over time, smallholder irrigators in the region discovered this latent demand for leafy vegetables and gradually tapped into it by producing a selection of these vegetables 'out of season'. The market for green maize evolved in a similar way. In the past, the window of availability of green maize was restricted by the rainfall pattern which determined when the crop could be planted. Irrigation water provided the opportunity for farmers to widen this window considerably, because the temperature regime in the area allows for year-round planting of maize.[7] Growing these crops was made possible by the slackening of state control over the farming system of plot holders on irrigation schemes, which, in accordance with the Trust System that applied on these schemes, was highly prescriptive during the first 15 years until the farmers settled on the scheme had learnt to irrigate. Expansion of the market for fresh produce occurred as a result of the creation of the town of Thohoyandou, which offered excellent opportunities for street traders to operate. A key point here was that the local government allowed the development of street trade, when this type of informal activity was still prohibited elsewhere in South Africa. Competition for trading places in the CBD of Thohoyandou gave rise to the township-pavement and door-to-door trade, further expanding the reach of this nested market. Farmers, in turn, responded to this new market by stretching the planting windows of these crops, making them available well outside the traditional season (Van Averbeke *et al.* 2007), thus driving additional market expansion.

It is difficult to say whether similar nested markets could crop up elsewhere in South Africa. At least one important lesson was learnt from the case study and other work in the region. A survey of the 48 smallholder irrigation schemes in the Vhembe District showed that closeness to town was the most important factor affecting the 'commercialization' of smallholder farming on these schemes (van Averbeke 2012). The important implication for (smallholder) irrigation development is that the old adage 'suitable land + source of water = irrigation scheme' should be modified by adding 'market' to the equation. For smallholder schemes, proximity to a town or city provides conditions that are favourable for 'nested markets' to develop.

Notes

1 The rate of unemployment in South Africa is amongst the highest in the world (World Bank 2012: viii). In the first quarter of 2012, the narrow rate of unemployment stood at 25.2 per cent and the broad rate, which included discouraged workers, at 33.8 per cent (World Bank 2012:7).
2 One of the plots is allocated to the extension officer for demonstration purposes, three plots no longer receive water, two plot holders have double plots, and three plots have been abandoned.
3 Trust tenure was first applied on land that had been bought by the South African Native Trust, later called the South African Development Trust (SADT) under the terms of the Development Trust and Land Act, No 18 of 1936. In the years that followed the specifics of trust tenure were gradually developed, refined and amended to suit particular circumstances, including smallholder irrigation schemes. Masiya and Van Averbeke (2013) provide detailed information on these regulations and their application over time at Dzindi.
4 Indigenization of the administration of the 'Native Areas' formed part of Apartheid policy and was aimed at transforming these territories into self-governing 'Bantustans', each being the 'home' of a particular cultural group of African people. The homeland in which Dzindi was located was created for Venda-speaking people (Van Averbeke, 2008).
5 In 2009 the exchange rate of the South African rand hovered around R10 for €1 and R7 for US$1.
6 Bakkie traders reported that cabbages could be kept fresh for at least three days, which made it less crucial to sell the entire load in one day than if they had been selling leafy vegetables and green maize.
7 The temperature regime allows maize to be grown all year round in the Thohoyandou area, but when planted between January and May the crop is severely affected by maize streak virus (Van Averbeke *et al.* 2013). Until now, this challenge has restricted availability of green maize to the period September through to March.

References

BENSO and RAU (1979) *The Independent Venda*, Pretoria: Bureau for Economic Research Cooperation and Development (BENSO).

Cousins, B. (2013) 'Smallholder irrigation schemes, agrarian reform, and "accumulation from above and from below" in South Africa', *Journal of Agrarian Change* 13: 116–139.

Crush, J. and Frayne, B. (2011) 'Supermarket expansion and the informal food economy in Southern African cities: Implications for urban food security', *Journal of Southern African Studies* 37: 781–807.

D'Haese, M. and Van Huylenbroeck, G. (2005), 'The rise of supermarkets and changing expenditure patterns of poor rural househouses case study in the Transkei area, South Africa', *Food Policy* 30: 97–113.

Du Toit, A. and Neves, D. (2007) 'In search of South Africa's "second economy"', *Africanus* 37: 145–174.

Hebinck, P. and Van Averbeke, W. (2013) 'What constitutes "the agrarian" in rural Eastern Cape African settlements', in Hebinck P. and B. Cousins (eds) *In the Shadow of Policy: Everyday practices in South African land and agrarian reform*, Johannesburg: Wits University Press.

Jansen van Rensburg, W.S., Van Averbeke, W., Slabbert, R., Faber, M., Van Jaarsveld, P., Van Heerden, I., Wenhold, F. and Oelofse, A. (2007), 'African leafy vegetables in contemporary South Africa', *Water SA*, 33: 317–326.

Louw, A., Madevu, H., Jordaan, D. and Vermeulen, H. (2004) *Regoverning Markets: Securing Small Producer Participation in Restructured National and Regional Agri-food Systems*, Pretoria: Department of Agricultural Economics, Extension and Rural Development, University of Pretoria.

Louw, A., Vermeulen, H., Kirsten, J. and Madevu, H. (2007) 'Securing small farmer participation in supermarket supply chains in South Africa' *Development Southern Africa* 24: 539–551.

Louw, A., Ndanga, L., Chikazunga, D. and Jagwe, J. (2008a) *Restructuring Food Markets in the Southern Africa Region: Dynamics in the context of the fresh produce subsector, a synthesis of country findings*, Pretoria: Department of Agricultural Economics, Extension and Rural Development, University of Pretoria.

Louw, A., Jordaan, D., Ndanga, L. and Kirsten, J. (2008b) 'Alternative marketing options for small-scale farmers in the wake of changing agri-food supply chains in South Africa' *Agrekon* 47: 287–308.

Madevu, H. (2006) *Competition in the Tridimensional Urban Fresh Produce Retail Market: The case of Tshwane metropolitan area, South Africa*, Pretoria: Department of Agricultural Economics, Extension and Rural Development, University of Pretoria.

Madevu, H., Louw, A. and Ndanga, L. (2009) 'Mapping the competitive food chain for fresh produce retailers in Tshwane, South Africa'. Paper prepared for the *International Association of Agricultural Economists Conference, Beijing, China*, August 16–22.

Manyelo, K.W. (2011) 'Street trader livelihoods linked to smallholder farming at the Dzindi canal scheme', unpublished M Tech. Agric. dissertation, Pretoria: Tshwane University of Technology.

Mohamed, S. (2006) 'Livelihoods of plot holders on a smallholder canal irrigation scheme', unpublished D Tech. Agric. dissertation, Pretoria: Tshwane University of Technology.

National Planning Commission (2011) *National Development Plan: Vision for 2030*, Pretoria: Department: The Presidency, Republic of South Africa.

Ortmann, G. and King, R. (2010) Research on agri-food supply chains in Southern Africa involving small-scale farmers: Current status and future possibilities', *Agrekon* 49: 397–417.

Ramabulana, T.R. (2011) 'The rise of South African agri-business: The good, the bad, and the ugly', *Agrekon* 50: 102–110.

Ramoroka, K.H. (2012) 'Participation and utilization of formal vegetable markets by smallholder farmers in Limpopo: A Tobit II approach', unpublished M Sc Agric. mini-dissertation, University of Limpopo.

Senyolo, G.M., Chaminuka, P., Makhura, M.N. and Belete, A. (2009) 'Patterns of access and utilization of output markets by emerging farmers in South Africa: Factor analysis approach', *African Journal of Agricultural Research* 4: 208–214.

Van Averbeke, L.L. (2009) 'A historic perspective on women, livelihoods and agriculture at Dzindi irrigation scheme', unpublished BHCS. Hons (History) essay, Pretoria: University of Pretoria.

Van Averbeke, W. (2008) *Best Management Practices for Small-scale Subsistence Farming on Selected Irrigation Schemes and Surrounding Areas through Participatory Adaptive Research in Limpopo Province*, Water Research Commission Report TT 344/08, Gezina: The Water Research Commission.

Van Averbeke, W. (2012) 'Performance of smallholder irrigation schemes in the Vhembe District of South Africa', in Kumar, M. (ed.) *Problems, Perspectives and Challenges of Agricultural Water Management*, Rijecka: InTech: 413–438.

Van Averbeke, W., Jansen van Rensburg, W.S., Slabbert, M.M., Chabalala, M.P., Faber, M., Van Jaarsveld, P., Van Heerden, I., Wenhold, F. and Oelofse, A. (2012) 'African leafy vegetables in South Africa', in A. Oelofse and W. Van Averbeke (eds) *Nutritional value and water use of African leafy vegetables for improved livelihoods*, Water Research Commission Report TT 535/12, Gezina: The Water Research Commission: 39–67.

Van Averbeke, W. Khosa, T.B., Mbuli, S.S. and Ralivhesa, K. (2013) 'Green maize production' in W. Van Averbeke (ed.) *Improving Plot Holder Livelihood and Scheme Productivity on Smallholder Canal Irrigation Schemes in the Vhembe District of Limpopo Province*, Water Research Commission Report TT 535/12, Gezina: The Water Research Commission: 213–284.

Van Averbeke, W. and Mohamed, S.S. (2006) 'Smallholder farming styles and development policy in South Africa: the case of Dzindi Irrigation Scheme', *Agrekon* 45: 136–157.

Van Averbeke, W., Tshikalange, T.E. and Juma, K.A. (2007) 'The commodity systems of Brassica rapa L. subsp. chinensis and Solanum retroflexum Dun. in Vhembe, Limpopo Province, South Africa', *Water SA* 33: 349–353.

Van der Heijden and Vink, N. (2013) 'Good for whom? Supermarkets and small farmers in South Africa – a critical review of approaches to increasing access to modern markets', *Agrekon* 52): 68–86.

9 Beyond land transfers

The dynamics of socially driven markets emerging from Zimbabwe's Fast Track Land Reform Programme

Prosper Matondi and Sheila Chikulo[1]

Introduction

The central argument of this chapter is that newly emerging markets in Zimbabwe have been boosted by land reform. Since independence in 1980, the country has implemented a programme to redistribute land more equally and to restructure the agrarian sector. Land reform has then gone through different phases. This chapter explores the developments initiated by the recent Fast Track Land Reform Programme (FTLRP), which was set in motion not just by the state and experts. A range of other actors, e.g. landless people, people from communal areas and war veterans, seized the opportunity to access land. For them, the FTLRP represented a new set of opportunities. The most visible outcome of the FTLRP is the radical redistribution of land and the consequent reform, and in some cases complete disappearance, of some large-scale and commercial farms in the country. Many observers have commented in detail about the post-FTLRP in Zimbabwe (Scoones *et al.* 2010, Matondi 2012, Hanlon *et al.* 2013). This chapter adds to these analyses an examination of a hitherto hardly described phenomenon: the newly emerging markets in the southern part of Zimbabwe, the Lowveld, which is being repeated with similarities elsewhere in the country. A plethora of markets have mushroomed in the Lowveld to support the endeavours of numerous social actors to build, rebuild and enhance their livelihoods. These markets were not planned and can at best be understood as the unintended consequences of the fast track land reform programme.

The construction of these new markets is significant in two ways. First of all, the markets that have emerged in the Lowveld in the wake of the FTLRP are *new* markets. These markets did not exist before as the previous landowners were embedded in markets designed and controlled by agribusiness companies and political interest groups. Second, the new markets are designed and constructed by new groups of actors (e.g. women from the neighbouring communal areas and landless people) who did not inhabit the area before as landowners. The analysis of the newly emerging markets shows the robustness of their experiences in constructing markets that fit their interests and how they are enhancing their livelihoods. We argue that these markets are structurally different from previously existing markets; the previous market structure of the

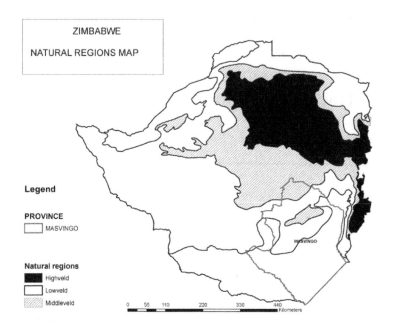

Map 9.1 Agroecological zones and the location of the Lowveld in Zimbabwe.

Lowveld that was predominantly attuned to the interests of a large-scale farming sector has largely disappeared. The new markets do not operate in a vacuum but incorporate experiences from the previously existing markets although reconstructed and following different livelihood calculi.

This chapter is structured as follows. We first describe the situation and construction of markets before land reform reordered the agrarian landscape in the Lowveld. Then we will shortly describe the dynamics of FTLRP and how and when it came about. The last part of the chapter provides an account of the plethora of emerging markets, characterizing them as an outcome of the social struggles of a range of actors in the Lowveld to make a decent living for themselves and their families.

Markets before land reform

Zimbabwe's agricultural markets prior to the FTLRP in 2000 were largely designed to support the large-scale commercial farming sector.[2] These markets had clear international linkages. They were dominated by firms and conglomerates operating at a global level, and served as inlets for inputs (seeds, fertilizers, chemicals and technologies),[3] and as outlets for the produce of the land. While government seemed to be far removed from these markets, it played an important role in preserving them by allowing their unfettered operations. It also created structures to support these markets through a range of policy interventions.

Smallholder farmers, which were largely of secondary importance benefited from this system by default (Rukuni *et al.* 2006) through having access to these markets for their inputs and outputs. A key problem for them was that they hardly had any influence on how these markets operated.

The large-scale commercial sector was highly organized and centralized. In fact, government went a long way to support the sector for its contribution to the country's economy. Large farmers too were advantaged, as their representative body, the Commercial Farmers Union (CFU), exerted enormous and unchallenged influence on the government. Not surprisingly, the government retained the colonial legacy of providing large white farmers with preferential access to economic incentives, such as foreign currency for their machinery and other import requirements, protection from competition against cheap imports, provision of cheap electricity tariffs, subsidized internal market stability, lower fuel duties and a series of export incentives. More importantly, the CFU used its political muscle to prevent large-scale compulsory land acquisition, based on economic arguments about markets operations. A clear manifestation of market control before 2000 shows that large-scale producers had a monopoly over the value chain, and were regulators of market prices, both directly and indirectly. In the agriculture sphere, market produce was determined collectively by the large farmers through the power of their unions to negotiate (Madhuku 2004) for favourable prices. In turn, the government, in contrast to its policy rhetoric, appreciated their economic contribution, and largely relied on them as the price pacesetters in any marketing season.

The provision of public infrastructure for production and marketing was a key measure through which support was provided to commercial agriculture. The private firms were beneficiaries of the Open General Import License policy that enabled them to import goods for the sector without restrictions. To facilitate such acquisitions, the state relied heavily on the Agricultural Finance Corporation (AFC), now the Agribank, to mobilize loans to firms and farmers (Zumbika 2006). While the loans were in theory open to everybody, the collateral requirements for accessing funds were fundamental in determining who could borrow or not. Commercial farmers with title deeds to their farms had leverage, while firms used their global structures to mobilize domestic and international capital to finance their operations. Through this process they entrenched their hold of the markets and production fields. The slow deregulation of the business environment in the 1990s, inherent bias in export promotion schemes, and the distortion of capital markets which gave some favoured access to credit had limited public support, which led government to consider reforms.

As poverty increased, the poor took action to reclaim control of resources, principally of land through illegal land occupations (Matondi 2001, 2012). During much of the 1980s and 1990s, the state politically sided with white farmers and the industrial sector to control picketing through strict laws and enforcement mechanisms. Yet the weight of these challenges was such that by the end of the 1990s, the state was politically overwhelmed by direct challenges from civil society and different interest groups (war veterans, peasants, farm workers, urban dwellers, industrial workers, women and youths) for reforms that would favour the smallholders. The target of dissent was not just the state, but also large business and farmers. By 2000, taking possession of land became widespread, giving way to the FTLRP (Sadomba 2008, Marongwe 2008, Scoones *et al.* 2010, Matondi 2012).

The dynamics of the Fast Track Land Reform

Emerging from social struggles instigated by poor farmers and later supported by the state, the FTLRP led to a re-ordering of the agrarian structure, which directly influenced the formation of new markets for agricultural inputs and outputs. Previous attempts at land reform from 1980 to 1999 had no effect on the structure of markets, which remained largely unreformed. While a transformation of people's livelihoods was noticeable in the Old Resettlement Areas (ODA 1988, 1996, World Bank 1991, Kinsey 1999), the functioning of markets did not change much. In fact, the 'old' actors, in the form of large industrial and commercial agricultural concerns, consolidated their hold on the markets, determining what all farmers could produce (or not), and acting as price trend setters in a variety of ways.

While the FTLRP was underpinned by social struggles, its expression was political. As people were allocated land, some started to produce and market their crops on their own account with hardly any support from the state. This was at a time when the formal markets had not been reformed, and were unable to respond. For instance, the parastatal company, Grain Marketing Board, was unable to buy maize from farmers, ostensibly because it claimed to have no money. Yet, before 2000, it had never reneged on payments to those who delivered maize to its depots. Smallholder farmers had to respond, and one way was simply to generate their own local exchange markets and to deal directly with small traders and maize milling companies. In this way the smallholders began to create new markets which, following the theme of this book, can be seen as nested markets.

Farmers who have been allocated land under the FTLRP are no longer just crop and livestock producers, but are playing a variety of roles in the agricultural value chain, and being very active on agricultural markets. A cursory examination shows that the FTLRP has replaced not just the 'old' actors, but also production and marketing systems formalized during and inherited from the colonial and post-colonial periods. Diverse smallholders now dominate Zimbabwe's rural agrarian landscape with 1.2 million communal farmers existing side by side with fast track farmers (162,750 A1[4] farmers and about 18,967 A2[5] farmers) and some 94,904 farmers in old resettlement schemes, with 8,000 farms with 18,967 farmers in the Small Scale Commercial Farms (SSCF) created in the 1930s (Team Zanu PF 2013). The large-scale commercial farming sector in its past form has been transformed and about 4,500 mostly white farms,[6] that were purely commodity producers, have disappeared (some had other forms of investments in markets, without playing an active role in agriculture). Though few in number, they largely controlled the agricultural markets and their levels of income and lifestyle far exceeded that of the local black population.

The significance of the land reform in market transformation is captured poignantly by Scoones *et al.* (2010:155), who noted the transformation of a 'tight, rather insular social milieu' that shattered the mostly white social and economic world with traumatic consequences. Whereas in the past, white business interacted with African producers and labourers on their own terms, this changed.

> Both the political and economic conditions have changed so radically that the functioning of the cosy, inward-looking social basis of business and trade is no longer feasible. Instead, new relations have to be brokered, with new entrants coming into these networks, and, indeed, wholly new networks being formed.
>
> (Scoones *et al.* 2011: 155)

These authors note that in Masvingo's beef sector, and elsewhere in the country, there has been a major shake-out of the integrated commodity chains of the past that were dominated by a few, mostly white, players. In fact, in the Mashonaland provinces, large beef entities such as Montana Meats, Koala Abattoirs and others are now forging business relations with many black cattle beef producers. This has spread entrepreneurial activities and provides producers with alternative market channels to better their earnings. After the land transfers, the large farmer unions lost many members, together with their power to influence markets and to set prices.

The new markets that emerged after FTLRP can be explained by the changed agrarian base which led to more producers, who through different means and strategies have exerted an influence on the value chain and markets. Fast track farms are now producing a variety of agricultural products, although not in such quantities as the large white farms who combined diversification and specialization, of agricultural commodities, depending on the scale of operations, market penetration and ability to meet international quality requirements (van der Ploeg, Chapter 2 in this book). In Masvingo and in Matabeleland and Midlands Provinces the large farms were mostly cattle ranches, and farmers specialized because of the received wisdom that the land was unsuitable for crop production without irrigation. However, in Masvingo, the new farmers are now producing a variety of agricultural commodities including sugar cane, citrus fruits, wheat, maize, cotton, sorghum and sunflowers, alongside livestock production. The A1 and A2 farmers in the new resettlement areas are also combining cropping with cattle production.

Thus, by engaging in dry land farming at a commercial level, the beneficiaries of the FLRP are challenging expert opinions on what can and cannot be produced on the land of the Lowveld. While there is some irrigated land, its production is complemented by diverse rain-fed crops. The production and marketing mix shows a new pattern of production and production relations not previously evident in the country's history. The market transformation of production and marketing relations has had knock on effects, leading to the expansion of small service centres and creating new opportunities for men and women to take produce to various types of markets.

While resettled farmers are breaking new barriers by producing a wider variety of agricultural products, the communal areas are also being transformed. This is because the large-scale commercial markets of which they used to be appendages have disappeared. The agrarian base, previously based solely on commercial farms, is now a new space that provides multiple livelihoods and allows for multiple land use systems. Chaumba *et al.* (2003) noted a variety of actors in new farms, and argued that they had different motivations, origins, identities and livelihoods for getting into the resettlement. Many of the players continued their previous livelihood patterns, while others adapted to their new circumstances. In the old resettlement areas of 1980–1997, the approaches were clinical in the sense that people were selected and at times were provided with a house and water. This was not the case with the FTLRP. In the old order, beneficiaries concentrated on farming, yet the FTLRP provided opportunities for the landless poor to engage in farming, for business people to expand their markets and for women to escape dominant cultural control systems (Mutopo 2012).

The result is that there are new multiple identities, shaped by how people eke out a living from the land, but more importantly, from the other opportunities associated with access to land. Many of the youths, disappointed by the slowness of making money in agriculture, have ventured into opportunistic activities offered by a transitional economy. Their activities range from selling fuel, providing transportation to new resettlement areas, foreign currency exchanges (US$/South African rands) and trading in commodities brought mostly from South Africa to the resettlement and communal areas. The youths, see the income from these activities as quicker, higher and less laborious than working in agriculture, which can be affected by weather conditions, and where (in dry land areas) returns are only seasonal.

Evolving new nested markets

Today these smallholder farmers find themselves operating in a new situation, defying scientific knowledge, departing from a communal farming repertoire, with limited support from experts and the extension service and developing a new marketing/infrastructural logic. They are struggling, and finding many ways to fight poverty. In order to survive a difficult and contracting economy, they have had to resort to the 'old' ways of business such as part-time work (*maricho*), labour migrancy to neighbouring countries, roadside vending and depending on natural resources for their economic livelihoods. These developments are clearly influenced by new bodies of knowledge based on redefined resources, reformed institutions and institutional arrangements, new landscapes and new crops for new farmers, new markets and new social relations that are still largely family/kin based. The opportunities afforded by land reform and new players may help reduce poverty, when taken in the context of opportunities availed through open markets, where poor households are seizing the new opportunities (de Janvry and Sadoulet 1993). There is an emerging pattern in which the new agrarian structure is giving rise to new social relations between actors, new cultural repertoires, and new knowledge, and thus the construction of new social material infrastructures.

Yet, people's ability to gain access to market spheres is greatly affected by their capabilities and the opportunities that arise through acquiring land through the FTLRP, the delinking of the state due to weak capacity and insufficient resources to implement legislation, and 'genuine' policy developments that promote market forces. For instance, people with significant endowments of land (natural capital) or financial resources (capital), or strong social networks (social capital) who are trained (human and social capital), are generally better able to gain access to the institutions of the state and market, and are therefore more powerful. In the market, one sees a variety of new physical structures of a temporary nature being constructed. These are often made from plastics, papers, wood boards, fence, iron and wooden beams. Local authorities have legitimized these temporary trade spaces, and charge for the use of the space (with amounts ranging from US$3 to US$25 per day/month). A variety of agricultural and non-agricultural goods are being traded in these markets. This encroachment of the state (in this case local authorities) has helped to create market fixation, at odds with what van der Ploeg (this book) terms as the permeability of nested markets. Yet, when faced with an encroaching state, smallholders create new markets of their own, which although regarded as illegal are very flexible in the way that they work. Below we will discuss a series of such emerging markets.

Roadside markets

Liberalization appears to have introduced both emancipation and chaos. Farmers have become traders in order to maximize their profits. Yet, their attempts are very similar to the farm-gate kiosks that were popular before the land reform programme, which were mostly dominated by large-scale commercial farmers. As a result the question of whether or not to permit these 'new' forms of roadside kiosks, which are a popular market arrangement, has been politically problematic for the state. The farmers say that they do not have adequate transportation to take their produce to sell by the roadside so they prefer selling at the farm-gate to hawkers who then resell at the roadside (or elsewhere). Farmers who do sell by the roadside are those whose plots are located close enough to the road for it to be convenient to do so. Roadside sales have a down side, the most notably being unhygienic conditions that increase public health risks. Vendors of edible products (both pre-cooked food or fresh vegetables and fruits) use a 'shouting and scrambling' method as they try to attract clients passing by in vehicles. The sites they sell from lack adequate sanitation facilities (such as toilets or points with running water) and for this reason are frequently 'raided' by local authorities. In addition, the competition for trade from passing vehicles places vendors (often young children) and passers by at the risk of accidents.

Farmers marketing their produce prefer to be paid cash on the spot because as harvest time approaches they will have run out of money. They often sell to the closest buyer who offers a acceptable price. Such farmers are typically desperate sellers, and often end up suffering significant losses. Even farmers who have contracts to produce for a buyer may go down this route and 'side-sell' their produce. If a middleperson comes along and offers a better price than the contracting company the farmer will be tempted to sell to the middleperson. Sometimes, when a contractor comes to collect 'his' produce, the farmer has nothing left and the contracting party takes a huge loss. Some farmers are alleged to have used political connections to avoid repaying their debts. As such the contract system is not working well, at least partly because of the highly politicized situation in which the farms were created. These factors have helped depress expected growth in the agricultural sector, where sales volumes have not increased as expected. Yet at the same time private sales of produce can also be risky for farmers as they can be tricked into unfair sales, such as selling maize or livestock with improper weight measurements, promises of payments that are not honoured (or at least not on time), and the absence of knowledge of prevailing market prices that would allow farmers to bargain competitively.

Street marketing

Vendors mostly sell their products to local people (residents of Mwenezi) and are able to supply most of what people need (maize, vegetables, onions etc.). This arrangement is more convenient when their clients are also their neighbours. These traders were often willing to offer credit when their customers did not have cash. Traders involved in transactions at community level were also willing to sell their products through barter trade, as some of the local people did not have money. This happened often and traders indicated that barter trade was much more profitable for them. For example one trader at Rutenga was ordering a 20 litre bucket of tomatoes against just 2 kgs of sugar, which would cost $2.30 giving her a profit on the tomatoes of about $15.

Commodity traders were also selling 2 kgs of sugar in exchange for a gallon of round nuts, groundnuts, maize or other crops. This kind of trading was also popular among clothing traders who could exchange cloths for chickens, crops, or even casual labour. This form of market has made life easier for the poor who may opt to offer their labour in exchange for a particular commodity they want. Many of these micro-entrepreneurs provide goods on credit to their clients, because they know each other. Trust and belonging to the community over a period of time qualifies one to borrow goods from the vendors. Credit is not subject to a fixed repayment period. At Neshuro Growth Point, the vendors said that they allow credit because '*dhora hariwori*' (a US$ does not rot, nor is it eroded by inflation, an adage stemming from the period of hyper-inflation in Zimbabwe before 2009). Yet the vendors and clients also forge specific relationships based on their mutual poverty, that reflect trust and understanding about what it means to have no money, while still needing goods for one's own use.

When agriculture commodities are critically examined, one notes that it seems that traders along highways and shopping centres are selling their own produce they are familiar in producing. In this case, the new producers benefiting from economies of specialization, which entail that they stick known commodities with familiar markets. A few are diversifying into tobacco, but such changes to choice of farming requires a longer learning curve that often has to be mastered through significant investments in training. Yet, when speaking with the traders, we found out that traders bring goods that respond to market demands. They tend to switch products based on shifts in supply of agricultural produce. Seasonal factors or trying to stay ahead of stiff competition was key. The location of the source of supply is also more important in determining the products traded than the volumes traded.

Transport networks

There has been a significant growth in the ownership of vehicles in resettlement areas, after a few seasons of marketing produce. Traders who own their own vehicles provide transportation services to farmers who lack the means of moving their crops to the market. Their ability to provide such services is limited because of the trade-off between earning revenue as a transporter and working as a commodity trader. Those with vehicles are also reluctant to transport crops from many parts of the rural areas where unmaintained roads increase the risk of breakdowns and damaging their vehicle. Repair services and spare parts are expensive and almost unobtainable in remote parts. In the majority of cases, producers still rely on foot, wheelbarrows and scotch carts for ferrying their produce to the market. Women who walk on foot and traditionally carry their commodities on their heads are the largest group. The producer-traders prefer to take their produce directly to market rather than to wait for buyers to come and purchase it.

Cross-border markets

Cross-border trade in both agricultural and non-agricultural goods has been one of the main effects of the opening up of markets brought about by the Fast Track and the Government of National Unity (GNU) from 2009 to 2013. There is a significant interface between the trade in agricultural and non-agricultural commodities. Masvingo province is the hub of such trade links because of its proximity to South Africa, Botswana and Mozambique. Another key influence historically has been the influence of waged labour relations, and many young people migrate to South Africa in search of employment opportunities. Cross-border trade, which evolved out of the economic hardships before and following the switch to the multi-currency system in 2009, is still a livelihood of choice for people. Scarce goods are being sourced within or outside Zimbabwe and resold on parallel markets.

A common response used by people to describe the nature of the activities they were engaged in was *Ndinongokiyakiya*. It literally means 'doing this and that' and means strategically sourcing and selling scarce commodities in an uncertain environment in which people have to constantly change how they make a living. The tradition of cross-border trade changed at the time of the FTLRP, as there were more people of different ages and ethnicities migrating to South Africa. Women are increasingly involved in trade and have become the main importers of goods into Zimbabwe. They also sell various products, including agricultural produce, such as bambara nuts (*nyimo*), ground nuts (*nzungu*), mopane worms, fresh and dried vegetables. The tradition of only the men going to South Africa has been broken (Mutopo 2012), and this has transformed gender relations.

The ability of small traders to negotiate their way past international borders is fundamental to their growing power in the market place. Yet, these small traders could also be farmers, who diverse their activities from the farm to the market. The need to survive difficult economic circumstances, mean that smallholders (as farmers and traders, or both) are becoming more astute and pushy, and have adopted several strategic methods of passing through visible and invisible roadblocks. Women traders of modest educational background have shown themselves to be adept at weaving their way through international borders, dealing with police authorities and at times corrupt officials seeking bribes. Some individual traders have developed strong ties with border officials who regulate the movement of goods between Zimbabwe and South Africa. Sometimes the women traders pay duty, or find ways of bribing officials. At other times, however, the authorities might be in no mood to negotiate passage, or the officers might abruptly change causing a loss in 'relations of understanding'.

This social connection with the authorities was a key, because they see each other as being part and parcel of a wider social and economic struggle for survival. Media reports show that women are particularly at the mercy of corrupt officials, and women who try to 'border jump' are at risk from crocodiles, thieves and rapists. Yet, there is a strong bond between the external and the internal markets of the Lowveld. The external markets have two dimensions: (1) foreign markets and (2) provincial markets in Zimbabwe. Different types of goods from elsewhere find their way through these markets to the agricultural communities, creating competition, in which anyone can fairly win or lose. It is the ability then of the smallholder to control resources for production (land and water), which provides them with the tools for being competitive. Though there is national rancour of imported products, this does not worry small producers and traders, the same way it does the large companies. In fact, international competition, induced by South African business importers has also created a new niche, as some Zimbabweans have become brokers, and in the process gaining significant incomes for their families. A new and dynamic market is emerging in which people of all genders, classes, political affiliations, ethnicity and ages are participating, changing the previous conception of rural development which was largely state-centred.

The social meaning of the new nested markets

The Fast Track has broken generations of gender-based division of labour, where women stayed at home and men engaged in productive income activities far away from home. Through an examination of economic engagement of men and women, it is possible to see how institutionalized regulations are being side-stepped, manipulated and even resisted by the new actors, and especially women (Mutopo 2011, 2012). While in the past, culture was conditioned and provided the arsenal, language and ideological space for controlling women, such practices are now crumbling. Men are more than willing to see their spouses becoming traders and connecting with different social networks that bring money to the families. The new resettlement areas created new communities, where people who hardly knew each other before (Matondi 2012) now live together. The bonding of people without kinship ties has created the space to side-step some obligations to kin, and the adoption of a business-like approach to living in the A1 schemes.

While in the past men migrated through economic necessity, women are now finding themselves heavily involved in family economies that sometimes reach distant places (Mutopo 2011). Therefore, while farming still continues to rely heavily on female labour still continues, this reliance has been weakened through new forms of market participation, a phenomenon that warrants further exploration. Mutopo (2011) observed that at Merryville farm, the A1 farmers were doing a variety of production activities that do not ordinarily fall within the ambit of commercialization. This was a result of a risk-spreading strategy based on the multiplication of the number of farming combinations: cultivating multiple plots, different ways of working the soil, combining varieties, staggering sowing dates etc. This was in addition to the selling of produce in the community, outside the local community (but within reach of the farm) and exporting beyond their district and sometimes out of Zimbabwe. The A1 farmers recognized that some of these combinations would be productive and that others would fail. Thus, the divergent yields of the various fields cultivated by the same family are a result of a strategy of risk spreading and the complementary use of different ecological environments.

Small-scale farming and informal vending continue to be the most common economic activities in Masvingo. One of the many strategies adopted by the people in Masvingo was the deliberate investment in both communal areas and A1 farms. Continued access to communal lands was a survival option, which was a pragmatic response to scarcity of resources, and the difficulties of practicing agriculture when there is tenure uncertainty. Some of the men allocated land in A1 farms are not only tenuring in the communal areas, but they also engage in informal non-farming employment. Some had left spouses on the A1 farms in order to eke a living from manual jobs in the estates being revived by the Zimbabwe Bio-Energy Company in Mwenezi.

In places such as Mwenezi and Chiredzi, the communal areas remain unchanged. The Ruzivo (2013) survey shows that a few people sell cattle and goats, while the majority still engage in casual labour, neither group realizing very much income. In most cases, peasants from Mwenezi and Chiredzi are dependent on remittances from relatives working in South Africa and other towns and cities, showing that kinship relations are still important for their live-lihoods and are more important than the effects of land transfers.

Most people have learnt to network on a daily basis and to build relationships that are crucial not only for business but for everyday life in general. Traders such as A1 farmers have a modest education, but have learnt to use the power of social networking as a basis for sustaining their trade business. Traders spend a lot of time at their trading place and regard this, their 'work place', as a place for raising income for their families. Yet, as they spend time at the market they get informal education, through learning about marketing (where to get inexpensive goods, how to negotiate with other traders and clients). Yet, the by spending a long time together at the market place, they also learn of social life matters, that are part and parcel of how they live and socialize beyond the market place. The reality is that kin are now only significant in relation to retaining the 'communal home' (*kumusha*), which is still visited on a regular basis.

Land reform beneficiaries are constructing new markets that are geograph-ically and commodity specific. These new, highly differentiated markets are built upon new social relations. This is because the new actors are relatively new to the production areas, and are also finding their way into the market arena in a context where the state has withdrawn.[7] Before the FTLRP the economy was tied to the wider large-scale markets controlled by agribusiness and white farmers in ways that extracted surplus value from rural areas, constrained smallholder access to resources (primarily land) and that involved unfavourable relationships between rural people and the market and state. Smallholders, particularly those who worked and lived in the communal areas remained at the margins of the markets, and only accessed markets at the benevolence of the state and large market players.

An emerging pattern is that a new agrarian structure is giving rise to new social relations between actors, new cultural repertoires, and new knowledge (and leading to the construction of new social material infrastructures). The introduction to this chapter defines 'new' actors as meaning those who were not major market players before, and who did not have significant decision-making control over the land. In less than 10 years Zimbabwe's new actors have become more prominent, and are shaping the landscape and markets in ways that defy logic within a state that is regarded as heavy-handed, technocratic and orderly. In Zimbabwe, smallholders in resettlement areas have graduated from backward-ness, marginality and vulnerability (Scoones *et al.* 2010, Hanlon *et al.* 2012). The emergence of small farms that are different from those in the communal areas, and not as excessively large as the earlier commercial farms, is reshaping the space of the poor in both agriculture and the markets. A new kind of family entrepreneur, connected to land and agriculture is now appearing, mostly from a new generation of smallholders. They are not only farmers who work on their plots but they also market their produce directly: they are farmer entrepreneurs relatively unfettered by geography or culturally defined gender roles. This represents a cultural shift within a normally conservative society: wives are now engaging in multiple activities beyond the farm and are earning income for the families. The resettled farmers are interacting with the markets in complex ways, which we will discuss later as providing a significant shift in our understanding of markets and rural development.

The new actors exhibit and demonstrate changing behaviour, which is influenced by a new culture. The changed situation and way of doing things in the market place shows that a high number of small producers achieve market power through quick penetration, logistical control, economies of scale, overcoming barriers to the entry of competitors, and/or the ability to remould the social and political environment to their own benefit. Smallholder production and market practices are not always in keeping with official norms and recommended technical behaviour nor do they adhere to formalized rules. The small producers are largely outside the reach of state regulation,[8] which provides them with some leverage to tacitly control markets. The effect has been that the monopolistic networks (van der Ploeg 2008) that previously controlled the production, processing, distribution and marketing of agricultural products have been largely swept away. However, in contrast to the earlier market sector, which the state subsidized and regulated so that the majority had little or no access to it, the new smallholder market players have established their own in the markets.

Struggles for autonomy in a new environment

Smallholders are penetrating markets without being influenced by complex formal structures (banks, local authorities). It seems that access to initial capital (often in very small quantities) to begin trading, which is often mediated through social money saving and lending in groups (*mikando*) and involvement in broader market networks that facilitate access to markets is key to their entry and participation. Theory has it that in areas where social structures are more 'vertical' and based on authority relations, this limits citizens' capacity for collective action, and their access to, and influence over, the state and markets are far weaker. However, in Zimbabwe, the state has delinked since 2008, letting market forces dominate, with the result that citizens are literally participating liberally in the markets. Fewer regulations may have created market chaos, but in the process smallholders have been emancipated from the heavy handedness and technocratic approach of the state.

Most of the marketers allocate themselves market places. This means that they may find themselves operating in prohibited spaces which may result in them being arrested. Most marketers conduct their business at undesignated points and as a result raids by the authorities are one of the main challenges that they face. Equally the authorities have failed to accommodate the growing number of fresh fruit and vegetable marketers whose number has expanded due to the worsening economic hardships and the shrinking labour market. The implications of this state of affairs for marketers is that they have become exposed to harassment from anyone who sees a reason to threaten them or extort some favour from them. The open conditions at markets are rife with bullying by middlepersons (*makoronyera*), and lack overnight accommodation and toilet facilities, factors that mostly affect women. Men and women usually just sleep in shop doorways before the market begins. This exposes them and (women in particular) to insecurity, the vagaries of the weather (rainfall, cold) or to thieves.

The state has not been able to construct a socio-material infrastructure that supports the new (small) landholders. Yet, this has given smallholders the opportunity to take advantage of the state vacuum and begin to create their own infrastructure. Some of their activities include redirecting cross-border trade and intensifying road side trading by farmers and traders. Much of the capital involved is raised autonomously, with hardly any funding coming from state programmes, as was the case before 2000 when large farmers and large market players were heavily backed by the state. Smallholders are opportunistically making use of the situation in which people need to make a living as producers and consumers.

The high proportion of marketers who are not under any regulation depicts a certain degree of institutional breakdown. While some of the places where they trade might be subject to regular raids by police (council) many marketers sell their commodities tactfully, in smaller lots and in market spaces where the police do not normally show up. The policing side is often ineffective in any case because of inadequate human resources. Marketers did allege that there was corruption by the police and council officials, who collect money from them without providing receipts, and if questioned, harass the marketers. The marketers prefer to accept this and pay a bribe rather than be denied access to the market place.

There are several issues here. In an emerging spontaneous economy where 87 per cent of the people are officially unemployed, marketing is a convenient livelihood option for many. Yet in Zimbabwe the authorities send out confusing signals about what is and is not permitted. First, local authorities have restricted their mandate to chasing vendors from the street. Yet, in a contradictory way, they also allocate the same vendors spaces to do business from and charge them for using those spaces. Second, the producers and marketers are rising as a powerful force. They may (and may be) unorganized but they are succeeding in invading public spaces, be it in the streets or in official open air spaces, to sell their wares. So far, they have won the battle simply because the government has been reluctant to implement another clean-up programme because of the political implications. Third, legislation in the form of national statutory instruments and bye-laws related to health and safety has not been implemented as the state lacks the manpower to do, or because of trader resistance. Often the marketers simply ignore the authorities. In some markets, we found, surprisingly, that informal groups have been able to organize these marketers and extract their own value out of them for their own benefit (and not that of the producers), usurping the supposed role of government.

In the last five years, the state has left the smallholders to do 'what they please in the new nested markets'. Yet, gaining this market niche is due to the strategies that smallholders used to collectively create a wedge for operational space in the markets. Scott's epic 1985 book defined the kind of behaviour and instruments they use as 'weapons of the weak'. In Chapter 2 of this book this is associated with the capacity to construct a 'socio-material infrastructure', that underpins and enables smallholders to enhance their space and livelihood. We argue that this partly comes through having control over assets (land and labour) but also through the new actors gaining some influence over state institutions.

Yet, the state has been unsure of smallholders, their political behaviour and its effects on broader governance (Matondi 2012). Trends show that before 2009, the government militarily intervened when agricultural production and marketing were threatened (Scoones *et al.* 2010) with the youth militia playing a regulatory role, whereby '...*the confiscation of produce and intimidation of traders were commonplace, highlighting the political tensions surrounding food production.... The politicization – and even militarization – of markets reached its height in 2008 ...*' (p. 151–152). However, in light of food shortages and inadequate production of staples, the control system imploded as farmers faced with food shortages improvised through making their own large-scale informal arrangements.

At present smallholders are both playing a new role in agriculture, while taking advantage of the retreating state and market players to enter the market space. In less than a decade, they have availed themselves of the markets, with demand and supply, rather than the state or unions, being the key price determinants. They do this in several ways that include: producing agricultural commodities and marketing, underpinning agricultural value chains through service provision (transport, information etc.), and forcing both domestic and foreign financial institutions to deal with them, as the people who are on the land and working in the markets.

We have seen the practices and processes that underlie smallholder engagements with the state and with markets and how they emerge in fascinating ways. Access to productive land, ability to secure finance through formal (state subsidies) and informal channels and their ability to find market outlets signify a shift in the 'normal behaviour' of smallholder farmers. These everyday practices are partly the result of the 'absence' of the state and formal markets. Yet at the same time the smallholders are negotiating for opportunities within the impositions of central and local regulations. The construction of nested markets, founded on social and state driven processes, has both benefits and drawbacks and is characterized by precariousness and fragility, often leading to unexpected outcomes. Yet, we know that in Zimbabwe, the exclusion of smallholders from the market has historical roots, shaped by colonial and post-colonial policies designed to underpin the economy in general, and agriculture in particular. The state played a significant role in the markets and used the technical and legislative instruments at its disposal to manage, and exclude others from the markets. The independence government in 1980 adopted the same instruments, with attempts at assuaging blacks through reforms[9] in smallholder areas, without tinkering with the large commercial farming sector. Yet, by ignoring questions of equity, the state impeded growth, as smallholders remained at the margins of lucrative markets, while the beneficiaries of post-colonial policies were protected. The unreformed markets marked the basis for the political problems that the government faced in the 1990s, which gave way to the political crisis that began in 2000.

Conclusion

The politics over land during the Fast Track Land Reform Programme changed the manner in which the state governed people and markets. The emergence of new nested markets, underpinned by small farmers, emerged by default rather than by (state) design. Nevertheless, in the process, the actions of the state can be seen as enhancing people's ability to access and defend resources and transform them into income, securing their livelihoods. The new markets emerged and evolved from changing land relationships, which involved the creation/construction of new/alternative social and economic (or socio-material) infrastructures that support local ways of earning livelihoods.

The reforms have changed the structure of wealth, which was largely skewed towards one racial group who had disproportionate control over the country's productive resources (finance, technology and skills). As these old actors were swept aside, the majority moved to exploit the opportunities offered by the 'liberation' of the market place. This is not to say that the old market ways have been removed, but that there has been a co-evolution of old and new markets, systems and processes – which benefits some and disadvantages others. Yet, while finding this freedom in the market, the poor continue to struggle because they have very little influence over the state whose existing institutional structures were largely created to serve markets than ordinary citizens. Meanwhile old actors are beginning to discover new forms of integrating themselves into the new nested markets by participating at different levels of the value chain. This is happening at a time when there seems to a degree of equity, with partnerships being built that are not based upon superiority (large scale) and inferiority (poor, black) which used to dominate. The rules and regulations and organized services have become more equal. This is not to say that the people-controlled markets are rigid: the people in these markets are dynamic and creative, but the systems are fragile, depending on speculation and (from a developmental perspective) a struggle to sustain a level of well-being and consumption that can help them overcome poverty.

In Zimbabwe smallholder farmers are attempting to construct new markets and redesign existing ones. This is a learning process, with people constructing a market culture essentially consisting of 'nested markets' in the making. People appear to be building up their capacities, learning from their experiences and establishing a marketing structure that fits what they do for a living.

The actions of small farmers are enhancing their ability to access and defend resources and transform them into income and secure livelihoods. The new players and actors have access to state institutions for their beneficiation on land.

However, in the spheres of markets they have seen an unusually predatory state being reluctant to interfere with market players, which in the past they would have done. Therefore, for the first time smallholders are not only accessing state resource access, but they are using the opportunity to defend their resource rights. Where resistance by bureaucrats is seen they force transformation through the political route. Yet, at other times, by simply ignoring powerful state institutions, they have new avenues through which they enhance their access to income. The people know very well that the state, if it so wishes, can erect barriers to such market activities. The state and local authorities in Zimbabwe have the legislative arsenal to interfere in such markets; however, the politics at present, with a transitional government in place with a limited mandate, is preventing this from happening. The new nested markets have the ability to enhance the autonomy of local social actors who are learning to master a market culture which differs significantly from the existing state-controlled agribusiness relations.

Notes

1 We sincerely acknowledge the data collection efforts of Elmon Mudefi and Wilbert Marimira.
2 Historically the assumption was that communal producers could only produce for subsistence. Yet, over a period of time they produced both for themselves and for the markets (local and distant, formal and informal). According to Rukuni *et al.* (2006) they overtook the large-scale sector in marketing commodities such as maize, cotton, and sunflower in the formal markets from the 1980s onwards.
3 While these were largely global conglomerates (Monsanto, Agricura, etc), the government also promoted local seed houses (Seed-Co, Pannar, National Tested Seeds) and an agrochemical corporation (Sable Chemicals) under Industrial Development Corporation (IDC) to produce fertilizers for the domestic and regional markets. Smallholders benefited from accessing such seeds and inputs.
4 A1 is defined by the government as the decongestion model for the generality of landless people. Beneficiaries have access to the following average land allocations: Agroecological Region (AER) I (12 ha.), AER IIa (15 ha.), AER IIb (20 ha.), AER III (30 ha.), AER IV (50 ha.), AER V (70 ha.). Each household is allocated 3 ha. of arable land with the rest being for grazing. Settlers have basic social services with administrative and social management systems. Twenty per cent of all resettlement land is reserved for war veterans (GoZ 2001).
5 A2 – this model is administered under the Agricultural Land Settlement Act (Chapter 20:01). The model is intended to increase the participation of black indigenous farmers in commercial farming through the provision of easier access to land and infrastructure on full cost recovery basis. The aim is to empower black entrepreneurs by giving them access to land, inputs, thereby closing the gap between white and black commercial farmers. The land is issued on 99-year leases with an option to purchase. Land is allocated in the following manner: peri-urban (2–50 ha.), small-scale commercial farm ranging from 20 ha. in AER 1 to 240 ha. in AER V, medium-scale farm ranging from 100 ha in AER 1 to 1,000 ha in AERV, and large-scale farm, ranging from 250 ha. in AER 1 to 2000 in AER V.
6 It is estimated that the remaining 300 white farmers are producing on less than 2 million hectares, compared to the 12 million plus that they commanded before the FTLRP.

7 State withdrawal is perhaps a literal metaphor, because it remains there but is invisible, as it has always been. People conform strictly to defined rules and regulations, though they do take advantage of the states' invisibility. The Zimbabwean government of ZANU PF is known to have the political capacity to largely control people in rural areas.
8 State technical and bureaucratic capacity has been eroded because of inadequate resources, a high attrition of experienced personnel and an incapacity to replace or train new officers. This means that rural people are frequently left alone, and participate in markets without hindrance.
9 Through broad rural development aimed at boosting market infrastructures, such as increasing the number of depots for grain and industrial crops (e.g. cotton), investing in research and extension and diversifying smallholder production through commercialization. This was underpinned by education and health delivery in the smallholder sector, contributing to Zimbabwe's second agricultural revolution (Rukuni and Eicher 1994, Rukuni *et al.* 2006).

References

Chaumba, J., Scoones, I. and Wolmer, W. (2003) *New Politics, New Livelihoods: Changes in the Zimbabwean Lowveld since the farm occupations of 2000.* Sustainable Livelihoods in Southern Africa. Research Paper 3.

de Janvry, A. and Sadoulet, E. (1993) Relinking agrarian growth with poverty reduction, in Lipton, M. and J. van der Gaag (eds) *Including the Poor*, Washington, DC: World Bank.

Hanlon, J., Manjengwa, J. and Smart, T. (2013) *Zimbabwe Takes back its Land*, Auckland Kumarian Press/Jacana Media.

Kinsey, B. (1999) Land reform, growth and equity: emerging evidence from Zimbabwe's resettlement programme. *Journal of Southern African Studies* 25: 173–196.

Madhuku, L. (2004) Law, politics and the land reform process in Zimbabwe, in M. Masiiwa (ed.) *Post Independence Land Reform in Zimbabwe: Controversies and impact on the economy.* Harare, Zimbabwe: Friedrich Ebert Stiftung, and University of Zimbabwe Institute of Development Studies.

Marongwe, N. (2008) *Beneficiary Selection in the Fast Track Land Reform Programme in Goromonzi District, Zimbabwe* Unpublished PhD thesis. Cape Town: Institute of Poverty and Agrarian Studies, University of Western Cape, South Africa.

Matondi, P. (2012) *Zimbabwe's Fast Track Land Reform*, London: ZED Books.

Matondi, P. (2001) *The Struggle for Access to Land and Water Resources in Shamva District, Zimbabwe*, unpublished PhD thesis Uppsala: Swedish University of Agricultural Sciences.

Matondi, P. B., Havenvik, K. and Beyene, A. (2011) *Biofuels, Land Grabbing and Food Security in Africa*, London/Uppsala: ZED books/Nordic Africa Institute.

Mutopo, P. (2012) *'Go Home and Solve the Conflict': Women's access to land and non-permanent mobility at Merrivale Farm, Mwenezi District, Zimbabwe*, Unpublished PhD thesis, Cologne African Studies Centre, University of Cologne.

Mutopo, P. (2011) Women's struggles to access and control land and livelihoods after fast track land reform in Mwenezi District, Zimbabwe, *Journal of Peasant Studies* 38: 1021–1046.

ODA (1988) *Land Resettlement in Zimbabwe: A preliminary evaluation*, London: Overseas Development Administration.

ODA (1996) *Report of ODA Land Appraisal Mission to Zimbabwe, 23 September to 4*

October, British Development Division in Central Africa. London: Overseas Development Administration.

Rukuni, M. and Eicher, C. (1994) *Zimbabwe's Agricultural Revolution*, Harare: University of Zimbabwe Publications.

Rukuni, M., Tagwirei, T., Munyuki-Hungwe, N. and Matondi, P. (2006) *Zimbabwe's Agricultural Revolution Revisited*. Harare: University of Zimbabwe Publications.

Sadomba, W. (2008) *War Veterans in Zimbabwe's Land Occupations: Complexities of a liberation movement in an African post-colonial settler society*. PhD thesis Wageningen: Wageningen University.

Scoones, I., Marongwe, N., Mavedzenge, B. Z., Mahenehene, J., Murimbarimba, F. and Sukume, C. (2010) *Myths and Realities. Zimbabwe's Fast Track Land Reform*, London/ Harare: James Currey/Weaver Press, Harare.

Team Zanu PF. (2013) *Taking Back the Economy: Indigenize, empower, develop and create employment*, Election Manifesto, Harare.

van der Ploeg, J. D. (2008) *The New Peasantries: Struggles for autonomy and sustainability in an era of empire and globalization*, London: Earthscan.

van der Ploeg, J. D. (2010) The peasantries of the twenty-first century: the commoditisation debate revisited, *Journal of Peasant Studies* 37: 1–30.

van der Ploeg, J. D, Jingzhong, Y. and Schneider, S. (2012) Rural development through the construction of new, nested, markets: comparative perspectives from China, Brazil and the European Union, *Journal of Peasant Studies* 39: 133–173.

World Bank (1991) *Zimbabwe: Agriculture Sector Memorandum: Vols. I and II* (No. 9429 – Zimbabwe). Washington, DC: World Bank.

Zumbika, N. (2006) Rural Finance: 1994–2004, in Rukuni, M., Tagwirei, T., Munyuki-Hungwe, N. and Matondi, P. (eds.) *Zimbabwe's Agricultural Revolution Revisited*. Harare: University of Zimbabwe Publications.

10 In the shadow of global markets for fish in Lake Victoria, Tanzania[1]

Modesta Medar, Paul Hebinck and Han Van Dijk

Introduction

This chapter explores the dynamics of the various fish markets that exist in and around Lake Victoria. As well as operating alongside each other, these markets also interact and shape each other in many ways. Lake Victoria's fish resources have over the years gradually been integrated in the global market for fresh water fish. This counts in particular for species such as the Nile perch and Tilapia, but increasingly also for the sardine like *Dagaa* which until recently were only available at local markets. The export industry, which is dominated by a few export factories, is an aggressive market player distributing the added value in highly unequal ways. The factories control most of the Nile perch catch through their control over the fishing networks. The intensification of fishing, notably for Nile perch, has triggered a range of controls to streamline and improve production and guard food safety aspects (discussed in this chapter). The processing sector is currently facing a structural over-capacity and the export factories have developed ways to control most of the productive fishing grounds, often at the expense of those local fishers who are not linked to the export processing industries.

In the shadow of the export market, however, there is a range of dynamic local, domestic and regional markets for fish. These are not well documented and are often ignored when the future and dynamics of the fishing sector in the lake region are discussed. The local markets have deep historical roots and respond to demand for fish from large sections of people, especially the poorer people living around and close to the lake. The local markets for fresh and open-air processed sun-dried, salted, smoked *Dagaa*, Nile perch, Tilapia and Haplochromine (*Furu*) are mostly found at the lake shores, near the landing sites and in the lake's hinterlands. Large proportions of illegal fish (that are too small), those that are rejected for export or escape the control of the export factories, are traded and processed here. There is also a substantial trade in *Dagaa* for human consumption and as chicken fodder across the border, mainly to the Democratic Republic of Congo (DRC) and Kenya. In addition, domestic markets specializing in the trade of frozen Tilapia and Nile perch have emerged in response to changes in the global market for Nile perch, brought about by concerns over food safety and the sustainability of fishing. This market has become substantial in recent years and has emerged as a serious competitor to the Nile perch export industry.

These processes and trends capture the contrasting and contradictory ways in which a classic common property resource, (fish) is being reshaped through opening up the lake to global markets. When the Nile perch, an exotic species, was introduced it transformed a common pool resource to a commoditized one. The export processing factories (EPFs) played a key role in this by creating networks of dependency that give them almost absolute control over the Nile perch caught in the lake. This does not mean that the Nile perch markets and business are not contested; on the contrary. By contrast, local species such as *Dagaa* and *Haplos* epitomize the characteristics of common pool resources: open access resources whose shared histories, nutritional values, prices and so on are known by consumers, traders and fishers. This said, the *Dagaa* networks and markets have undergone several transformations over the years and have taken on some of the traits of export markets.

The various markets discussed in this chapter are dynamic and together provide substantial livelihood opportunities for a broad range of local and regional actors. However, the social relationships within these markets and the way that they distribute the added value are structurally different. Equally, these markets do not simply co-exist; the local, national and export markets are continuously interacting and mutually transforming the socio-ecological spaces and networks that surround them. The way the market, notably the export market, operates has a tremendous and significant impact on the way fish resources are accessed, protected and traded at the local level. Local markets are not only intrinsically interwoven with the local economy, culture and history, but also exist within a broader set of markets that give them their locally specific dynamic and practices of value adding. Understanding their 'nested' nature (see Chapter 1) thus requires exploring how, and the extent to which, local markets are shaped by the global, regional and national markets for Lake Victoria's fish resources and the changes that have been brought about by their expansion. The nature of the local markets and, to an extent, the regional and national markets, is shaped by the struggle of the local population, fishers and traders seeking to escape the relationships of dependency and aggressiveness that characterize the export market. These nested markets are clearly the result of a social struggle and interaction with the export markets. The chapter also highlights the ambiguities of these markets. Both are driven by gender inequalities and this is also transforming the common property nature of the fish resource.

The data for this study is derived from detailed qualitative work undertaken by Modesta Medard at Mwanchimwa sub-village and Shinembo Village (Magu District), Makobe Island and Mihama Village (Ilemela District), Chikuku and Ikulu Island (Sengerema District) and Ghana Island (Ukerewe District) between 2009 and 2011. Some data on markets span from 2009–2013.

The chapter proceeds as follows. The first section provides background data on Lake Victoria and the fishing sector, showing how it provides unequally

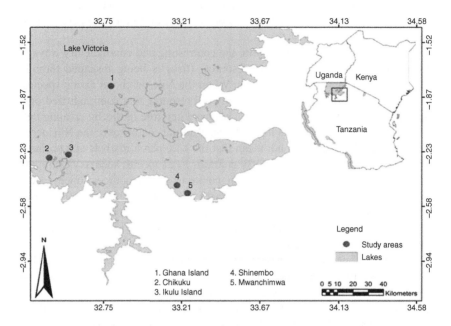

Map 10.1 Lake Victoria and the location of field research sites.

distributed opportunities for a range of social actors to make a living from the lake's resources. Escaping dependency relations is an essential part of actors' strategies. The sections that follow focus on the way different markets have emerged over time and how these shape, and are shaped by the configurations of the socio-material networks of actors and fish.

Lake Victoria's fisheries

Lake Victoria is the largest freshwater lake in Africa and the second largest in the world, covering approximately 68,800 km². It is spread across three countries: Kenya, Tanzania and Uganda. The lake contains many fish species and generates tremendous income opportunities, food, employment and foreign exchange. Some 4 million of the 40 million people that live and work in the lake basin derive their livelihood directly from the lake (Mkumbo 2012: 8). The lake is also used to generate hydropower, is a water reservoir for human consumption and irrigation and generates revenue through lake transport and tourism. In recent years the lake region has experienced rapid population growth, at approximately 2.6 per cent per annum (LVBC/EAC 2008). The region is predominantly rural, although migration to towns is increasing. Along the lakeshore 'boom towns' have sprung up in response to demand for fish and services (e.g. markets, transport, bars, guest houses, recreational facilities) to sustain the fishing industry both economically and materially). Not all services are up to standard and most 'boom towns' resemble shanty towns. Fishing camp owners (boat owners), boat crew members, fish agents and handlers, fish traders and processors, cooks, net mounters and repairers and bait fishers and suppliers make a living directly from the exploitation of the lake's fish resources. In contrast to the vibrant fishing economy the traditional agrarian economy is suffering from a downturn in the production of its major cash crops (e.g. rice and cotton). One of the most booming business sectors along the Lake is bars and sex work, responding to the demand from *matajiri*,[2] fishing crews and other labourers seeking to spend their earnings from a day's fishing. Mama Tabia who owns a bar and guest house in Ntama at Kome Island explained the interaction between fish and non-fish businesses in an interview '...with fish we make business and the villages grow to towns and small cities'.

From local to global markets

The lake has long been a source of many fish species harvested for local consumption. Eating fish is deeply embedded both culturally and historically. For traditional fishers, fishing provided status – a good fisherman could marry more than one woman – and fishing laid the foundation for wealth and reputation (Medard 2014). It is estimated that Lake Victoria once had over 500 different fish species (Seehausen 1996). This picture dramatically changed during the 1950s and onwards when the Nile perch (*Latesniloticus*) was introduced. A dramatic increase in the numbers of the predatory Nile perch combined with the eutrophication from agricultural and waste runoff (Pitcher and Bundy 1995) has reduced the lake's fisheries from multiple species to three commercially important ones: Nile perch, Nile Tilapia (*Oreochromisniloticus*) and the sardine-like *Dagaa* (*Rastrineobola argentea*). The *Haplochromines* which was the most abundant fish species[3] in the lake before the Nile perch's introduction declined substantially. Today, 60 per cent of the lakes' species are said to be on the brink of extinction due to predation by Nile perch (Witte *et al.* 1992a, 1992b). The Nile perch, its introduction and the emerging fishing industry drastically transformed an enormous amount of bio-mass that used to be used for local protein consumption (notably the *Haplochromis* species) into bait for a global commodity. Haplos have been indirectly commercialized: they have been transformed into a bait fishery for Nile perch, an input for producing and reproducing a globally marketed commodity (Medard 2014). The Nile perch has vastly expanded the economic value of the fishery sector over the years (see Figure 10.1). The rapid expansion is legitimized by the assertion that the Nile perch is economically far more efficient and profitable than local species (Kadigi 2007:1; Pollard 2008). This, in turn, supports and legitimizes the neo-liberal policies of the Tanzanian government to not intervene in any way, except for ensuring compliance with WTO and global safety requirements. The expansion of the fishery sector, particularly of Nile perch, occurred overwhelmingly as a result of a spontaneous working of 'market forces', and local communities have had to accommodate themselves to the changes brought about by the appropriation of the lake's fish

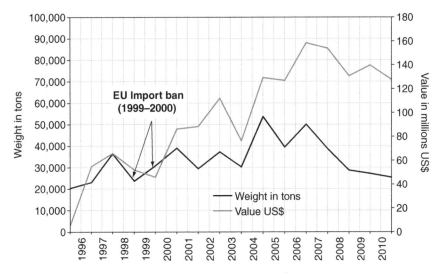

Figure 10.1 Nile perch export weights (fillets) and export earnings (in US$) in Lake Victoria, Tanzania (source: URT/MLFD 2012).

resources by global markets and consumers. By the mid-1990s, thousands of young men had found employment as fishers, workers in the fish processing industry and fish handlers. However, the main beneficiaries have been the owners of the export processing factories (EPFs) (mostly of Asian origin) and, to an extent, the fishing camp and boat owners. Fishers have nicknamed the Nile perch '*mkombozi*' – the saviour (Reynolds *et al.* 1992; Gibbons 1997). Exports of Nile perch, show its regional economic significance: they represent a significant portion of East Africa's export earnings, generating about $370 million per annum (i.e. 68 per cent of the region's export earnings) (Mkumbo 2012: 8).

In the last three decades, the fishery sector has attracted many, and above all, new entrants. An export oriented industrial processing and marketing infrastructure to industrially process fish for export has emerged along the lakeshore towns of Kisumu (Kenya), Musoma and Mwanza (Tanzania) and Entebbe and Jinja (Uganda).

In 1978, before the Nile perch came to dominate Lake Victoria, there were about 11,100 boats on the lake. By 2010 there were 65,578 boats and 194,172 fishers (LVFO/LVEMP 2010). Since then the number has risen to 71,138 boats and 205,249 fishers (LVFO/EAC 2013). About 101,250 (49 per cent) of the fishers are from Tanzania and of those, 53.7 per cent target Nile perch, 31.3 per cent *Dagaa*, 9.5 per cent Tilapia and 5.5 per cent other species (URT/LVFO/ LVBC 2012). Table 10.1 clearly indicates that fishing has intensified in recent years, although it peaked between 2005 and 2007.

Intensified commercialization on Lake Victoria

The Nile perch export processing industry currently suffers from a structural over-capacity. Most factories operate at less than 50 per cent of installed capacity (Lukanga and Mgaya, 2005:214); a number have ceased operating or reduced production because of supply problems.[4] The closure and reduced processing capacities of EPFs is, however, also due to the pressure to upgrade the quality of the factories in order to meet EU quality regulations (World Bank 2009). The changing global demand for Nile perch also explains and adds to the overcapacity. Import companies such as Icemark in Belgium and Nieterlof in the Netherlands ceased trading Nile perch in 2008 because the business was no longer profitable and in recent years they have only imported Pangasius from China and Vietnam (Pollard 2008:17). In other markets, such as Germany, fresh sea perch (Redfish) is preferred to Nile perch which usually arrives frozen. Fish investors, the Lake Victoria Fishery Organization (LVFO) and governments in the region say that the over-capacity and factory closures are due to declining catches (shown in Figure 10.1). The lake, it is argued, is being overfished, both in terms of quantity (due to increased and intensified fishing activities) and in terms of size. The latter is important for the long term sustainability of Nile perch and other fish stocks.

Accusations of overfishing are directed at specific groups of actors; in most cases the finger is pointed at local fishers who fish illegally and harvest fish that are too small. These fish are sold to markets beyond the control of the processing factories. On 1 November 2012, a Tanzanian daily newspaper reported that 'a huge catch of prohibited fish species' had been seized at the jetty of one of Mwanza's export processing factories. The chairman of the Tanzania Industrial Fishing and Processing Association is on record as saying:

> If it is proven that the said factory is involved in the scam, it will be banned from exporting processed fish for one week and subjected to a one-month export ban if it commits the same offence for the second time.

The factory responded and claimed that the fish had not been received and had remained in the hands of the supplier. The controversy then quietly disappeared.

Scientists, notably fish biologists, and governments have called for a concerted effort to curtail overfishing in order to prevent the collapse of lake's fishery which has brought such enormous fortunes to the area (FAO/LVFO 2005). 'Operation Save the Nile perch' (LVFO, 2010:4), and 'Implementation of Zero Tolerance to Illegal Fishing and Trade to 100 per cent with a focus on Nile perch' (Okware 2009) are examples of such governance endeavours. Fishing gears are now subject to strict controls and certain seines are banned (see Table 10.1) and classified as illegal as these catch fish that are too small. The banning includes the very long nets set out by boats and then pulled to shore (beach seines). *Dagaa* nets of less than 10 mm and gillnets of less than 127 mm (5 inches) have also been classified as illegal (gillnets look like large tennis nets suspended in the water and ensnare fish by their gills). Beach Management Units

Table 10.1 Intensification of fishing in the Lake Victoria Fishery, 2000–2012

Indicator	2000	2002	2004	2006	2008	2010	2012
Landing sites	1,492	1,452	1,433	1,431	1,327	1,443	1,481
No. of fishers	129,305	175,890	167,466	196,426	199,242	194,172	205,249
No. of boats	42,519	52,476	51,592	68,836	67,513	64,595	71,138
Outboard motors	4,108	6,552	9,609	12,765	13,721	16,188	20,229
Sails	6,304	9,620	8,672	10,310	9,811	8,424	7,871
Paddles	32,032	35,720	33,405	45,753	43,553	39,771	41,392
Gillnets <5"*	113,177	178,205	142,618	215,049	207,954	159,013	200,689
Gillnets > 5″	537,475	724,879	1,090,434	1,007 258	805,678	708,292	832,295
Hand lines	53,205	58,123	40,953	71,636	65,717	48,681	49,679
Long line hooks	3,496,247	8,098,023	6,096,338	9,044,550	11,267,606	11,472,068	13,257,248
Dagaa: small seines	3,588	7,795	8,601	9,632	10,276	13,514	15,064
Beach seines*	7,613	3,491	3,355	3,653	4,187	3,743	4,375
Cast nets*	5,887	1,095	803	775	1,174	1,282	1,551
Monofilament nets*	0	0	5,944	2,293	20,194	16,488	35,253

Source: LVFO/LVBC/LVEMPII (2012:6).

Note
* Illegal types of gear.

(BMUs), local representatives of fisher-folk, have been established to manage the governance of fisheries. But these BMU's have not been successful, due to the interests of fisheries managers and because of corruption (Medard 2014).

In November 2007 (Kayungi 2011), the Tanzania Industrial Fish Processors Association (TIFPA) formed their own monitoring teams to inspect the size of Nile perch destined for their factories. They found that a number of factories were still buying small fish below the recommended slot size (55–85 cm).[5] Despite these controls and management system, illegal fishing, that is to say, fishing with forbidden gears that allow smaller fish to be caught and traded,[6] continues, although it has been curbed somewhat.

Governance efforts thus far have focused on banning beach seines. Some observers (e.g. Pitcher and Bundy 1995) argue that restrictions on fishing intensity would be more effective. However, restricting access to fishing grounds is very unpopular and rarely discussed by fisheries managers. For instance, proposals to close fishing grounds for a period of six months from January until 30 June in more than 145 bays and islands (URT 2009) to allow fish spawning never got beyond paper.[7] The reality is that the fishing grounds are beyond government control. Rich camp owners (*matajiri*) and EPFs have identified[8] the 'hot spots' (rich fishing grounds) and excluded local fishers. Armed guards on fast boats protect these fishing locales around the clock. This is symbolic of the degree of control that the export factories and *matajiri* have over the fishing grounds as well as camps (capital equipment and labour) and even the fishing organizations At a stakeholder's meeting for the launch of one factory's 'eco-labelling project'[9] for Nile perch a factory director said:

> Our factory intends to work with 2,300 commercial fishermen who own fishing camps. We have mapped all the potential island and mainland sites. Now we have 500 fishermen and we need 1,800 more to meet our target. We will facilitate them.
>
> (name withheld, 29 July 2010, Mwanza)

This clearly shows the intention of the export factories to economically tie large numbers of fishing boats and fishing camps to them. Over time the better and larger fishing areas (fishing ground) and fishing camps (mainland and islands) are coming under the control of the factories.

The main driver of the 'Nile perch boom' has been international demand for fresh and frozen Nile perch fillets. Initially it was largely fuelled by demand from Europe for high-quality white fish meat. The export market has since expanded away from Europe towards the Middle East, the United States and Australia. Europe is, however, still the main market for the Nile perch and imports about 60–70 per cent of Tanzanian Nile perch. This means that the industry is subject to European Union health and safety regulations and inspectors. The EU initiated import bans in the late 1990s because of unsatisfactory hygiene at factories and cholera outbreaks on the lakeshores (Lukanga and Mgaya 2005; Kadigi *et al.* 2007). The effect of this import ban can be seen in

Figure 10.1. Such bans have had a negative impact on the fishing communities around Lake Victoria and a major adverse impact on the Tanzanian economy.

The future of the fishery sector and the export industry is currently at stake. Export market restrictions due to global safety concerns and the effects of global competition are seriously challenging its current position. However these two factors alone do not fully explain the crisis facing the industry. Over-capacity, a reduction in production and competition and counter tendencies from local, regional and national markets also play a role. In recent times, fishermen and traders have been gradually redirecting their activities away from the export processing factories which they think exert too much control over prices, materials and offer credits on unfavourable terms. The factories are also known for cheating on fish tonnage and falsely rejecting fish.

Nile perch and the reshaping of fishing and fish trade

The 'Nile perch boom' is not a neutral phenomenon. The increasing integration of Nile perch and the lake's fishing locales in the global economy has not only profoundly redirected the fish trade from predominantly local to global markets and contributed to a significant commoditization of the lake's biomass resources; it has also transformed the way in which fishing is organized. New actors that were attracted to invest in the fishery because of the Nile perch initiated new relationships that affected the distribution of the added value. The marketing of fish to global markets redefined the fishing landscape through the emergence of new sets of social relations and practices, both in trading and in fishing. This quote, from an interview with Bibi-Meng'wa, a 90-year-old woman, captures some of the transformations in and around Lake Victoria.

> I started trading fish when I was 11 years old but now I can't. The fish trade has changed because of *soko la Ulaya* (European markets). To make a profit you need financial sponsorships. It is only powerful actors, young and beautiful women who can manage that. Trade is now done through personal contacts. To be successful you need to be at the beach all the time and show your presence. As committed mothers and old people we are totally excluded. Today's trade is impossible without fraud, aggression, theft and sex and it traps many.

The Nile perch factories and trade business involve a number of intermediaries (middlemen and women in direct contact with fishers at the landing sites) who operate as commissioned agents for the processing factories and their fish collectors and suppliers. Male traders, known as *chingas*, predominate and are directly connected to the agents of EPFs. They own small weighing platforms along the beaches and receive cash loans from factory agents and materials such as ice flakes, weighing scales and storage bins. In turn, they are obliged to sell fish to the loan providers at reduced prices. Fish are traded and weighed on two separate scales; one provided by the EPF agent and one by the *chinga*. Their main fish suppliers are gill net fishers and bicycle traders who purchase fish mainly caught with (illegal) beach seines. BMUs and government fisheries officials are often bribed to protect seiners so that their nets and fish are not confiscated. This structures their relationships and makes them implicit in these illegal activities. Beach seiners are interested in prompt cash (to settle bribes) for their catch; the *chinga* reward them instantly together with advances (to be sure of steady fish supply). This is in contrast to the factory agents, who usually pay between 5–14 days later at reduced prices. In addition to the *chinga*, camp and boat owners sell their fish directly to EPFs. They are also financed with cash and materials by the EPFs.

Figure 10.2 summarizes the flow of fish from the fishing grounds and camp intermediaries to the EPFs. These are the main buyers, accounting for between 80–90 per cent of Nile perch caught in Lake Victoria. The market is a buyer's market: EPFs determine the price and their control over the supply chain enables them to keep it as low as possible. Fishermen, traders and agents are firmly incorporated in networks that, ultimately, are almost fully controlled by the export processing factories. The EPFs seek to control the supply of fish, notably through the armed guarding of the productive fishing grounds – which in the light of the assumed overfishing and reduced Nile perch catches – is key for them maintaining their central position and power in the value chain. The grip of factory owners over the chain also extends to most boat owners. Those outside these networks find it difficult to access the credit needed to purchase boats, petrol and nets. Most, if not all, of the credit is supplied and controlled by the factories which lend money on strict conditions that tie boat owners (capital) and crew (labour) to the factories. These controls are imposed to reduce the risk of

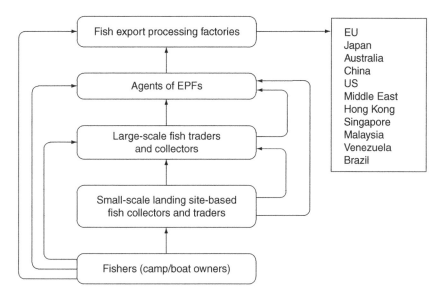

Figure 10.2 Nile perch export supply flow diagram (source: Field study Medard (2009–2011)).

anyone absconding the 'system' and preventing fish from ending up with their competitors on the export, national or numerous small lakeshore markets. Those who defy the system have less room for negotiation and have to endure price fluctuations, inflated costs for materials and equipment, higher (and potentially false) rates of fish rejection at the factories, false weights and measures and ambiguous business contracts.

Two accounts underline the nature of this dependency and the near impossibility of escaping it. An agent for an export factory underlines some of the dynamics:

> When fish is delivered to the factory doors, we are not allowed to enter. We just remain at the factory doorway and witness the weighing of our catches. Later, rejects (unwanted size and rejects) are verified by factory selectors in our absence. We are finally given a form that is written in English to sign. The factory form has three main parts of delivered fish: (i) rejected fish (ii) net cutting and (iii) gross cutting. Such professional jargon confuses us. They always claim to reject some fish, but surprisingly, they keep the rejects and we get paid at the reduced price of TShs[10] 300–500 per kilo. They never give the fish back to us and we never get the chance to verify the grounds for rejection. Later, they fillet reject fish or sell them at Kirumba market to wholesale *kayabo*[11] traders from DRC for between TShs 2,800–4,000 per kilo, depending on the season. They get a lot of benefits by cheating on the weight and falsely rejecting fish.... We are not united; we are totally disorganized.
>
> (Interview No. 600122; Ghana Island, 8 August 2010)

The account by a rich camp owner shows that the dependency relationship goes beyond class per se. A prominent *tajiri* from Sengerema attests that resisting these dependencies is risky, and perhaps impossible:

> My fishing charter is big.[12] I own three camps in Sengerema, one in Ukerewe and several other sub-camps. I supply my fish to one of the factories here in Mwanza. One lesson I have learnt is that factory owners do not want to work with someone who is well-informed. They want us to be submissive and agree to whatever they say. A few months ago, fuel was selling at TShs 1,600 per litre, but the factory charged me TShs 2,000 per litre. I was so annoyed. When I called the manager, he told me that the excess of TShs 400 was for fuel transportation costs to my fishing camps. I complained and told him I could find another person to supply me fuel at a cheaper price. He became worried and invited me to come and discuss the matter further. It was agreed I should pay TShs 1,750-a litre. This means that for every litre I bought, I was paying more than the current market price, and all of this was being added to my loan, and against my name. Since then, in all my camps, when they give me fuel I keep the delivery note and later countercheck when they deduct my loans. This has been my

principle. But it has not been easy. Initially, when I showed them my copies of the delivery notes, they were furious and I was told keeping fuel delivery notes was not my job. But I never stopped. (…). Cheating on the weighing scales is another drawback. At one time in 2008, I got fed up and decided to bring my own weighing scale to weigh my fish, but the manager refused. I decided to take the fish to another factory. Since then, when they know it is my fish cargo, they become more attentive. But I know a number of *matajiri* who are subject to such losses because factories control all undertakings unfairly. This business is not ours. We labour for the Indians.

(Interview no. 600123; Ikulu island, 8 August 2010)

These unequal relations of power extend to isolated locales, along the lake's shores and islands (e.g. fishing camps) and the centralized market and landing sites in or near major towns and cities such as Mwanza.

In addition *matajiri* sometimes steal each other's Nile perch and smuggle them (as an alternative way of selling) to the agents of the processing factories near the lake. This is due to the intense competition for fish, not only because of access problems and high prices, but also differences in prices, taxes and market fees in East African states.

Contesting dependency: local and national markets for fish

Over the years many of the actors involved in the fishing sector have developed an antipathy to the power concentrated in the hands of the export factory owners, the dependency relations embedded in this position of almost absolute power and the aggressive way in which the trade is organized. 'Everyday forms of resistance' are emerging around the lake. A major expression of resistance revolves around creating alternative market practices. This shows that the market is a major driving force of social and ecological change in the fishery sector and Lake Victoria. Below we focus on the emergence of local, regional and national markets, arguing that this can only be partly understood as countertendencies (Arce and Long 2000) to the dominant mode of organization of the export sector. These are newly emerging markets which are continuously seeking fish for export or local and/or national markets. This struggle goes beyond generating an income per se and involves escaping dependency relations and the unfair distribution of benefits. This underscores the social and political meaning and importance of local markets: they are the expression of the desire for development through a self-controlled and self-managed market, which allows actors and living nature to interact with the market on their own terms, thereby reducing their dependency on the factory-dominated relations that tie them to export markets. However, these local markets are situated in socially and ecologically fragile environments, because of competition and the lack of power to compete with more powerful actors in fish trading chains.

In contrast to the export Nile perch markets, where quality and value addition play a role (eco-label, fish size, hygiene standards) in setting prices, the availability of fish and whether the consumer can afford to purchase fish are the major determinants for Nile perch prices in local, national and regional markets (Medard 2014). This means that the prices consumers pay for products do not necessarily reflect quality. During the study, Nile perch prices in export channels ranged between TShs 3,600–4,000 (US$2.4–3) per kilo, whereas a bag of *Dagaa* (36 kg) was priced at TShs 42,000 (US$28), a price which most local people could hardly afford (Medard 2014). In local markets, fish is sold in small and affordable portions,[13] and bargaining and different weights and measures (depending on fish type) are commonly used.

In order to understand the strategic actions of the actors involved, their practices and social ordering of the market, we need to examine the social relationships of power and gender that shape the different markets. The following section shows what is happening in the shadow of the global markets.

Different markets in the shadow of the global one

This section describes and differentiates the fish markets that have evolved over the years in and around Lake Victoria. As said, some have clear historical, cross-border roots, while others are more recent. In this section, we seek to go beyond making distinctions between markets in terms of their scale (local, regional and national) or the fish species traded. A further, more relevant distinction is between the categories of actors (traders) who shape these markets. Here we focus on the owners of the export processing factories controlling the export chain, the owners of cold store facilities that process fish for the domestic market as well as serving particular niches of the export market, and those that shape the regional markets. These markets do not operate independently; they co-exist and are interconnected. Each influences the other. Illegal trade, fishing methods and evasion of the authorities cut across these market categories.

The local retail, lakeshore and hinterland fish markets

The label 'local' does not mean locality per se. At local fish markets a range of fish species is traded; some fish (e.g. *Dagaa* and other local fish species, but also Nile perch) are traded at local, lake shore markets, where rejected and undersized Nile perch is also traded. Some of the Nile perch that is caught outside the influence of the export processing factories is also traded at local markets. Nile perch by-products from the EPFs (e.g. belly flaps, fins, heads, skeleton and trimmings or off-cuts) are also sold in the weekly markets in the hinterlands and the permanent village markets. Some lakeshore markets are founded upon barter. Fish is exchanged for chicken, firewood, cereals, fruits, grains, cassava, rice, tomatoes, sweet potatoes or legumes. The peak period for the fish barter trade is during the harvesting periods between May and August, when most rural families harvest their rice, cotton and other crops. In this way the agricultural production cycle shapes the fish trade. This is also the time that roads are passable, offering good opportunities for large numbers of full-time and part-time fish traders to generate

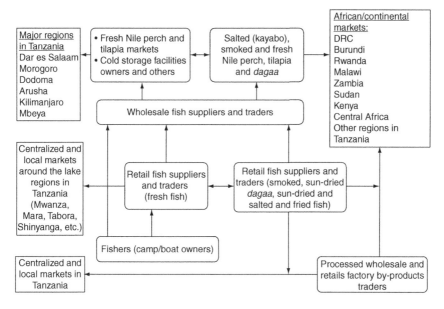

Figure 10.3 Local, regional and continental fish supply and distribution networks (source: Field study Medard (2009–2011)).

additional income. This also results in increased competition and higher fish prices and high(er) incomes. During the rainy season, part-time traders switch from trading fish to fresh farm produce. Roads become almost impassable during the rains, fish is easily spoiled and little income can be derived from trading fish.

Retail markets (small-scale fish collectors and traders) mainly operate on the lakeshore, weekly markets, permanent village markets and centralized markets. The latter are found in towns and in smaller urban centres where there is a concentration of buyers and sellers. While the lakeside markets are dominated by women, the others are dominated by men.

These markets are clearly shaped by asymmetries of power between men and women in the fish trade. Men (e.g. camp owners, camp supervisors and crew) through their 'traditional' dominance and cultural representation engage socially and sexually with women to create stability in their fishing camps and an environment in which they can be treated as a 'husband'. It is important for women to maintain such social ties in order to secure access to fish which they can trade themselves. During a group discussion with six women who maintained sexual relationships with camp owners, supervisors or crew members at Mwanchimwa, it emerged that men and women had unequal control over the fish resource. Men could reap greater benefits because they controlled the supply of fish for lucrative markets. Women fish traders handle less lucrative fish that are of less interest to men. The quote below from Mary Simon clearly shows how fish for local and export markets are intertwined:

We rely on fish which are not in the export category but if we happen to get one we sell to the export channel. The major buyers for our fish are local people from this village, neighbouring and faraway villages – mainly bicycle and foot traders. In order to protect our market we also campaign for the BMU leaders who can protect our interests and we protest against any fisheries officer who confiscates small fish or illegal fishing gear. What we do is not only for our own desire, but also for our men – the fishers, agents of the export factories and the entire community. People are suffering as there is not sufficient food in many homesteads and the impact falls on women and children. Not only that, if men in the export category go out of business, we shall go out of business also because they will take our markets and we can't compete with them. (…). In this case, our struggle against law enforcers is also to obtain some share of our men partners' income in order for both of us to co-exist.

(Mwanchimwa, 11 June 2010)

Women are aware that, as access to the export market becomes increasingly restrictive, men may also seek income from the local fish trade. Women at Mwanchimwa are strategically trying to curb the influx of men into what they consider their market. Their strategy partly consists of ensuring that the use of illegal fishing gear, particularly beach seines, is continued. Women at Mwanchimwa hostilely campaigned against restrictive law enforcers banning illegal gears. The significance is that beach seines are mostly used to catch fish for the local markets. The women feel that their activities serve the local markets and the larger community by supplementing family incomes and contributing to the welfare of the community which has limited alternative livelihood options. Women also supply undersized (below the slot size) Nile perch fish for the local and domestic markets and provide small capital assets such as beach seines (Medard 2014). When a seine is confiscated or worn-out, they join forces and piece together a replacement. Such actions reflect a diverse type of counter tendency and resistance to being excluded from the fish trade. Lake shore markets can be further subdivided by the type of traders that operate these markets. The majority of small-scale traders are women but they operate in different ways. As a result, markets of a rather different nature are emerging. Most but not all, interact with men in different ways to access fish to trade. Some maintain sexual relations with camp owners, camp supervisors or crew as a means to access fish. Such women are also known as *chingas*. Others operate more independently.

The first category is women traders that maintain sexual relationships with men. They gain the status of 'semi-permanent wives' (*nyumba ndogo*[14]) (Medard 2012: 562) which gives them prestige and influence; the latter is important as this enables them to access the Nile perch rejected by the export processing factory agents and handlers. The rejected fish is returned to their partner's boats or simply given to the boat crew members as an incentive (*madabulo*). Through this, fish is not sold or given to any other trader (*chinga*) without the woman's consent. Moreover, these women can exercise some power and influence the firing of camp staff (e.g. crew, cooks and even supervisors) if their interests are not taken into account. Juma, a fisherman from Mwanchimwa, had this to say:

> I have two women, one is in my home village and another is 'nyumba ndogo'. She stays here and we help each other. She is a 'chinga'. Having her around, I get a place to eat and rest because my home village is far. She takes all spoilt and small fish from my boats. In that way, she makes money for her own income. She also helps to support my camp labourers and provides them with small loans. In this way, my crew don't get tempted to join another fishing camp. This is how we try to make our camps independent.
>
> (Mwanchimwa, 10 June 2010)

A second group are women traders who try to avoid sexual conduct but befriend those who have a relationship with either *tajiri* or supervisors. In so doing they can access a few fish with their friend's permission. Over time, some women have ended up having secret relationships with crew members, enticing them to steal and sell fish at reduced price in return for sexual favours. An interview with Justa from Mwachimwa, testifies to this:

> (...) our friend is now out of the fish business. She tried to inform *tajiri* about fish that had been stolen by a crew member. Since then she has not been able to take part in the fish trade. If you want to survive in the fish business at Mwanchimwa you don't inquire how someone is getting fish. We are all searching for money. Our male partners have many plans in their head but they don't share them with us. We are just another one of the labourers and they show us little respect compared to their wives back in their home town and villages. I am aware and I know how to go about my business.
>
> (Justa Simon, 6 June 2010)

A third category is the *chinga*, who operate independently in the fish trade and do not rely on men. Knowing the nature of the 'fragile sexual and marital style'[15] from their past experiences, they strive to become independent, accumulate capital assets and open complementary businesses (e.g. shops, bars and guest houses). They also combine selling fresh, smoked and salted Nile perch (*kayabo*) to gain additional income. Some women own fish stores and accumulate small quantities of salted fish over a period of time before selling them to mobile *kayabo* buyers and collectors. The fourth category of women traders are old women who grew up as fish traders but were marginalized and excluded when the fishing business and markets became more complex and aggressive. They usually buy a few pieces of *nyambole* which they sell on the local markets. Bibi Meng'wa, quoted earlier in the chapter, is typical of this category. The fifth category of traders comprises those involved in the barter trade of fish. These are rather independent, semi-permanent traders as described earlier. Trading occurs on the beach, largely with lake shore and hinterland villagers and is largely seasonal.

Domestic wholesale fish suppliers and traders

In Tanzania, the wholesale fish suppliers and traders deal largely with Nile perch and *Dagaa*, and a few Tilapias. At the national level, the market is dominated by male traders who are supplied directly by fishers or by retail traders. Most Nile perch sold in these channels are spoiled[16] or undersized but in recent times some fresh Nile perch for export is being sold here to gain better prices and reduce dependence on export markets. Fish in these market are sold in different forms – smoked, sun dried (*Dagaa*), sun dried and salted (*kayabo*), fresh and fried. Nile perch by-products from the EPFs are also traded in domestic markets through this channel.

Cold stores, niche export and domestic markets

The national market in Tanzania for frozen fish is expanding rapidly. A growing economy has generated and expanded a middle class who increasingly look for quality fish, especially Nile perch. The demand has generated the establishment of a number of cold store facilities that are concentrated in Mwanza. The domestic market has rapidly gained in popularity because it offers better prices and fewer rejects.

The owners of the cold store facilities and their suppliers set the quality criteria for the fish as well as the prices to be paid. There are two distinct price categories: one with high prices, particular for fish with maws (swim-bladders),[17] and another one with significantly lower prices for fish without maws. This price differentiation attracts many fish suppliers because Nile perch with maws can be

Table 10.2 Nile perch and Tilapia cold store and selling facilities in Mwanza

Name	Year started	Location	Freezing containers	Freezing capacity (tons)
Katarama	1996	Mlango mmoja	1	1.5
Mama Furaha	2005	Pasiansi	2	2
Mugulusi storage	2007	Kirumba	3	6
Pius Shilatu	2007	Nyakato	4	4
Chobo Investment	2008	Sabasaba	4	44
Mohamed storage	2009	Mkuyuni	3	6
Makapa co. Ltd	2011	Kirumba	3	4
Kishari Investment	2012	Nyakato	5	30
Makapa co. Ltd	2013	Kirumba	4	5
Osward Ltd	2013	Sabasaba	2	6
Teddy storage	2013	Mkuyuni	3	6
Swedy storage	2013	Mkuyuni	2	3
Hilali Khalifa	2013	Mkuyuni	3	1
John Salia	2013	Nata	3	6
Hondo	2013	Mkuyuni	3	1.5
Yahaya store	2013	Mwananchi	2	10

Source: Nyamagana and Ilemela District Fisheries office, 2012/2013.

sold separately to mobile and fixed premise collectors.[18] Fish maws are the most lucrative Nile perch parts and are exported to the Far East as delicacies; a small portion is sold to the European markets (URT 2003). Whereas the export processing factories prioritize fish suppliers supplying large quantities, the cold stores buy fish in all quantities and will store and freeze fish for traders for a small fee. Many new investors are being attracted to this sector: the number of facilities approximately doubled in 2013 (see Table 10.2). Most owners of the cold stores are local fish traders, *matajiri*, former agents of EPFs and other businessmen. Their main goal is to free themselves from depending solely on export markets and other forms of subordination by the EPFs. The cold stores transport the frozen Nile perch and Tilapia to different areas of Tanzania by jointly hiring trucks.

Intra-regional fish markets

Most of the cross-border traders are local and foreign traders, commonly known as 'regional fish traders' who combine fish trading with other economic activities. Salted Nile perch (*kayabo*)[19] and *Dagaa* are transported from the beaches to Kirumba International Market (in Mwanza) for sale in dried form. This business is facilitated by domestic and regional Commercial *Dagaa* and *kayabo* traders. They use local residents and migratory fish and *Dagaa* collectors who travel to various fishing locations to buy *Dagaa* and *kayabo* on their behalf, giving them direct access to fish which is caught both using both legal and illegal methods. *Dagaa*, *kayabo*, factory by-products and fried *Dagaa*, Nile perch and Tilapia are sold in border, cross-border and national markets. While most dealers in national markets are men, in the regional markets men compete equally with women from DRC and Kenya, and a few Tanzanians. The DRC is the major recipient of Nile perch by-products from Kirumba market, accounting for 70–80 per cent of sales.

Kirumba Market is an African trading hub. It is an extremely busy market where fish is salted, dried, packaged (often in unhygienic conditions) and loaded onto trucks. *Dagaa* are sold for human consumption and chicken fodder. Some 30 per cent of total export of *Dagaa* meant for human concumption is sold to the DRC, followed by Rwanda (20 per cent), Burundi (10 per cent) and Zambia (5 per cent). About 35 per cent of *Dagaa* catches remains in Tanzania. Medard (2014) found that about 60 per cent of the Dagaa from Tanzanian waters sold through Kirumba Market was destined for fish meal factories in Kenya, making Kenya the major buyer of *Dagaa* for animal feed from Tanzania. Bokea and Ikiara (2000) also found that 50–65 per cent of *Dagaa* from Kenyan waters were used for fishmeal. *Dagaa* from Kirumba for animal feed from is also traded within Tanzania (30 per cent).

Conclusion

This chapter has shown that the market, both global and local, is the driving force of social, ecological, economic and political transformation of the fishery sector in and around Lake Victoria. It has explored how the global market has reconfigured the social and natural environment of the lake in dramatic ways. The demand for Nile perch made it a much desired commodity which has simultaneously restructured the ecology of the lake and the organization of fisheries into a complex and aggressively managed sector. From a historical point of view, power has shifted from many points of coordination and decision making into the hands of a few who own the export processing factories. Illegal fishing and trading are widespread and corruption is rife to safeguard individual interests. These factors shape the local practices of Lake Victoria.

There is evidence that the most powerful players are exploiting and marginalizing fishers and fish traders. This manifests in fishers and fish agents being contractually and morally obliged to sell their catch to the buyers to whom they are indebted. But there is also a degree of mutual benefit and dependence between sellers and buyers. This leads the fish buyers to market the catch, something that the sellers would find difficult to do.

The chapter also shows that the power of the export factories and their control over the fishing sector is not absolute. It points to the emergence of everyday forms of resistance as expressions of counter-tendencies to the workings of global connections. Local markets, national/domestic markets, and the persistence of regional (in-country, border and cross-border) markets are examples of nested markets that operate within, and are partly shaped by, the larger global market. The markets are different in many ways but share a common aim of protecting their market share and redistributing the added value from Lake Victoria's fish resources in structurally different ways. This chapter, *inter alia*, has also pointed out some of the ambiguities of these markets. Unequal man–woman relationships are part and parcel of these markets. Most of them continue to rely upon 'illegal' fishing and trading and condoning these illegal practices. Corruption is rife and bribery is a normal practice. This case study of local markets has also shown that these do not always escape the characteristics of mainstream and global markets and that they mutually transform each other.

Notes

1 This chapter draws on Ph.D. research that is part of a larger project, 'Disentangling Social and Ecological Drivers of Ecosystem changes on Lake Victoria, Tanzania', which was funded by a grant (W01.65.304.00) from the Netherlands Organization for Scientific Research (WOTRO/NWO).
2 *Tajiri* (singular) and *matajiri* (plural): *Tajiri* means 'rich'. Camp/boat owner is called *tajiri* which expresses employer (*tajiri*)–employee (labour) relationships. *Matajiri* own fleets of boats and other capital equipment and are financed directly by EPFs and indirectly through agents of EPFs.
3 The *Haplochromis* was estimated to account for 80 per cent of total fish stocks (Kudhongania and Cordone 1974).
4 The Mwanza-based factory of the ALFA group of companies, one of the largest freshwater fish processing factories, has enough capacity to process 120 metric tons per day. From 2005–2009 it processed just half of that on average. By 2010, production had declined to 30–35 tons. Their Musoma factory with an average daily capacity of

40 tons, only produced between 20–25 tons in 2010 (Vedagiri 2010). In Kenya some firms attempted to export Tilapia, but this failed to take off due to limited supplies of the fish and high competition from low-cost Tilapia aquaculture producers, such as China, Egypt, Thailand, Philippines and Indonesia.

5 This is to protect immature fish, harvest mature individuals and the large females which would be expected to replenish the stocks. It was gazetted with 'harmonized enforcement' in 2007 for the three East African states (Kenya, Tanzania and Uganda. (LVFO/IFMP 2007).

6 In 2008 and 2009 fish quality inspectors confiscated between 100,000 and 300,000 tonnes below the slot size measure: by 2010–2013 the average was below 50,000 tonnes.

7 Many breeding and nursery grounds are now heavily fished. Bait fishers also fish both day and night.

8 Hot spot islands and mainland sites have been geo-referenced through Nile perch eco-labelling projects.

9 The EU requires eco-labelling to ensure the quality of Nile perch products. Eco-labelling initiatives are led by individual factories and are seen as providing them with long-term market access to the Nile perch fishery sector. They also require that consumers are prepared to pay a premium for eco-labelled Nile perch products. There is an assumption (not necessarily justified) that the fishermen involved will adopt better management practices and share in the added value (see Medard 2014 for more details).

10 At the time 1US$ was equivalent to TShs 1,500.

11 Local name for sun dried and salted Nile perch.

12 Meaning that he has many boats and big investments.

13 For instance Dagaa are sold in small piles, tins, cups, buckets and sacks.

14 Meaning 'small home or sub-house'. The same men would have no qualms about pursuing other women than their wives. Some men abandon their first wives while others maintain both their homes.

15 Most of them had lived with more than one man by co-habiting, traditional and/or formal marriages.

16 Spoiled fish is fish whose meat has turned a greenish and/or blackish colour. It is a classic case of post-harvest losses. Locally it is known *nyambole* or *samaki aliyechina*.

17 An organ in most fish species which is filled with air, which keeps the fish buoyant should it stop swimming. In some fish, such as Tilapia, it is a sealed organ, and the amount of air within it cannot be regulated. However in the Nile perch, it is linked to the outside of the fish and the amount of air in it can be regulated, depending on the depth at which the fish is.

18 One kilo of the biggest size of fish maw is sold at TShs 450,000 ($300) per kilo; the large size is sold at TShs 220,000 ($138) per kilo, medium-large at TShs 105,000 ($66), medium at TShs 72,000 ($48), small at TShs 42,000 ($28) and the smallest size between TShs 5,000–9,000 ($3–6) per kilo.

19 Mostly *nyambole* (see footnote 17) and *madegele*. The later is the local name for small size fish.

References

Arce, A. and Long, N. (2000) *Anthropology, development and modernities: exploring discourses, counter-tendencies and violence*, London: Routledge.

Bokea, C. and Ikiara, M. (2000) The Macroeconomy of the Export Fishng Industry in Lake Victoria (Kenya). Socio-economis of the Lake Victoria Fisheries. IUCN Eastern Africa Programme. The World Conservation Union (IUCN). Report no. 7, Nairobi: IUCN.

FAO/LVFO (2005) Report of the First Lake Victoria Fisheries Organization and FAO Regional Technical Workshop on Fishing Effort and Capacity on Lake Victoria. FAO Fisheries Report No. 796 SAFR/R796 (En). Dar Es Salaam, United Republic of Tanzania. 12–14 December 2005: 30.

Geheb, K., Kaloch, S., Medard, M., Nyapendi, A., Lwenya, C. and Kyangwa, M. (2008) 'Nile perch and the hungry of Lake Victoria: Gender, status and food in an East African fishery', *Food Policy* 33: 85–98.

Gibbons, P. (1997) Of saviours and punks: the political economy of the Nile perch marketing chain in Tanzania. CDR Working Paper 97.3. Copenhagen, Centre for Development Research.

Kadigi, R., Ntengua, S., Mdoe, E. and Mpenda, Z. (2007) The Effect of Food Safety Standards on the Livelihoods of Actors in the Nile Perch Value Chain in Tanzania. Copenhagen-Denmark: Denish Institute for International Studies (DIIS).

Kayungi, J. (2011) Effectiveness of Slot Size Self Monitoring. Mwanza: TIFPA and EAIFFPA. Report Presented to the Stakeholders Round Table (SRT) for Eco-Labeling Project of Fish Landing sites in Mwanza, Tanzania. Esamo Hotel. 22 January, 2011.

Kudhongania, A. and Cordone, A. (1974) 'Batho-spatial distribution patterns and biomass estimate of the major demersal fishes in Lake Victoria', *African Journal of Tropical Hydrobiology and Fisheries* 3: 15–31.

Lukanga, S. and Mgaya, Y. (2005) Fish quality assurance, in: Y. Mgaya (ed.) *Synthesis Report on Fisheries Research and Management. Lake Victoria Environmental Management Project (LVEMP)*. Jinja-Uganda: LVEMP/LVFO. Final Report Submitted to LVEMP/LVFO.: 212–227).

LVBC/EAC (2008) A Project to Prepare Investment Plans for 15 Secondary Urban Centers under the LV Basin Water and Sanitation Initiative in Kenya, Tanzania, Uganda, Burundi and Rwanda (p. 23).

LVFO/LVBC/LVEMPII (2012) Regional Status Report on Lake Victoria Biennial Frame Survey Between 2000–2012. Kenya, Tanzania and Uganda. Report funded by Lake Victoria Basin Commission and Lake Victoria Environmental Management Project Phase II. p. 65.

LVFO/EAC (2011) 'Technical Report: Stock Assessment Regional Working Group. East African Community (EAC)' Partnership Fund Support to LVFO for Resource Monitoring Studies. Lake Victoria Fisheries Organization of the EAC. 22 to 25 November 2011. Ridar Hotel, Seeta, Uganda. p. 26.

LVFO/EAC (2013) Regional Status Report on Lake Victoria Biennial Frame Surveys between 2000–2012 for Kenya, Tanzania and Uganda.

LVFO/IFMP (2007) LVFO Fisheries Technical Report. Measures taken as a result of the Regional Plan of Action to prevent and eliminate illegal, unregulated and unreported fishing. Jinja-Uganda.

LVFO/LVEMP (2010) Regional Status Report on Lake Victoria Biennial Frame Surveys Between 2000 and 2010. Jinja, Uganda: LVFO and LVEMP.

Medard, M. (2012) 'Relations between people, relations about things: gendered investment and the case of the Lake Victoria Fishery, Tanzania', *Signs* 37: 555–566.

Medard, M. (2014) 'A social analysis of contested fishing and fish trading practices in Lake Victoria, Tanzania'. Wageningen: Wageningen University, Unpublished Ph.D. thesis.

Okware, P. (2009) Review Implementation of Zero Tolerance to Illegal Fishing and Fish Trade. Country Report (Uganda). Regional Workshop to Develop District Fisheries Management Plan in Mwanza. March 2010, Monitoring Control and Survillance Groups (MCS National and Regional Working Groups): 4 pp.

Pitcher, T. and Bundy, A. (1995) 'Assessment of the Nile perch fishery in Lake Victoria', in T. Pitcher and P. Hart (eds) *The Impact of Species Changes in African Lakes. Fish and Fisheries*, London: Chapman and Hall.

Pollard, I. (2008) Description and Analysis of Value Chain of the Lake Victoria Nile Perch Fishery. Consultancy Report No 42. Funded by EU/IFMP Project. Report submitted to IFMP/LVFO. Implementation of Fisheries Management Plan (IFMP) and Lake Victoria Fisheries Organization (LVFO) of the East African Community. Jinja-Uganda.

Reynolds, J., Greboval, D.F. and Manning, P. (1992) Thirty Years on: Observation on the Development of the Nile Perch Fishery in Lake Victoria UNDP/FAO Regional Project for Inland Fisheries Planning (IFIP) Rome: FAO.

Seehausen, O. (1996) 'Lake Victoria Rock Cichlids: Taxonomy, Ecology and Distribution, Zevenhuizen: Verduijn Cichlids'.

URT (2009) *The Fisheries Regulations (G.N. No. 308 of 28/8/2009). Government Printer*, United Republic of Tanzania (URT). Dar Es Salaam, Tanzania. 246pp.

URT/LVFO/LVBC. (2012). National Status Report on Lake Victoria Biennial Frame Survey Report. Frame Survey National Working Group. The United Republic of Tanzania. Ministry of Livestock and Fisheries Development. Funded by Lake Victoria Fisheries Organization (LVFO) and Lake Victoria Basin Commission (LVBC). September 2012. 110pp.

URT/MLFD (2012) Annual Statistics Report for 2011. Ministry of Livestock and Fisheries. Fisheries Development Division. May 2012.

Vedagiri, G. (2010) Stakeholders Workshop on First Standard 'Round Table Meeting' for Eco-labelling Project for Tanzania. Workshop organized by Tanzania Fish Processors (TFP Ltd) and Musoma Fish Processors (MFP Ltd). Workshop Held at Bank of Tanzania (BoT), Mwanza. 29–30 July, 2010.

Witte, F., Goldschmidt, T., Goudswaard, P. C., Ligtvoet, W., Van Oijen, M. and Wanink, J. H. (1992a) 'Species extinction and concomitant ecological changes in Lake Victoria', *Netherlands Journal of Zoology*: 214–232.

Witte, F., Goldschmidt, T., Wanink, J.H., Van Oijen, M., Goudswaard, P., Witte-Maas, E. and Bouton, N. (1992b) 'The destruction of an endemic species flock: quantitative data on the decline of the haplochromine cichlids of Lake Victoria', *Environmental Biology and Fish*, 34: 1–28.

World Bank (2009) LVEMP II Project Appraisal Document. Report No. 45313.

11 Reconsidering the contribution of nested markets to rural development

Sergio Schneider, Jan Douwe van der Ploeg and Paul Hebinck

A plethora of markets

The different contributions that make up this book make it abundantly clear that, while we often talk about one market, there is more often a plethora of co-existing concrete markets in any given situation. These markets differ from each other but are interlinked. They compete with each other and often there is tendency for one to take over or marginalize the others. They also create and reproduce each other. In Brazil, for instance, food is commercialized through both traditional street markets that have existed for a long time and through newly created ones (or *feiras*) as well as shops, delivery systems, the internet, supermarkets and institutional markets (which are established by public policy and their operation involves considerable state intervention) (see Chapter 4 by Schmitt *et al.*). The chapters about Africa detail contrasting examples of real existing markets. In South Africa, mainstream markets are copying from local and informal street markets (Chapter 8 in this volume by Mayelo *et al.*), but in Tanzania the dramatic expansion of global markets for Nile perch has created opportunities for new markets to emerge and reshape the existing local and cross-border markets for fish (Chapter 10 in this volume by Medard *et al.*). The Zimbabwean case is a good example of how new markets has been created in the wake of the much debated Fast Track Land Reform in the southern part of the country. Land reform brought new actors onto the land who are actively constructing markets that did not exist previously; it also led to the opening up of new cross border markets (notably with South Africa) (Chapter 9 in this volume by Matondi and Chikulo). In China one single product – glass noodles – can flow through circuits defined by food processing industries and supermarkets, through informal networks that link migrant workers to their home villages and through newly built circuits defined by local farmers who grow the sweet potatoes (from which the noodles are made), process them artisanally and distribute them to specific groups of urban consumers (see Wu *et al.*, Chapter 6 in this volume). Although dairy farmers in the Netherlands are linked to the main milk market (controlled by Friesland Campina), they simultaneously operate in a range of new, nested markets that includes care provision, agro-tourism, regional specialties and green educational activities (Oostindie and Broekhuizen, Chapter 7 in this volume).

One intriguing theme that emerges from many of these empirical chapters is that products (and services) and market circuits are often strongly linked together. Each helps to define the other. The Chinese glass noodles that flow through supermarkets are both materially and symbolically different from the ones that migrant workers bring with them and these differ again from those distributed through the newly emerging nested markets (Wu *et al.*, Chapter 6 in this volume). Radomsky *et al.* (Chapter 9 in this volume) argue that different market circuits turn seemingly similar products into different entities. Similarly in Thoyandou (South Africa) (Manyelo *et al.*, Chapter 8 this volume), street markets make a product (cabbages) into something that *differs* from the similar product in supermarkets. It might be the price, or the trust, or the joy of going to a street market (or the 'distinction' derived from not going there but, instead, to the more 'classy' supermarket), or the personal contact or something else. We see here that material exchanges are embedded in and co-defined by social definitions of quality and symbolic exchanges (van der Ploeg, Chapter 2 in this volume). But then, as Radomsky *et al.* (Chapter 5 in this book) remind us, there is also the 'risk of de-characterization'.

These concrete markets are specific spaces in which specific transactions and economic exchanges take place. As the different contributions to this book show, these markets differ in their nature, dynamics, prices, the distribution of value added and the relations between producers and consumers. They harbour distinct forms of interaction. They are spaces in which individuals seek to discover traces of their own identity in the merchandise they acquire and the ways in which they acquire it. As concrete spaces the markets make individuals remember where they come from and who they want to be.

Is there an 'underlying' general market system?

Can this plethora of market places be viewed as constituting one overarching market that is governed by an underlying and self-regulating abstract system ('the invisible hand') which assesses price levels, provides equilibria between supply and demand, and generates a specific distribution of value added, etc.? Are we just talking about different segments of one and the same market? Or, are there more fundamental differences between these markets?

At the symbolic level, the neo-classical discourse reduces the enormous heterogeneity encountered within today's markets to just one abstract system. Equally, at the material level the neo-liberal project tends to eradicate all elements and relations that run counter to hegemonic market forces. However, there are contrasting views and we believe that these are badly needed to construct an alternative market narrative.

First, as the contributions in this book show, the rich mixture of contrasting and interlinked market-places does not reflect just one ordering principle (i.e. 'the market' as defined by neo-liberal and neo-classical views). There is, instead, a wide range of ordering principles that co-order, through complex interactions, the variegated morphology of market places. Such ordering principles include the strong public support for the principle of Food and Nutrition Security that translated into new public policies that allow for new 'institutional markets' in Brazil (Schmitt *et al.*, Chapter 4). Peasant struggles to achieve more autonomy in the face of the power of dominant market players (Schneider and Niederle 2010; Radomsky *et al.*, Chapter 5 this volume) seem to function in the same way, helping to create new, nested markets. Consumer interest in searching for genuine food products can equally help to create and then sustain new market circuits for products such as glass noodles or Texel lamb (examples from two very economically and geographically contrasting parts of the globe). In short: the market as a concrete phenomenon is not structured by just one ordering principle – instead it is a theatre, defined by a wide range of interacting, and often changing, ordering principles. This implies that within 'one market' there are actually different marketplaces, each built upon its own socio-material infra-structure and each having its own form of governance. Some of these forms are 'less market', others 'more market' – they are, as neo-classicists and neo-liberals would argue, more, or less, 'disturbed' by non-market elements. In some market circuits the interests of say the food industry and large retail organizations provide the main ordering principle. In others the main ordering principles may be provided by peasants' struggles for autonomy and/or consumers' search for food that better fits with their own definitions and needs. This is what Polanyi (1957) meant when he coined the term 'double movement' (going from more market to less market and then back again). He used this concept to catalogue changes over time, but as argued in the introduction of this book, this 'double movement' can also be seen within the same location in time and space. Different market circuits, each reflecting a specific combination of ordering principles, represent ever-so-many expressions of the 'double movement', some tending to be subject to the hegemony of dominant market forces, others reflecting the needs and struggles and ambitions of producers and consumers.

Second, to represent the large plethora of concrete market places as just being part of one market neglects the reality that the actors operating within and between these different places do not regard market places as indifferent, neutral and exchangeable entities in which only the lowest price and/or the most convenience matter. The same applies to the products that circulate through these markets. As argued above, the circuits through which they flow are not neutral to products and services – they contribute to the concrete nature of the latter. This suggests that actors and products will move in particular strategic ways through the system called 'the market' and that these particular ways of moving may well change over time.

Third and finally, neo-classical and neo-liberal views obscure the fact that markets become the object of socio-political struggles. As we have seen throughout this book, markets increasingly exist as *arenas* within which struggles take place – struggles that aim to modify the dynamics of the market itself. Markets are both the locus and the focus of socio-political struggles.

In the introduction to this book we argued that socio-political struggles have partly shifted from the sphere of production to the sphere of circulation. This is not to say that such struggles have ever have been absent from the sphere of circulation (from 'the market') but over recent decades we have witnessed a strong increase in markets being both the arena and the object of socio-political struggles. The accelerated differentiation of markets (as documented by Oostindie *et al.*, 2010 for Europe; Schneider *et al.*, 2010 for Brazil and Ye *et al.*, 2010 for China) into contrasting marketplaces is a clear expression of the intensification of these struggles.

If we want to understand – and to support – the trajectory of current socio-political struggles we need to re-conceptualize the market along the lines suggested above. We need to recognize that concrete markets are shaped through the often complex and variable interactions between *a range of ordering principles*; markets cannot be understood without *referring to the concrete actors, products and services* that circulate within them. And, finally, markets are not only the object of socio-political struggles, they are also the *arena* in which such struggles (partly) take place.

The richly chequered whole constituted by different markets raises several pertinent questions. We will discuss four of these in this synthesis.

First, we will re-discuss the concept of nested markets. Although previous publications contain tentative definitions that functioned remarkably well in the first debates about rural development and the construction of new nested markets (see van der Ploeg *et al.* 2010, 2012, Polman *et al.* 2010), the plethora of markets presented and discussed here provides grounds for further theoretical elaboration. What are nested markets? In what respects do they differ from other markets? And what about the biography of nested markets, i.e. their development over time? (see in this respect Milone and Ventura, Chapter 2 in this volume) In short: what are the main features of the nested markets covered in this book? And what is their novelty?

Second, where are they located and how are they constructed? Third, how do nested markets (and notably the newly constructed ones) contribute to rural development? And fourth, what is the actual and potential role of public policy (more specifically, rural development policy) in the making of new nested markets?

What are nested markets?

Not all market segments that make up the plethora of markets can be typified as nested markets. Nested markets share certain characteristics with other markets, but also have unique features that are not found in other markets. It is these unique features that make a market segment a nested market.

The first characteristic that a nested market shares with other markets is that it is a market *segment* that functions alongside (and is interlinked to) other segments. Even the global market is only a segment out of a whole that embraces all the differentiated flows and associated transactions of products and services.

Second, all markets are *institutionally embedded*. In places where stability reigns this institutional embedding translates into a seemingly self-evident order.

Thus people forget about the institutions involved and 'the market' emerges as a kind of natural order – as, indeed, an abstract system that is self-regulating. In more turbulent places and periods things look very different. The situation described by Medard *et al.* (Chapter 10 this volume) is a point in case. It shows how different market segments are each dependent on particular actors, rules and practices. The 'global' market (i.e. the segment that produces for export) is dominated by highly unequal power relations which are imposed and maintained through aggression, bullying, the threat of exclusion, tied sales, etc. 'Local' markets critically depend on bribery and sex, whilst the national market requires cold storage facilities, owned by *matajiri*. Nested markets are, of course, also embedded. But the *form* of embedding differs: nested markets are embedded in (and thus delineated by) a mutual understanding of, and agreement between, producers and consumers. This mutual understanding concerns product attributes such as where, how and by whom the product is produced, its qualities, the correct price, the way it is to be consumed, etc.

Third, all markets require a *socio-material infrastructure* that makes the products flow in a specific way, from specific origins to specific destinations. This infrastructure also raises the issue of control: who decides about the flows, their volume, their timing, etc.? When we look at the *form* this infrastructure takes, it turns out that nested markets are once more distinct: production (and services) are rooted in ways that differ from those of other market segments (e.g. circular versus radial patterns; short versus long distances; decentralized and flexible versus centralized and rigid). Needless to say that the 'mutual understanding and agreement' discussed above is an important element of the wider socio-material infrastructure of nested markets.

So much for the characteristics that nested markets share with other markets. There is a fourth characteristic that makes nested markets unique. Nested markets involve and are (partly) grounded upon *Common Pool Resources* (CPRs) (van der Ploeg *et al.* 2010: 176). Indeed nested markets critically depend on CPRs (Polman *et al.* 2010). CPRs create and delineate nested markets in that the latter are based on the former and as such represent a specific expression of CPR. CPRs are made up of specific resources (e.g. fishing grounds, jointly owned networks for seed exchange, communal land, scenic landscapes etc.) and a commonly shared set of rules that specify the use of these resources. It is these rules that turn a specific resource into a CPR. Shared experiences, bodies of knowledge, organizational patterns and so on, can form part of such sets of rules, helping specify how things are to be done. The rules might equally be materialized, e.g. in a specific irrigation scheme (with a set pattern of water inlets, primary, secondary and tertiary canals, devices for division and distribution, etc.).

A nested market is *in and by itself* a CPR.[1] It is a resource in as far as it helps to add value to a specific economic activity. By channelling their products through a nested market (such as those discussed in this book) producers retain more value added. A nested market allows products to flow in a way that allows this to happen.[2] However, this resource, i.e. the nested market, is not privately owned (in the way that a supermarket is privately owned). A nested market, like other CPRs, is jointly owned. Usually it is *jointly* owned by both producers and consumers. And it is not for sale. A nested market cannot be bought, sold and re-sold (again in the way a supermarket might be bought and sold). This is an important feature in today's economy as it means that nested markets cannot be taken over by outside capital, or at least not easily. The CPR nature of nested markets acts as a strong line of defence in a world in which everything seems to have become fluid and absorbable by capital. This does not exclude the danger that nested markets might be copied and/or imitated.

In summary then: a nested market is a common pool resource that is (a) grounded in a commonly shared set of rules. This set of rules (b) links specific producers and consumers (through shared expectations, quality definitions, specific infrastructure, reputation, trust, etc.). It (c) specifies resource use (also beyond the nested market) and thus (d) allows for the transaction of specific products.

Nested markets are shaped by the people who constitute and use them. This explains a *fifth* feature. Nested markets are created for a purpose. They are, directly or indirectly,[3] the outcome of social struggle. They can derive from the active search for more value added (or a more just distribution of it), for greater autonomy and/or the intent to avoid paralyzing patterns of dependency (see Medard *et al.*, Chapter 10 in this volume).[4] They may also emerge from the search for more social justice and/or the fight against hunger and malnutrition (see Schmitt *et al.*, Chapter 4 in this volume) and thus make an important contribution to wider social struggles. Nested markets are constructed with the aim of providing an alternative to the dominant ways of trading, markets and distribution. In short, '*they are actively constructed responses*' (van der Ploeg *et al.* 2012: 140). 'Nested markets often emerge out of a critique on the relations that dominate the general food markets' (ibid.: 141).

Taken together the second, fourth and fifth characteristics lead to a sixth characteristic. Whereas markets typically belong to the private sphere (i.e. the realm of commodity exchange and labour), nested markets typically belong to the *public sphere* as defined by Jürgen Habermas (1989). Habermas distinguished between the *public sphere* and the official economy; the public sphere is an arena of discursive relations rather than market relations. It is a space for debating and deliberating, rather than for buying and selling. In short: the public sphere is the area in social life where individuals can come together to freely discuss and identify societal problems, and through that discussion they may influence political action. It is '*a discursive space in which individuals and groups congregate to discuss matters of mutual interest and, where possible, to reach a common judgment.*' (Habermas 1989: 30). The interesting point here is that the public sphere does not operate just through 'talk'[5] – it also operates through culturally embedded[6] *transactions*. Thus we may further specify the aspect of social struggle discussed above: *nested markets represent the intervention of social movements, debate and reciprocity into the market*. Nested markets allow civil society to conquer (admittedly small) parts of the economy instead of continually being driven out of it. Milone and Ventura's contribution to this book (Chapter 2) discusses this aspect of the *public sphere* in more detail. They indicate that nested markets have a strong component of public good and that this relates to public values (such as, to echo the different contributions to this book, the right to food, culinary traditions, poverty alleviation, the maintenance of landscapes and biodiversity, creation of employment, fair trade, etc.).

The cases reported in this book show considerable differences in the degree to which specific market segments operate as nested markets. The more a market segment is the outcome of social struggle (and the more it is sustained through different forms of social struggle), the more it is a nested market. The more it is structured as a CPR and the more that different elements constituting it (brand, mode of production, reputation, certificate, knowledge, use of natural resources, etc.) are CPRs, the stronger the nested market is. This implies that a nested market is not constructed at one single moment or through one single decision. It requires an ongoing process of strengthening the different 'commons' that are part of the game. This might be a progressive process, although it can also be reversed. If it is a progressive process the specific market segment (increasingly grounded on and structured as a CPR) will become increasingly nested through being 'nested' in a widening range of CPRs, constituting itself as a CPR and being continuously supported and driven forward by social struggles and pressures.

Where are nested markets located and how are they constructed?

Currently, new nested markets are emerging at places that are the focus of social struggle.[7] These are places that do *not*, for example, provide enough food to the hungry and undernourished, or do *not* deliver food with the desired (and sometimes even promised) qualities. Such places are 'structural holes' (Burt 1992; van der Ploeg, Chapter 2 in this volume) that epitomize 'market failures'. These 'failures' become the focus of critique which subsequently translates into the construction of new markets. Where the existing markets fail to deliver, the new markets do deliver, by 'bridging' and cross-cutting the hierarchies of the hegemonic markets, by-passing distances (between, for example, the prices paid to farmers and those paid by consumers) and connecting what was separated. Thus, newly created nested markets may, for instance, link the productive potential of local family farmers and the need for meals to be delivered to local schools and poor people (as in the case of the 'institutional markets' created in Brazil). They reground trading on ecological principles (only bringing in from elsewhere what cannot be produced locally and only transporting local produce to *feiras* elsewhere when there is a surplus) as is the case in the ECOVIDA experience (Radomsky *et al.*, Chapter 5 this book). They bring the qualities (taste, appearance, background and memory included) that the hegemonic market segments can no longer provide in a metropolis (as in the case of *glass noodles* in China).

One striking feature of nested markets is that they are not constructed by hegemonic players. The markets are grassroots initiatives emerging from the

undergrowth. They are arrangements and channels developed by small producers, petty traders and/or small and medium entrepreneurs who see they cannot
survive, let alone prosper, in impersonal globalized markets. In a sense, these
markets emanate from 'out of the blue' as the mainstream discourse clearly suggests that one can only 'survive' through participating in the large dominant
'value chains'. However, this is not the only, nor perhaps even the most interesting finding, to emerge from this process of renewing and redefining rural and
agri-food markets. A key element is that consumers are emerging as important
drivers in the construction of these new channels of access to agri-food products.
The reasons for this are varied, as the different chapters of this book show. There
are consumers who are looking for differentiated products because of their
higher added value, and who are willing to pay higher prices. But there are also
consumers who are looking for products with an identity that carry a 'sense of
place', or were produced by certain types of producers (organic or agroecological ones), with whom they establish interfaces. But there are also casual consumers, who are looking to reduce their expenditure in order to satisfy their other
immediate needs. Therefore, although consumption is needed to create demand,
it is also creating the market itself, as a concrete space of exchange and interaction between people. In that vein, consumers create markets where distinction
involves dimensions such as shape, location and the type of exchange involved.

As suggested by Milone and Ventura (Chapter 3 this volume) 'de-nesting'
can also occur, particularly when nested markets evolve into undifferentiated
segments of the general markets (i.e. when their distinctive features disappear)
One possible example of de-nesting in this book is the development of the
Dagaa market (around Lake Victoria) into a segment of the export market for
fish meal (often to be used as poultry feed) (Modesta *et al.*, Chapter 10 in this
book).

How nested markets contribute to rural development

Rural development exists of a set of evolving and more or less coherent
responses to failures of the dominant markets. Ironically, these responses sometimes occur as and through the construction of new, i.e. nested markets (van der
Ploeg, *et al.* 2010). These newly constructed, nested markets sustain processes
of rural development that differ sharply from continued and/or accelerated modernization based on scale-enlargement, specialization and technology-driven
intensification. The contribution of nested markets to rural development is
considerable, as has been documented for specific food markets (Karner 2010,
Low and Vogel 2011, UNDP 2012, European Commission 2013 and Farming
Matters 2013) and for different continents (Oostindie *et al.* 2010, Ye *et al.* 2010,
Schneider *et al.* 2010).

The relevance and importance of newly constructed nested markets for rural
development can be elaborated through the four central questions of political
economy synthesized by Bernstein (2010): who owns what, who does what, who
gets what and what is done with the surpluses? Using these questions the general

agricultural and food markets (mainly, though not exclusively, ordered by food empires) and the newly emerging nested markets (driven by very different socio-political forces) can be compared systematically. Table 11.1 summarizes the results.

First the table shows that the inter-linkages that make food products flow (or more specifically: the points of entry, conversion and exit through which product flows have to pass) are, in the case of the large commodity markets owned and controlled by food empires. That is to say the decisive socio-material infrastructure is owned and controlled by the main capital groups operating in the food domain. This is in sharp contrast to most nested markets where the main infrastructural elements (the certificate, the market-place, its reputation and the trust relations it harbours) are all Common Pool Resources. They belong to (are co-owned) by the producers and consumers who participate in these markets. They are not private property. They cannot be taken over, or at least, not easily. This evidently represents a main line of defence in an era in which take-overs are the main instruments for establishing and re-confirming power relations within markets.

Second, there is a remarkable contrast in the role that farmers play in the two systems. In the general food and agricultural markets the role of the farmer is limited to the delivery of raw materials produced according to a script dictated by food processing industries and/or large retail chains. In the case of newly con-

Table 11.1 A comparison of the general agricultural and food markets and the newly emerging markets

	General agricultural and food markets	Newly emerging markets
Who owns what?	Most linkages between production, processing, distribution and the consumption of food are controlled by food empires.	Short circuits that interlink the consumption of food. These short circuits are owned or co-owned by farmers (and sometimes) consumers.
Who does what?	The role of farmers is limited to the delivery of raw materials for the food industry.	The role of farmers is extended to embrace on-farm processing, direct selling and the redesign of production processes that better meet consumers' expectations.
Who gets what?	The distribution of value added is highly skewed: most wealth is accumulated in food empires.	Farmers get a higher share of the total value added.
What is done with the surpluses?	Accumulated wealth is used to finance the ongoing imperial conquest (take-over of other enterprises).	Extra income is used to increase the resilience of food production, to strengthen multifunctional farming and to improve livelihoods.

Source: van der Ploeg *et al.* 2010: 142.

structed nested markets this is very different. The farming families are *also* engaged in processing, designing, selling, evaluating and re-organizing. Consequently, they are also engaged in far more social encounters. Whilst the producers of raw materials are often very socially isolated, the providers of nested markets frequently and systematically meet other farmers and, especially, many consumers. This helps them to counter the atomization of social life that is so characteristic of modern day societies. It also explains why the new roles (and involvement in nested markets) are highly attractive to young people.

Third, there is considerable documentation that the value added (VA) per unit of produced product tends to be considerably higher in nested markets. This helps farmers engaged in these new markets to sustain their income and, in particular, to counterbalance the pressure to continuously enlarge the scale of their operation. The different patterns for VA distribution are both associated with, and to a degree lead to markedly different agricultural patterns. One pattern is large-scale, intensive and specialized and is developed in an entrepreneurial way, while the other is far more diverse and peasant-like.

Finally there is the question of the use of the surpluses (i.e. the social wealth produced through food production). In the case of the general agricultural and food markets these surpluses are increasingly centralized within the large food empires and they are subsequently used to strengthen the position of the latter. In the case of newly emerging (and long established) nested markets this is different. Here the surpluses are mainly used to strengthen the resilience of farming, food processing and marketing and to improve the livelihoods of those involved.

What is the role of public policy?

The main question we asked ourselves in the Porto Alegre seminar (2011) out of which the current collection of papers emerged, centred on *the importance and role of public policy* in the construction and further unfolding of nested markets.

However, before trying to answer this specific question, it is worth noting that one of the conclusions that emerges from the chapters of this book, is that the role of the state should not be limited to only correcting market failures (the state as the second best principle); neither should the state confine its actions to legal regulation and control. This has been the relatively 'comfortable' role of the state since the mid-twentieth century, when planned and over-controlled markets became subject to much criticism. Since then, the state has treated 'the market' as if it were one single entity, with its own will and intention, which needs to be treated with reverence. This attitude has led to half-hearted and ineffective state control of the market.

The current era is one in which market failures are resulting in ever more structural holes and therefore the need for more pro-active action has become urgent and necessary. We can no longer accept the market as the most effective method of exchange in capitalism, at least not when it based around the capacity of the 'invisible hand' to provide the optimal allocation of wealth, according to the relative abilities of market agents. It is clear that highly heterogeneous and dynamic agricultural systems that contain a range of often fragile balances[8] *cannot be governed by markets alone.*

In this book we demonstrate that the state's role should not be conceptualized in relation to 'the market' as an idealized entity. Instead, the role of the state needs to be elaborated in relation to markets as concrete spaces where interactions and transactions take place. The state should play a role in these concrete spaces simply because the state is a political space in which civil society projects are also being carried out. According to this Gramscian perspective the state comprise the *political society* and *the civil society*, which include, ensure, regulate and control the hegemonic interests and not those of a single group, stratum or even a class (Gramsci 1975: 811, Mouffe 1979: 48–79, Coutinho 2003: 121). In that sense, the interests of the civil society is part of the interest of the State, and this makes that state policies for the markets have to have a public and social sense (Jessop 2008: 101).

Looking at the different contributions to this book and the issues they raise we can conclude that policy is very important – for better and for worse. However, it is not decisive. If anything holds the key it is the *interactions* between well-tuned policy programmes, socio-political processes, movements in wider society and local initiatives that aim to translate emerging opportunities into new practices.

What is the current role of policy in supporting (or hindering) the construction of new, nested markets? And what might policy potentially do?

What policy actually does varies greatly over time and space. In China the role of the state is often decisive in the construction of new markets. However, this does not imply a disconnection with peasant realities. In their chapter Wu *et al.* (Chapter 6 in this volume) clearly outline how the construction of new markets for agro-tourism followed on from peasant initiatives. In Brazil social movements are perhaps the most important social drivers and their proposals are often, partly or completely, accepted and institutionalized by the state, after which the social movements often play a role in implementing the resulting programmes. In the European Union the gravitational centre also clearly resides in civil society: it is farmers, consumers, activists, small traders, etc., who – mostly through specific forms of cooperation – are engaged in constructing nested markets. They are often supported by local authorities (and hindered by the central state and vested interests). It is interesting though despite this some initiatives have been institutionalized at the level of the European Union (through regulations issued by the European Commission and supported by the European Parliament).[9] A case in point is the 'territorial cooperatives' that have delineated a nested market for maintenance of landscapes, natural values and biodiversity. This new institutional arrangement was developed in the north of the Netherlands and – finally, after some 20 years – incorporated in the new Rural Development Regulation for 2014–2020. In Africa we observe states which have gradually adopted laissez-faire attitudes. The South African, Tanzanian and Zimbabwean states refrain from interfering with the market through (e.g.) price setting and matching demand and supply. Most states in

Africa strongly believe in a market-oriented economy and see the mainstream market as the central and ideal institution to solve problems of poverty, unemployment and food insecurity. There is little 'peoples' perspective and no concept of newly emerging markets which are ignored in official development planning.

Despite these clear differences between places there is, nonetheless, a clearly discernible pattern. The introduction to this volume (van der Ploeg, Chapter 1 in this volume) refers to the 'policy cycle', which starts with new institutional arrangements (nested markets being an expression of such arrangements) that are developed within 'institutional voids', i.e. in as yet unregulated social fields, with no discernible relations, no flows taking place. Hence there are no rules (formal or informal) in place about how to behave or operate, which justifies us in referring to them as 'institutional voids' (ibid.). These voids are breeding grounds for innovations, the development of novel arrangements and the specification of nested markets. These voids[10] allow novel elements to be designed, tested and improved, precisely because there are *no* rules (and, in particular, the paralyzing regulatory schemes that govern today's worlds of production and marketing and the regimes they represent, which inhibit deviations and slow down (radical) innovation, hold no sway here). All this newness represents a *deviation* from 'the standard'.

The building of 'institutional markets' (Schmitt *et al.*, Chapter 4 in this volume), the operation of the Ecovida Network (Radomsky *et al.*, Chapter 5 in this volume) and the invention of agro-tourism in China (Wu *et al.*, Chapter 6 in this volume) all took place in what initially were institutional voids. This first 'stage', then, is followed by a second one which involves the innovators (be it a region or farmers' organization) and civil servants involved in policy design building dialogue and trust. Transformative capacity of new institutional arrangements is decisive here (Oostindie and Broekhuizen, Chapter 6 in this volume). In a third 'stage' policies are mainstreamed. This allows for a wider dissemination of the newly found (and consolidated) solutions, but often also neutralizes the quite often radical and transformative potential of the new solutions. This is turn may provoke the emergence of a new cycle. As before the first stage of the new cycle might be seen as a nuisance, especially for vested interests, since it disrupts established routines. Nonetheless, these repeated cycles are much needed: without them dynamic innovations would come to a stop.

In order to allow such disruptive but necessary policy cycles to occur it is crucially important that rural policies are constructed as *multi-level rural governance* in which policy design and delivery operate as multi-chequered and differentiated 'processes that work across multiple levels, involving multiple policy frameworks and multiple actors' (Oostindie and Broekhuizen, Chapter 7 in this volume). Such mechanisms, as Oostindie and Van Broekhuizen put it, are the only possible way to allow a 'wide variety of new institutional arrangements' to emerge. That is to say that only through such multi-level rural governance can the different 'stages' of different policy cycles emerge, co-exist and to unfold without too much friction or turbulence.

Not all societies have effective or fully functioning frameworks for multi-level rural governance. Establishing them can take time and involve fundamental changes in power relations. So the question emerges: *what can public policy do in the absence of (effective) frameworks for multi-level rural governance?* If we summarize the insights from the chapters in this book we can identify a few ways forward.

1 Public policies can be used to define and operate an institutional market. As Schmitt *et al.* (Chapter 4 in this volume) make clear this can occur because of strong shared popular and political support for issues surrounding the production, quality, availability, price, circulation and/or consumption of food.

2 Public policies may define, support and, if needed, defend mechanisms for participatory certification that allows food flows to be decentralized and is more inclusive of marginalized farmers, as the certification costs are lower.

3 Specific target groups (school children, people in need of food assistance, family farmers willing and able to deliver food) can be linked by public policy, in order to make food flow in specific ways and according to specific conditions.[11]

4 Public policy can make attractive spaces available to be used as marketplaces (the *mercati contadini* in Rome, located in old industrial architecture are a point in case) that are located at places where people gather. In doing so, public policy makes cities more attractive by offering consumers new shopping opportunities and/or upgrading poor urban areas (and countering the 'food desert' effect) by offering selling points for fresh produce. They can also (as in the case of South Africa) ensure that informal markets have the necessary sanitation facilities (waste disposal, running water, toilet facilities etc.)

5 Public policies can allow NGOs and farmers' organizations greater (and longer term) access to rural development programmes so that they can sustain and expand their activities (thus indirectly enlarging their nested markets).

6 Public policy can establish legal frameworks that allow for self-regulation of specific market segments (e.g. agro-tourism in Austria) and help protect Common Pool Resources.

7 Public policy can recognize the specificity of products, processes, markets and flows as well as the inter linkages that exist between them. This can be very important for hygiene prescriptions, especially when artisanal methods of production do not confirm to the norms expected in industrialized production. It can also be very important for the (non-) implementation of anti-trust rules.[12]

8 Public policy can also be used to create space for experiments and/or temporary deviations (e.g. kitchen spaces that meet hygiene requirements where fledgling businesses can experiment with developing new products/lines).

9 Public policies can also contribute to supporting the material infrastructure (by supporting local food markets, transport facilities, storage facilities, etc.) in order to access markets.

10 Public policies can play an important role in devising new ways to reduce transaction costs and asymmetric information by creating an institutional environment in which communication technologies and news services play a greater role. This is currently happening in many parts of the world (Armijo and Michalczik 2014).

11 The performative capacity of state apparatuses might in some cases need be to improved.[13] This can be done directly, but also through 'outsourcing' specific activities to NGOs and/or farmers' organizations.

We believe that rural development policies have much potential and offer great promise. The opportunities we identify here should be carefully explored – including through comparative research – and further developed. However, and this is a fundamental difference to 'conventional' agricultural policy, the successful implementation and further development of *rural development* policies critically requires a permanent and multi-layered involvement of civil society. The agrarian policies of the past were basically designed by experts ('seeing like a state' thus became a chronic feature characterizing such policies) and coercively imposed by the state. By contrast, rural development policies involve, and need to include, civil society in all its aspects: peasants, traders, consumers, rural inhabitants, social movements, etc. This has two methodological consequences. First, it implies that rural development *practices* are always placed centre stage. Rural development is not a meta-narrative to be translated from policy into practice. It is wrought in and through a multitude of heterogeneous practices that are initiated and developed in responses to market failures. Policy making is one of these practices – and the more it interacts with the other practices (of single farmers, cooperatives, social movements, civic initiatives, etc.) the more effective it becomes.[14] In short: the study and analysis of RD policies should regard these policies not as the starting point of rural development, but as one of the often highly contradictory *outcomes* of the complex encounters between many different practices. More specifically, RD policies are co-produced through the many, multi-level encounters between the heterogeneous practice of policy makers and the many RD practices entailed in civil society. The second methodological consequence follows from this first one. If we focus on the multiple interfaces between different *practices*, we necessarily have to focus on the role of the involved *actors*. It is not possible to study rural development policies, their mechanisms and their impact if we ignore the farming families who design and create novel ways of producing food and managing environmental resources in order to aggregate value and produce wealth. The same applies to those actors (consumers included) who are engaged in new, nested markets and to social movements without the ability to change socio-political horizons.

Notes

1 This applies to the nested market itself as well as its constituent elements, i.e. the brand, the certificate, the infrastructure, the joint reputation, etc.
2 This extra value evidently is not surplus value. It cannot be appropriated by a single actor who excludes others from the benefits. It is shared (although not necessarily in an equal way) by those who participate in the nested market.
3 When e.g. socio-political struggles are translated into new legislation that allows for 'institutional markets'.
4 Medard *et al.* in Chapter 10 of this volume expressed it as 'escaping dependency relations is an essential part of actor strategies'.
5 A public space is '*a theatre in modern societies in which political participation is enacted through the medium of talk*' (Asen 1999: 115).
6 See the foregoing discussion on the second characteristic of nested markets.
7 Some nested markets may be longstanding and have roots in the distant past (see e.g. the discussion on the market for Chianina meat in van der Ploeg *et al.* 2012). Such longstanding markets also clearly figure in Chapter 8 (Mayelo *et al.* in this volume) and, to a lesser degree, in Chapters 4, 5 and 6. Chapter 10 on the other hand shows the *Dagaa* markets as historical trading systems that are currently being reconstituted.
8 For instance, local ecosystems might be overexploited and destroyed; forms of local cooperation needed to meet the requirements of the agrarian calendar which might be disrupted, etc.
9 There is a good illustration of the complexities and surprises entailed in this in what Oostindie and Broekhuizen (Chapter 7 in this volume) term 'multi-level rural governance'.
10 Or strategic niches as they are called in transition theory. See Rip and Kemp (1998).
11 In more general terms it can be argued that points 1, 2 and 3 imply that seals, certificates, definitions of beneficiaries and participants and/or specific funds jointly define how products are going to flow (through which 'gateways') and between whom and where.
12 The cooperation of producers in a nested market cannot be considered as an anti-trust violation in the same way as oligopolistic cooperation between food empires. Although two cases may be identical from a strictly formal point of view, substantially there is a huge difference.
13 This is especially important when vacuums emerge within the context of rural development. In Europe only 60 per cent of the available RD funds on average are effectively used. Many regions lack the institutional capacity to effectively utilize such funds. In other regions there might be an unwillingness to do so. And, many funds are used in such a way that the transaction costs (associated with planning, administration and control) consume far too much of the available budget. In Brazil we encountered similar problems: 50 per cent of family farms do not have access to the funds and programmes that are designed to assist them. Here we are facing complex interfaces that entail many particular problems. Sometimes such programmes are not adequately targeted to the potential beneficiaries. Sometimes the potential beneficiaries are not able to articulate their needs to those representing the programmes. Sometimes there is no adequate negotiation mechanism in place. All these factors can obstruct the development of transformative capacity (see Oostindie and Broekhuizen, Chapter 7 in this volume).
14 We have to keep in mind, though, that the practice of policy making might relate to the other RD practices in very different ways. Policy making might aim to control or even curtail ongoing RD processes (or to regain lost political momentum). On the other hand it might aim to facilitate or strengthen them. Often there will be a confusing mix of such objectives. It is the encounters and interactions with other practices that is decisive for the relative weight of the different objectives.

References

Armijo, M. and Michalczik, L. (2014) ICTs for agriculture, *Ecology and Farming*, (forthcoming February 2014).

Asen, R. (1999) Toward a normative conception of difference in public deliberation, *Argumentation and Advocacy*, 25: 115–129.

Coutinho, C. (2003) *Gramsci: um estudo sobre seu pensamento politico*, Rio de Janeiro: Editora Civilização Brasileira, Scnd edition.

European Commission (2013) *Short Food Supply Chains and Local Food Systems in the EU: A State of Play of their Socio-Economic Characteristics*, JRC Scientific and Policy Reports, Brussels.

Farming Matters (2013) *New Markets, New Value*, special issue, June 2013.

Gramsci, A. (1975) *Quaderni del carcere* (edited by de Valentino Gerratana, C. 4 Volumes), Turim: Einaudi.

Habermas, J. (1989) *The Structural Transformation of the Public Sphere: An Inquiry into a Category of Bourgeois Society*, Thomas Burger, Cambridge MA: The MIT Press.

Jessop, B. (2008) *State power: a strategic-relational approach*, Cambridge: Polity Press.

Karner, S. (2010), Local Food Systems in Europe, Case Studies from Five Countries and what they imply for policy and practice, Graz: Facilitating Alternative agro-Food Network (FAAN).

Low, S. and Vogel, S. (2011) *Direct and Intermediated Marketing of Local Foods in the United States*, Economic Research Report, number 128, Washington: USDA.

Mouffe, C. (ed.) (1979) *Gramsci and Marxist theory*. London: Routledge & Kegan Paul.

Polanyi, K. (1957, 1st published 1944) *The Great Transformation*. Boston: Beacon Press.

Rip, A. and Kemp, R. (1998) 'Technological change', in Rayner, S. and Malone, E. (eds) *Human choice and climate change, resources and technology*, Columbus, Ohio: Batelle Press.

UNDP (2012), *The roles and opportunities for the private sector in Africa's agro-food iIndustry*, UNDP African Facility for Inclusive Markets, Johannesburg: UNDP.

van der Ploeg, J.D., Jingzhong, Y. and Schneider, S. (2010), Rural development reconsidered: building on comparative perspectives from China, Brazil and the European Union, *Rivista di Economia Agraria* 65: 163–190.

van der Ploeg, J.D., Jingzhong, Y. and Schneider, S. (2012). Rural development through newly emerging, nested, markets, *Journal of Peasant Studies* 39: 133–173.

Index

Page numbers in *italics* denote tables, those in **bold** denote figures.

Abruzzo, Italy 49, 50, **51**
active learning communities 126
advertising 22
Africa 2, 6, 200–1; *see also* Fast Track
 Land Reform Programme (FTLRP),
 Zimbabwe; Lake Victoria fisheries,
 Tanzania; South Africa
agri-environmental services, Netherlands
 126–8
agri-marketing system 43
Agribank, Zimbabwe 151
Agricultural Finance Corporation (AFC),
 Zimbabwe 151
agricultural insurance, Brazil 69
agro-tourism: China 100–7, *106*;
 Netherlands 126
agroecology: Ecovida Agroecology
 Network, Brazil 79–80, 81–6, **82**, **83**,
 88, 90, 91–2, 93–4; institutionalization
 of 87–9; *see also* organic production
Allaire, G. 86
alternative food circuits *see* short food chains
ANA *see* National Alliance of
 Agroecology (ANA), Brazil
artisanal processing, glass noodles 108–10
Australia 2
autonomy 90, 109, 161–4, 195
availability, as distinction 20

back door strategies 127–8
Baili Gallery, China 103
bakkie traders, South Africa 137, *137*, 138,
 141–2, 143
barter trade: Lake Victoria fisheries 180,
 183; Zimbabwe 156–7
Beach Management Units (BMUs), Lake
 Victoria 173–5, 177

beach seines, Lake Victoria 173, *174*, 175,
 177, 182
Beijing 102–3, 107, 110–11
biodiversity 45, 101
Botswana 157
Bourdieu, P. 31
Brandenburg, A. 87, 88
Branson, R. 43
Brazil 2, 200; Ecovida Agroecology
 Network 79–80, 81–6, **82**, **83**, 88, 90,
 91–2, 93–4; emerging markets for
 organic food 86–9; Food Acquisition
 Programme 62, 63, 67, 69, 70–2, 75n23,
 82, 89; government procurement
 policies 7, 61–2, 63, 65–73, 82, 89, 90,
 91; National School Meals Programme
 7, 61, 62, 63, 67, 70–2, 73, 82, 89;
 social movements 6, 87–8, 200
Brazilian Association of Organic Food 87
bridging 29–34, 89, 196
Broad Based Black Economic
 Empowerment, South Africa 132, 144
Burt, R.S. 29, 30
Burundi 185

cabbages, white 133, 138
Canada 2
CAP, European Union 115–17, **116**, 128
carbon credit markets 48
carbon footprints 48
care farms 45, 46–8, **47**, 53–4, 126
Carneiro, M. S. 89
central business district (CBD) traders,
 South Africa 137, *137*, 138, 141, 142,
 143, 146
Chandler, A. 42
Chaumba, J. 154

China 2, 99–113, 200; agro-tourism 100–7, *106*; Communist Party 6; glass noodles 108–11
China Agricultural University (CAU), Beijing 110–11
Chinese cabbage 133, 136, 138, 141
circuits, short food 4
civil society 7, 195–6, 200, 203; Brazil 61, 68, 69; Europe 6; Zimbabwe 151–2
Coase, H.R. 42
cold stores, Tanzania **181**, 184–5, *184*
collaborative innovation 9
collective action 35, 55–6, **55**, 145
collective branding 49
College of Humanities and Development Studies (COHD), Beijing, China 110–11
Commercial Farmers Union (CFU), Zimbabwe 151
common-pool resources (CPRs) **18**, 19, 34–6, 194–5, 196, 198; and agro-tourism 105, *106*, 107; Lake Victoria fisheries 169
Communist Party, China 6
community level marketing, Zimbabwe 156–7
competitive advantage 22
CONSEA *see* National Food and Nutrition Security Council (CONSEA), Brazil
contract sales system, Zimbabwe 156
conventionalization 4, 5, 93, 94
cooperating farm shops 24
counter-development dynamic 5, 13, 91
CPRs *see* common-pool resources (CPRs)
cross-border trade 2; Lake Victoria fisheries 168, **181**, 185; Zimbabwe 157–8, 162

Dagaa 168, 169, 171, 172, **181**, 184, 185
Declaration of Aptitude to PRONAF (DAP), Brazil 70–1, 73
Democratic Republic of Congo (DRC) 168, 185
dependency 195; Lake Victoria fisheries 169, 176–80, **177**
deregulation 2, 5
direct selling 3, 13n4
distinction 18, **18**, 19–22, **21**, 23, 35, 80; organic production 20, 80, 89; traditional glass noodles 108–10
distribution 23, 24, 32; local–local delivery system 32–3, 35
door-to-door traders, South Africa 137, *137*, 138, 141, 142, 143, 146
double movement 5–6, 94, 192

Dzindi, Limpopo Province, South Africa: irrigation scheme 133–4, **134**; marketing of fresh produce 134–6; smallholder irrigators 131–3, 136, 138–46; street traders 132, 136–44, *137*, 146

eco-labelling 80, **83**; *see also* participatory certification, organic farming
ecological agriculture: China 101; *see also* agroecology; organic production
Economic and Social Partners (ESPs), European Union 120
Ecovida Agroecology Network, Brazil 79–80, 81–6, **82**, **83**, 88, 90, 91–2, 93–4
environmental benefits, nested markets 45
environmental sustainability: Netherlands 126–8; reducing greenhouse gas emissions 45, 48, **49**; sheep and goat farming 49–50, **51**; sustainable public procurement (SPP) 63–4, 65, 66, 67, 72
environmentally friendly farming practices 116
EPFs *see* export processing factories (EPFs), Tanzania
Europe: civil society 6; ETUDE programme 9; 'low mileage' food 48; multifunctionality 17
European Union 2, 200; new institutional arrangements 115, 117–23, 124, 126, 127; Nile perch ban **172**, 175–6; RUDI project 118–23; rural policy performance triangle 115, 123–8, **124**; state rural development policies 115–17, **116**, 119–23; structural funds 119–20, 121; sustainability in public procurement 63, 64
exclusive supply agreements 90
exotic products, as distinction 20
export processing factories (EPFs), Tanzania 169, 172, 173, 175, 176–9, **177**

family farmers: Ecovida Agroecology Network, Brazil 79–80, 81–6, **82**, **83**, 88, 90, 91–2, 93–4; and emerging markets for organic food in Brazil 86–9; and government procurement policies, Brazil 62, 66, 67, 69–73, 90, 91
farm-gate kiosks, Zimbabwe 155
farm shops 22, 24, 31
farmers' markets 31; Brazil 91–3; Rome 19–20

Fast Track Land Reform Programme
(FTLRP), Zimbabwe 7, 149–65, **150**;
dynamics of 152–4; evolution of new
nested markets 154–8; markets before
land reform 150–2; social meaning of
new nested markets 159–61; struggles
for autonomy 161–4
fish markets, Lake Victoria: alternative
169, 179–85, **181**; dependency 176–80,
177; exports 168–9, 171–2, **172**, 173,
175–9, **177**; intensified
commercialization 173–6, *174*; from
local to global 171–2
fish maws 184–5
folklore tourism, China 101–2, 103–5,
106, 107
Fome Zero (Zero Hunger Program), Brazil
61, 68–9, 70, 74n1
Food Acquisition Programme (PAA),
Brazil 62, 63, 67, 69, 70–2, 75n23, 82,
89
Food and Nutrition Security (FNS), Brazil
61–2, 68–73; Food Acquisition
Programme 62, 63, 67, 69, 70–2, 75n23,
82, 89; National School Meals
Programme 7, 61, 62, 63, 67, 70–2, 73,
82, 89
food safety problems: China 99–100, 106,
108, 110; Lake Victoria fisheries 168–9,
175–6
food sovereignty 63, 65, 72
forward movements 8–9
France 49–50, **51**
freshness: as distinction 20; local–local
delivery system 32–3, 35
frozen fish, Tanzania **181**, *184*
FTLRP *see* Fast Track Land Reform
Programme (FTLRP), Zimbabwe

GATT negotiations (General Agreement
on Tariffs and Trade) 62–3
Germany 119–20, 125
glass noodles, China 108–11
global agri-food system 62–5
global markets 53
globalization 2, 5, 41
goat farming 49–50, **51**
Goodman, David 23
goods and services, production of new
1–3, 17
governance: Lake Victoria fisheries 173–5;
multi-level rural 201–2; *see also* rural
governance, European Union;
transactional governance

Government Procurement Agreement
(GPA) 63
government procurement policies: Brazil 7,
61–2, 63, 65–73, 82, 89, 90, 91;
international context 62–5; South Africa
145; sustainability in 63–4, 65, 66, 67, 72
government rural development policies *see*
state rural development policies
GPP *see* green public procurement (GPP)
Granovetter, M. 29
green maize 133, 136, 138, 141, 145
green public procurement (GPP) 64, 65
greenhouse gas emissions, reducing 45, 48,
49
Grisa, C. 91
Grosseto province, Italy 120–1, 125
Gujia Village, China 104–5

Habermas, Jürgen 195
Hajer, M.A. 9, 127
Haplochromines 168, 169, 171
hi-tech sightseeing farms, China 102
High Level Group on Corporate Social
Responsibility 64
Hirschman, A. 51
Hodge, I. 117
home delivery systems, organic food in
Brazil 89
Household Responsibility System, China
99
human right to adequate food 61
hybrid governance 43–4, **43**; emergence of
nested markets 44–50, **47**, **49**, **51**;
organizational innovation cycle 53, **54**

illegal land occupations, Zimbabwe 151–2
incentives, government 53–4, **55**
information asymmetries 44–5, 85
infrastructures *see* socio-material
infrastructures
institutional embedding of markets 193–4
Institutional markets *see* government
procurement policies
institutional voids 9, 127–8, 201
institutionalization of agroecology 87–9
Integrated Local Development Companies
(ILDCs), Ireland 122, 125
international trade rules 62–3, 65
internet, organic food sales 88–9
invisible hand metaphor 41–2, 56n2
Ireland 121–2, 125
irrigation, South Africa 131, 133–4, **134**;
see also smallholder irrigators, South
Africa

Italy: care farms 48; Grosseto province 120–1, 125; quality products in Abruzzo 49, 50, **51**

kayabo (salted Nile perch) **181**, 183, 185
Kenya 168, 172, 185
Keynes, J.M. 42
King, R. 132
Kirumba International Market, Tanzania 185
Kyoto Protocol 48

Laag-Holland region, Netherlands 126–8
labour migration: China 99, 104, 110; Germany 119; Zimbabwe 157–8
Lake Victoria fisheries, Tanzania 168–86, **170**; alternative fish markets 169, 179–85, **181**; dependency 176–80, **177**; fish exports 168–9, 171–2, **172**, 173, 175–9, **177**; intensified commercialization 173–6, *174*; from local to global markets 171–2
Lake Victoria Fishery Organization (LVFO) 173
lamb marketing, Texel 24–7, **25**
land occupations, Zimbabwe 151–2
land reform, Zimbabwe *see* Fast Track Land Reform Programme (FTLRP), Zimbabwe
landscape management 45, 126
landscapes, China 101, 102, *106*
LEADER programme, European Union 121–2
leafy vegetables 133, 136, 138, 141, 145
liberalization 5
limited rationality 44–5
local government, China 107
local–local delivery system 32–3, 35
local markets 53
local origin, as distinction 20
local quality products: sheep and goat farming 48–50, **51**; traditional glass noodles 108–11
local supermarkets 32–3, 35
'low mileage' food 48
loyalty 143–4

market protection instruments, European Union 116
market research 22
marketing: glass noodles, China 110–11; of new goods and services 2, 3, 17; organic food in Brazil 88–9, 91–3; smallholder farmers in Zimbabwe 154–8

markets 3–4, 16–17, 19, 27–8; construction of new 2, 3, 17, 19, 45, 112–13; early theories of 41–2; exogenously controlled 41; failure of 5, 44, 196; social construction of 70, 80, 89–93; *see also* nested markets
Marxism 4
McCrudden, C. 64
Mecklenburg-Vorpommern region, Germany 119–20, 125
mercati contadini (peasant markets), Rome 19–20
Morgan, K. 64, 65, 71
Mozambique 157
multi-annual contracts 43
multi-level rural governance 201–2; *see also* rural governance, European Union
multi-tiered chains of exchanges 20–2, **21**
multifunctionality 1–3, 13n1, 17, 18–19, **18**, 45, **46**; China 99; Netherlands 126
multilateral agreements, on government procurement 62–3
multiple actors, agro-tourism, China 106–7
multiple livelihoods 1–3, 13n1

National Alliance of Agroecology (ANA), Brazil 87
National Catalogue of Green and Blue Services, Netherlands 127–8
National Development Plan: Vision for 2030, South Africa 131, 144
National Food and Nutrition Security Council (CONSEA), Brazil 61, 68, 70, 71
National Fresh Produce Market, South Africa 144
National Geo-park of Petrified Wood, China 103, 104, *106*
National Programme of Sustainable Development for Rural Territories, Brazil 69
National Rural Technical Assistance and Extension Policy, Brazil 69
National School Meals Programme (PNAE), Brazil 7, 61, 62, 63, 67, 70–2, 73, 82, 89
nature management, Netherlands 126
neo-classical economics 41–2, 56n2
nested markets 3–4, 5, 7, 16–36; characteristics of 50–3, 193–6; common-pool resources **18**, 19, 34–6, 194–5, 196, 198; construction of 196–7; contribution to rural development 197–9, *198*; and distinction 19–22, **21**;

nested markets *continued*
emergence and development of 44–50,
46, **47**, **49**, **51**, 52–3, **52**, **54**; locations
196; magnitude and strength of 27–8;
ordering principles 191–2; overview
17–19, **18**; role of public policy
199–203; socio-material infrastructures
18–19, **18**, 23–7, **25**, 29–34, 35, 194;
and state rural development policies
53–6, **55**; structural holes 16–17, 18, 19,
29–34, 89, 196
Netherlands: care farms 47, 53–4; Laag-
Holland region 126–8; performance
contracts 122–3, 125; Texel lamb
marketing 24–7, **25**; walking patch-
sellers 29; Willem & Drees 32–3, 35
new institutional arrangements 51, 53,
58n14, 201; European Union 115,
117–23, 124, 126, 127
New Zealand 2; lamb exports to Europe
25, 26, 27
niche markets 23
nightshade 133, 136, 138, 141
Nile perch 168–9, 171–2, **172**, 175–9, **177**,
180, **181**, 182, 184–5, *184*
nongjiale (happy peasant home), China
101, 102, 104
Norvell, D. 43

O'Connor, D. 6
OECD *see* Organization for Economic
Cooperation and Development (OECD)
online organic stores 88–9
Open General Import License policy,
Zimbabwe 151
ordering principles 191–2
organic baskets 89
Organic Law of Food and Nutrition
Security, Brazil 61
organic production 4; Abruzzo, Italy 49;
China 101, *106*; as distinction 20, 80,
89; Ecovida Agroecology Network,
Brazil 79–80, 81–6, **82**, **83**, 88, 90,
91–2, 93–4; emerging markets in Brazil
86–9; and government procurement
policies, Brazil 72, 82, 89, 91;
participatory certification 80, 81–6, **83**,
89–90, 94; third-party certification 81,
84, 89–90, 94
Organization for Economic Cooperation
and Development (OECD) 63–4
Ortmann, G. 132
Ostrom, Elinor 34, 117
overfishing, Lake Victoria 173–5

PAA *see* Food Acquisition Programme
(PAA), Brazil
Pareto, V. 42, 56n2
participatory certification, organic farming
80, 81–6, **83**, 89–90, 94
peer monitoring, organic production 84
Perez-Cassarino, J. 91
performance contracts, Netherlands 122–3,
125
PNAE *see* National School Meals
Programme (PNAE), Brazil
Polanyi, Karl 5, 13, 192
policy cycle 9
pollution, China 99
post-apartheid agrarian policies, South
Africa 7
poverty reduction: Brazil 67, 68; China 110
preferred supplier networks 131–2
price, as distinction 19–20
product differentiation 45–6; *see also*
distinction
production process, as distinction 20
PRONAF (National Programme for
Strengthening Family Farming), Brazil
69–71
Provence, France 49–50, **51**
Public Bidding Law, Brazil 66
public goods 45, 50, 51
public-private partnerships: Netherlands
126; quality schemes 50; Sweden 119
public rural development policies *see* state
rural development policies
public sphere 195–6
pumpkin 133, 136, 138, 141

Qianjiadian Township, China 102–5
quality: as distinction 20; organic
certification 80, 81–6, **83**, 89–90, 94;
sheep and goat farming 48–50, **51**; as
socially shared value 86; traditional
glass noodles 108–11
quasi-market governance *see* hybrid
governance
quasi-organizational governance *see*
hybrid governance

RDPs *see* Rural Development Programmes
(RDPs), European Union
Real Texel's Lamb 24–7, **25**
regulatory policy 53–4, **55**
reputation 22, 37n7
roadside markets 2; Zimbabwe 155–6, 162
Rome, *mercati contadini* (peasant markets)
19–20

RUDI project, European Union 118–23
Rural Development Programmes (RDPs), European Union 115, 116, 117, 119, 120, 121, 122–3, 124, 128
rural governance, European Union: new institutional arrangements 115, 117–23, 124, 126, 127; rural policy performance triangle 115, 123–8, **124**; state rural development policies 115–17, **116**, 119–23
rural groups 9
rural policy performance triangle 115, 123–8, **124**
rurality, China 101, 105, 107, 108, 110, 112
Rwanda 185

Sanggang Village, China 108–11
Savara, A. 30–1
school food programmes, Brazil 7, 61, 62, 63, 67, 70–2, 73, 82, 89
School Meals Law, Brazil 71, 72
Scoones, I. 153, 163
Scott, James 7–8
semi-permanent wife status, Lake Victoria 182–3
sexual relationships, and Lake Victoria fisheries 182–3
sheep farming 49–50, **51**
short food chains 4, 17, 24, *198*; Brazil 93, 94; Netherlands 126
sightseeing farms, China 102
Small Scale Commercial Farms (SSCF), Zimbabwe 152
smallholder farmers *see* Fast Track Land Reform Programme (FTLRP), Zimbabwe
smallholder irrigators, South Africa 131–4, 136, 138–46
Smith, Adam 41–2, 56n2
social benefits of nested markets 45
social capital 115, **124**, 125, 127
social construction of markets 70, 80, 89–93
Social Control Organizations (SCO), Brazil 81–2
social costs 44, 51, 57n9
social justice 74n3, 195; and government procurement policies 64, 65, 67–8
social movements 8, 9; Brazil 6, 87–8, 200; food sovereignty 65
social network based exchanges 22, 37n7; glass noodles, China 108, 109–10
social relations 29

social struggles 3, 4, 5, 192–3, 195, 196
socio-material infrastructures 18–19, **18**, 23–7, **25**, 35, 194; participatory certification of organic farming 80; and structural holes 29–34; Zimbabwe 151, 155, 162, 164
Sonnino, R. 65, 71
South Africa: cross-border trade with Zimbabwe 157–8; Dzindi Irrigation Scheme 133–4, **134**; marketing of fresh produce 134–6; post-apartheid agrarian policies 7; public policies 200; smallholder irrigators 131–3, 136, 138–46; street traders 132, 136–44, *137*, 146
sovereignty, food 63, 65, 72
special treatment, of consumers 143–4
spot markets 28
SPP *see* sustainable public procurement (SPP)
Spring Festival, China 108, 110
standardization 9
state rural development policies 6–8, 53–6, **55**; China 99, 100, 102, 103–5, 106–7; construction of new markets 46; European Union 115–17, **116**, 119–23; and family farmers in Brazil 88; next generation of 8–9; role in nested markets 199–203; *see also* government procurement policies
street markets 2; Brazil 88, 91–3; Zimbabwe 156–7
street traders, South Africa 132, 136–44, *137*, 146
structural holes 16–17, **18**, 19, 29–34, 89, 196
subsidies 63, 116
supermarkets 24; local 32–3, 35; South Africa 131–2, 144
support, government 53–4, **55**
surpluses *198*, 199
sustainable public procurement (SPP) 63–4, 65, 66, 67, 72
Sweden 119, 125
sweet potatoes *see* glass noodles, China

Tanzania 200; *see also* Lake Victoria fisheries, Tanzania
Tanzania Industrial Fish Processors Association (TIFPA) 173, 175
territorially-based rural policy 118–23, 124–5, **124**, 126–7, 200
tertius gaudens (laughing third party) 30
Texel lamb marketing 24–7, **25**

texiles, Netherlands 29
third-party certification, organic farming
    81, 84, 89–90, 94
Thohoyandou *see* Dzindi, Limpopo
    Province, South Africa
'*Three Nong*' issues, China 100–1
Tilapia 168, 171, 172, **181**, 184, *184*
time and space 20, 23, 24, 32
tourism *see* agro-tourism
township pavement traders, South Africa
    137, *137*, 138, 141, 143, 146
tractors, United States 30–1
traditional products, glass noodles 108–11
transaction costs 22, 42, 43, 44, 45, 56n3,
    144, 145
transactional governance 43–4, **43**;
    emergence of nested markets 44–50, **47**,
    49, **51**; organizational innovation cycle
    53, **54**
transportation: smallholder farmers in
    Zimbabwe 157; street traders in South
    Africa 137
Tregear, Angela 23

Uganda 172
unemployment, South Africa 131
United States 2, 30–1
urban–rural duality, China 99

value added (VA) 2, 23, 111, 191, 195,
    198

Västerbotten region, Sweden 119, 125
vehicle-based markets 2
village agro-tourism, China 101–2, 103–5,
    106, 107
visible hand 44

walking patch-sellers, Netherlands 29
Walras, L. 42, 56n1
Water Land & Dykes Agri-Environmental
    Cooperative, Laag-Holland 128
wholesale fish markets, Tanzania **181**, 184
Willard, G.E. 30–1
Willem & Drees, Netherlands 32–3, 35
windows of opportunity 30–1
women traders: Lake Victoria fisheries
    176, 181–3; South Africa 137–44, *137*;
    Zimbabwe 158, 159
world market 27–8
World Trade Organization (WTO) 63, 65

Xinshanzi Village, China 103–4

Yanqing County, China 102–5, 107
Yixian County, China 108–11

Zambia 185
Zimbabwe 200; *see also* Fast Track Land
    Reform Programme (FTLRP),
    Zimbabwe

For Product Safety Concerns and Information please contact our EU
representative GPSR@taylorandfrancis.com Taylor & Francis Verlag GmbH,
Kaufingerstraße 24, 80331 München, Germany

Printed and bound by CPI Group (UK) Ltd, Croydon, CR0 4YY
01/05/2025
01858418-0001